# AMY HERZOG'S
# ULTIMATE SWEATER BOOK

# AMY HERZOG'S
# ULTIMATE SWEATER BOOK

## THE ESSENTIAL GUIDE FOR ADVENTUROUS KNITTERS

..............................................................

## AMY HERZOG

### PHOTOGRAPHY BY BURCU AVSAR

ABRAMS ▪ NEW YORK

# CONTENTS

# INTRODUCTION

∙∙∙∙∙∙∙∙∙∙∙∙∙∙∙∙∙∙∙∙∙∙∙∙∙∙∙∙∙∙∙∙∙∙∙∙∙∙∙∙∙∙∙∙∙∙∙∙∙∙∙∙∙∙

Clothes have been a passion of mine for as long as I can remember. As a child,
I sketched endlessly, and then spent hours spelunking in my grandmother's sewing
room for fabric scraps to turn those sketches into clothes for my dolls.
(There were a lot of ruffles involved.)

As a teenager, I spent hours in secondhand stores looking for unusual pieces I could afford on my meager "budget." When I got my first "real job," I used the bounty of regular paychecks to invest in pieces I still love more than twenty years later. And when I picked up knitting again in my mid-twenties, my heart went immediately to sweaters.

Since then, I've knit hundreds of garments and helped thousands of knitters make clothes they love to wear. My previous books (*Knit to Flatter, Knit Wear Love,* and *You Can Knit That*) have all touched on different aspects of helping you move your sweater knitting beyond "what a great project" territory, and into the promised land of "this is my favorite top!" It's my passion, and the reason I do what I do.

But those books, as much as knitters have loved them, left a gap. They were each focused on specific aspects of sweater knitting: Here are the lines clothing can paint on your body; here's how to use yarn you love to make something that will fit into your closet, style-wise; here's how to make sweaters a little easier than you thought. And once you've gotten over the hurdle of your first fantastic sweater, your mind explodes with the possibilities! You don't *need* a single step-by-step walkthrough for your garments anymore. You've mostly got a handle on what you like and how to get it—with the exception of whatever burning design question you have at the moment.

*"I love that cardigan I made last month, but I think now I want one with pockets. How do I make pockets, again?"*

*"My latest fuzzy pullover has a great fit, but now I want one that's A-line and longer, and made out of a lighter-weight yarn. How do I make an A-line, again?"*

*"I've just seen the most amazing sweater in a store, except I want to make it out of something with silk in it and add this great lace I used to make a scarf last year. How do I do that?"*

In other words, once you've fully embraced the sweater, you need a *reference guide.* One that's written in clear terms, with an index, so you can quickly look up this month's burning sweater question and get knitting.

My *Ultimate Sweater Book* is that reference guide. My goal is the same as ever—to help you create garments that are the best clothes you've ever worn. But in these pages, I start with the premise that you already *know* what you *want* to wear and just need a little help making it a reality. I'll give you the same clear, gentle, and straight-up-honest advice of my previous books, never fear! But instead of weaving it all through a single theme or narrative, I've broken it up by sweater topic so you can easily dive in, get the information you need, and get out again. I want you to spend more time knitting.

I start out in part 1 (pages 9–107) with all the basic information you'll need to draft your own sweater pattern from scratch. From measurement, to swatching to sweater construction basics (chapter 1) to detailed guidance on the four major sweater constructions (chapters 2 to 5), you'll be ready to make a great, basic garment with any yarn you might have. (And if drafting your own pattern doesn't sound awesome to you, no worries! I've included basic cardigan and pullover patterns in each of these chapters—in twelve sizes, and three gauges.)

Once you've got a starting point, changing up the fit or shape of a garment is a great way to make it your own. In part 2 (pages 109–121), I offer guidance on fit and silhouette adjustments—either for a pattern you're writing or one you've purchased. I go through the basic shapes of sweater bodies, sleeves, and necklines—and how to draft or modify them. Along the way, I guide you through the *whys* as well as the hows. Want to change up (or draft from scratch) the body of your sweater, or the sleeves, or the neckline? Learn what adjustments you might need to make for a larger bust, or how to lengthen something? I've got you covered.

In part 3 (pages 123–147), I get to the fun part of design: embellishments. Learn how your yarn's construction and fiber mix affect your hand-knit fabric (chapter 10) and how to incorporate stitch patterns into your sweaters. I'll give you options for every sweater you knit, from edge shaping (chapter 11) to buttonholes (page 142), and everything in between. Whenever you're ready to move beyond a basic, you'll turn to this section.

And, of course, I've included garments to help guide your path. Twenty in all, they cover all the constructions, adjustments, and embellishments I describe in the rest of the book. But they're more than just technical exercises: From stylishly boxy (page 33) to scrumptiously pocketed (page 147) to elegantly shaped (page 177), the sweaters in these pages are truly ones you (or your loved ones) will love wearing every day.

And in my mind, there's no higher aspiration for a hand-knit.

*Note:* Centimeters are rounded to the nearest half centimeter throughout the book.

......................................................................

# PART ONE

# BASICS

Unusual stitch patterns and crazy constructions are fun, to be sure. But a well-fitting basic sweater made out of a yarn you love is one of the best gifts you can give yourself as a knitter. These sweaters are versatile, work with a wide range of yarns, and can be made to perfectly suit the kinds of clothes you wear every day.

In this section, I'll teach you how to take your measurements properly for sweater knitting and draft your own sweater pattern in four major construction styles. I'll also provide comprehensive twelve-size, three-gauge patterns for basic sweaters in case you're not feeling like writing your own pattern at the moment.

These patterns are the starting point for all specific garments later in the book, but they are equally gorgeous on their own—and you can tame the numbers while you're knitting by using one of the handy fill-in-the-blank sweater worksheets available for download on my website, amyherzogdesigns.com.

But before you dive in, we need to lay some groundwork. Three things form the basis of every sweater, and you'll need to figure them out before you can get knitting: Which construction you'd like to wear, how to swatch predictively for gauge, and which measurements you'll need to ensure your sweater *fits like a dream*.

# 1

## Sweater Basics, Measurements, and Ease

There are *tons* of different kinds of finished sweaters out there. High necks, low necks, long sleeves, flutter sleeves, cables and collars and tunics and A-lines . . .

But when you're thinking about sweater *design*, it's helpful to start by focusing on the core place a garment will fit: the shoulders. Add a basic outline of the shape of the sweater's body and arms, and you've got a blank canvas onto which you can paint stitch patterns and trims.

For the vast majority of sweater designs, there are four basic ways to attach the sleeves to the body of a sweater. Let's talk about them from the simplest math (and least precise fit) to the most complicated (and most precise fit):

- **Drop-Shoulder** sweaters are made with straight lines everywhere: The body is worked straight (or slightly notched in for a modified drop) to the shoulder, and the top of each sleeve is bound off all at once to create another straight line. To assemble the sweater, the sleeves are folded in half widthwise and seamed to the side of the sweater body. They are either worked in pieces from the bottom up and then seamed together, or worked in-the-round, with sleeves picked up and worked top down.

- **Raglan** sweaters can be worked bottom up, top down, in pieces, or all in one. The defining characteristics of a raglan sweater are that the sleeve and body have the same number of rows in the raglan shaping section, and that all shaping happens along four distinct lines. The top of the sleeves, top of the front, and top of the back form the neck edge, and you can see angled but straight lines of shaping from the armhole to the neck. Sweatshirts and baseball jerseys are raglans. Saddle-shoulder sweaters are sometimes built off the raglan construction.

- **Yoke** sweaters are worked in a single piece, either from the bottom up or the top down. Like raglans, the sleeves and bodies have the same number of rows in the top section of the garment; unlike raglans, the shaping is spread evenly around the entire circle of the yoke.

- **Set-In-Sleeve** sweaters are the most precise fit you can get in a hand-knit sweater. They're typically worked in pieces from the bottom up and then seamed, although there are alternatives to this traditional approach. In a set-in-sleeve garment, the armhole is curved, and the top of the

Drop shoulder          Raglan                    Yoke             Set-in sleeve

sleeve (called the sleeve cap) is shorter and also curved—like a horseshoe or bell curve. Unlike sewn garments, hand-knit set-in-sleeve sweater patterns are symmetrical: The front and back armholes are the same, and the two sides of the sleeve cap are the same. A saddle shoulder is often created from a set-in-sleeve construction.

You can see a schematic-style view of how the different constructions compare to one another above.

There are no right or wrong ways to put a sweater together—each of these main sweater constructions makes a great sweater. However, each definitely produces a different look and feel, and they all have different needs in terms of the fabric used to make the garment. We'll talk about all those things in this book.

### BASICS: SWATCHING FOR SWEATERS

The most important reason to swatch for a sweater is that swatches give you a chance to "test run" your fabric before you spend months creating it. That fabric can take all sorts of forms, from filmy and float-on-air to tough-as-iron and impossible-to-felt. The fibers and yarn constructions you choose make a tremendous difference to the look and feel of your sweater, and I'll talk more about them in chapter 10 (page 124). (How large or small your stitches are doesn't matter a whit if you don't like the fabric.)

Assuming you do like the fabric, though, before you start knitting, you'll need a swatch that gives you two things:

- An accurate prediction of your gauge.
- A gauge that's well suited to the demands of a sweater.

Notice I *didn't* say you need a swatch whose stitches are the same size as the pattern's. You can't possibly change the way your hands naturally knit over the course of an entire garment, so it's best not to try. Instead, swatch so that you know how large your stitches *will* be, and whether your yarn and needle choice will work for the sweater you have in your mind.

I'll say it again: It doesn't matter if you get *exactly* the gauge some designer had in mind. What matters is (a) whether your swatch represents how large your stitches will be when you knit a sweater, and (b) whether the swatch represents the fabric you want for your garment.

Here's how I go about swatching for sweaters:

- Cast on between 35 and 50 stitches. Fewer than 35, and you won't have enough fabric to evaluate; more than 50, and your soul will wither and die. (I'm kidding about the soul withering. Mostly. You're definitely likely to run out of steam before you make the swatch large enough.)

- Work in your stitch pattern of choice (I like to swatch all new yarns in Stockinette first) for about 5" (13 cm), then bind off all stitches.

- Wash your swatch, and let it air dry flat, with no pins.

At this point, you're ready to evaluate your swatch and decide whether it will work. In my opinion, there's actually a fairly narrow range of gauges at which a given yarn will make a good sweater. Sweaters work best when your fabric strikes a delicate balance: It should be flexible enough to move with you as you move, while at the same time being strong enough to stand up to gravity, motion, and the rubbing likely to happen at a few key points.

In a perfect world (we'll talk more about alternatives later), your swatch will pass something I call the "poke test": Try, fairly vigorously, to squirm the entire tip (or more) of your finger through the space between the stitches. You shouldn't be able to.

Obviously, the size of your yarn has something to do with this—for a bulky yarn, use your thumb and don't try *super* forcefully. For a worsted yarn, use your pinky and try to get the entire tip of your finger through. For a sport or fingering yarn, see if you can get the tip of your pinky nail through the space between the fabric.

If your fabric is loose enough for your finger to slip through, your gauge is fundamentally a little (or a lot) *unstable*. The stitches aren't well connected to their neighbors, so the knit fabric can't react appropriately to stress.

Think about your stitches as a line of dancers, all linking arms and trying to move together. To get a strong, flexible knit fabric, each dancer's movement should be passed on to the next—one dancer's kick or step being followed closely by everyone else, down the line. When your gauge is too loose for the yarn you're using, movements don't get passed along to the next "dancer," and the whole routine falls apart.

Back to sweater terms: When your sweater is subject to gravity, or an unstructured construction, or a lot of friction, there's a chance bad things (growth, pilling, sagging) will happen.

If you find you can easily worm your finger between your stitches, swatch again with needles that are a size (or two) smaller. If that still doesn't help, consider taking a class in knitting technique to firm up your fabric. Your sweaters will thank you.

***When you can break the rules.*** Sometimes, it's less important that your fabric pass the poke test for stability. *(Shhh, don't tell anyone I said that!)* If you're in one of the following situations, you can probably get away with a looser fabric without problems:

- **YOU'RE WORKING WITH MOHAIR.** If you can't rip out mistakes, you don't need to worry about stability— no matter how far apart the stitches are!

- **YOU'RE WORKING WITH A REALLY GRIPPY WOOL OR YARN TEXTURE.** This is a less-extreme version of the mohair situation. Generally speaking, if your yarn's fiber or texture causes a lot of "stickiness" between the stitches, it's OK to knit the yarn more loosely than you would if the yarn were slick.

- **YOU'RE WORKING A GARMENT WITH A LOT OF SEAMS.** Seams are the skeleton of your garment—they hold the rest of the sweater up and keep the fabric in place. You can get away with a slightly less-than-stable fabric if you reinsert that stability into the piece via seams.

***When you can't break the rules.*** Those guidelines come with flip sides: There are times when it's *vitally important* that the fabric you're working with passes the poke test, to avoid serious sweater issues. These include when:

- **YOU'RE WORKING WITH SUPERWASH WOOL, BAMBOO, OR ANYTHING THAT'S ESPECIALLY HEAVY AND SLICK (LIKE ALPACA).** You'll be counting on the stability of your fabric to counteract the tendency of these fibers to slip and slide around.

- **YOU'RE KNITTING A GARMENT WITHOUT SEAMS.** Seams add structure—so if you don't have seams, make sure your fabric can give the garment all the structure it needs!

**If you pass the test,** or are OK failing it, you're ready to answer the second most important question: Does this fabric match the garment you have in mind for it? This question is definitely qualitative, so the answer is up to you: Do you like the way the fabric moves? Feels? Do you like the texture of the yarn, its sheen, its halo (or lack thereof)? Does it look good in the stitch pattern you've selected for the sweater?

One way to get a sense of how your fabric will behave at sweater scale is something I call the *movement test*—place your swatch on a slippery surface, put your index fingers in a corner of the swatch, and move them around each other in half circles. If the entire swatch moves with minimal rippling, you'll get a sweater with a stiffer, sturdy fabric (just the thing for that cabled hiking sweater you've been dreaming about). If there are ripples and pools of fabric instead, and the rest of the swatch doesn't move, you've got an extremely drapey fabric (just the thing for that super-oversize drop-shoulder pullover with slim sleeves).

**If you're good,** then *you can measure for gauge.* I've waited this long to talk about measuring gauge for a reason—it's far more important to have a great fabric than for your stitches to be any particular size.

That said, it's tough to write a pattern (or knit one!) if you don't know how big your stitches will be when you knit the garment. So once you've settled on a great fabric, here's how to measure the size of your stitches as accurately as possible:

- Mark the maximum number of stitches you think are "good data" for predicting your gauge. This probably means you're not including a few edge stitches on each side. Mark nearer the top of the piece, since it's more likely that you've settled into your knitting groove by the time you're nearly finished with the swatch.

- Measure the precise width of those stitches with a ruler. This way, instead of estimating a fraction of a stitch (e.g., 22.25 stitches in 4" [10 cm]), which is difficult and error-prone even for very experienced knitters, you're letting the ruler tell you exactly how many fractions of an inch your stitches measure. You'll wind up with a number that's something like "26 stitches in 4⅞" (12.5 cm)."

- Do the same for rows. In this case, you might not want to count the rows closest to your cast-on edge. A typical set of measurements for rows might be "18 rows in 2.875" (7.5 cm)."

- Now divide to get your per-inch stitch and row gauges. In this case, our stitch gauge is 26 stitches in 4.875" (12.5 cm) = 5.33 stitches per inch (2.5 cm), and our row gauge is 18 rows / 2.875" (7.5 cm) = 6.26 rows per inch (2.5 cm).

Here's how that winds up looking in practice:

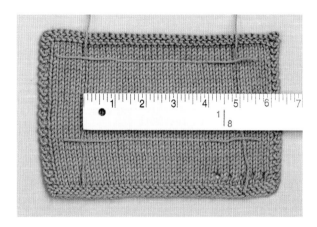

Measure a whole number of stitches and rows

If you're writing your own pattern, this is all you need. If you're working from a traditionally written pattern, these numbers may not exactly match the pattern's! That's OK—it's much more important to know what your gauge will be. Divide stitch counts for the size you've chosen by your true, accurate gauge to see how large your garment will be. If it's close to your desired size, you're good to go. If not, knit the instructions for a size up (or down).

## BASICS: MEASUREMENTS FOR SWEATERS

Taking accurate measurements for the sweaters you'll produce is the final step before you're ready to tackle a pattern. You might be tempted to choose a pattern style that lets you "try things on as you go," but I promise you'll be happier with the result when you start with actual body measurements and your very own gauge.

There are a few really simple measurements you'll need for any kind of sweater, and a few more (that are still fairly simple, I promise) that you'll need if you want to add waist shaping or fiddle around with different sleeve lengths or sweater lengths. You can download a photocopy-ready sheet from my website with a comprehensive list.

Circumferences should be taken level to the ground, evenly at the point specified, and pulled snug enough that the measuring tape doesn't slip, but not so tightly that the skin spills over the tape. Lengths should generally be taken against the flattest part of the body you can find—along the back for body lengths, and along the inside edge of the arm, with the arm held straight, for sleeves.

*(Please note that these instructions are for hand-knit sweaters only! There are a few cases where these measurements differ from measurements taken for sewn garments.)*

### *Sweater-Friendly Measurements and How to Take Them*

Basics that you need for everything:

- **UPPER TORSO CIRCUMFERENCE (FOR WOMEN).** Measure the circumference of the body with the tape as high in the armpits as it will go (the top edge of the tape should touch the armpit).

- **BUST/CHEST CIRCUMFERENCE.** Measure the circumference at the fullest part of the bust (for a woman) or at the nipple line (for men/kids).

- **HIP CIRCUMFERENCE.** Measure the circumference at the widest part of the hips.

- **TOTAL SWEATER LENGTH (FOR AN AVERAGE SWEATER).** Measure from the top of the shoulder straight down the body to where the wearer prefers their average sweater hem to fall. It's a good idea to double-check this length against a favorite top (store-bought is fine).

- **SET-IN-SLEEVE ARMHOLE DEPTH.** Measure from the top of the shoulder straight down the body to the place where armhole shaping should be located on a set-in-sleeve sweater. For women, this is typically ½–1" (1.5–2.5 cm) below the actual armpit; for men, this is typically 1½–2" (4–5 cm) below the actual armpit. *But preferences vary widely for this measurement!* So it's a good idea to sanity-check this length against the shaping in the shirt you're wearing when you take the measurements.

- **BICEPS CIRCUMFERENCE.** Measure the circumference around the largest part of the biceps.

- **WRIST CIRCUMFERENCE.** Measure the circumference around the wrist, at the wrist bone.

- **SWEATER-FOCUSED SLEEVE LENGTH.** Since the height of the top part of the sleeve varies both with construction and from person to person, it's more reliable to measure sleeve length from the cuff to the point the sleeve attaches to the body. The attachment happens at the underarm seam—so place the zero point of your measuring tape at the armhole depth point and then measure straight down the arm to *wherever you like your long-sleeve cuff to fall*—whether that's your finger knuckles, the break of your thumb, your wrist bone, or anywhere in between.

One additional bit of work: Subtract your armhole depth from your total sweater length to get your hem-to-armhole length. You'll need this to compare

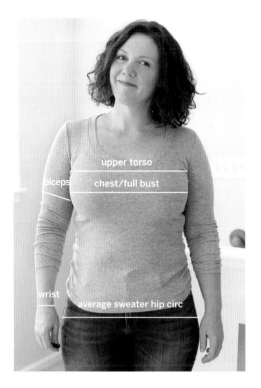

your measurements against a sweater schematic. See images above to locate these measurements on a body.

If you're after a basic, long-sleeve, average-length sweater without hourglass-waist shaping, you're now good to go. Here are the other measurements you might need, for sweaters with waist shaping and/or different sleeve/sweater lengths.

### IF YOU WANT WAIST SHAPING:

Waist shaping works best when it's located at your natural waist. To find it, bend sideways—just like when you sing "I'm a Little Teapot." Your natural waist is at the point of the deepest bend.

- **WAIST CIRCUMFERENCE.** Measure the circumference of your natural waist.

- **LENGTH FROM ARMHOLE POINT TO NATURAL WAIST.** Measure, straight down the back, from the armhole depth point to your natural waist.

These two measurements will help you size the waist of your sweater appropriately and center your waist and bust shaping on your waist. Which is what you want—the curve of the fabric should match your body's pivot points.

### IF YOU WANT OTHER SLEEVE AND/OR SWEATER LENGTHS:

- **ADDITIONAL HIP CIRCUMFERENCES (MAYBE).** If you're making a longer or shorter sweater, you might find it helpful to take additional hip circumferences:

    One higher on the hips, to include the lower tummy.

    One at the lowest point of the hips, if this isn't where you took your standard hip measurement.

    One below your bum, at the tops of your thighs— this is only useful for body shapes with slimmer hips and larger legs.

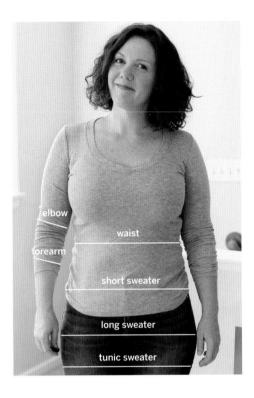

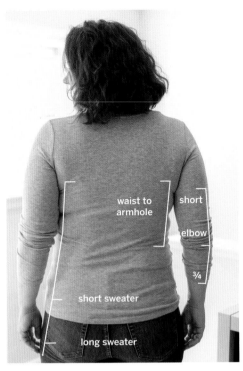

- **ADDITIONAL SWEATER LENGTHS.** If you'd like a shorter or longer sweater, take additional sweater lengths—either on your body, from store-bought sweaters whose lengths you like, or both. As with your standard sweater length, subtract your armhole depth from the total length to get your hem-to-armhole length for other sweaters.

- **FOREARM CIRCUMFERENCE.** Measure the circumference of your arm at the widest part of your forearm. This will help you determine a cast-on width for three-quarter sleeves.

- **ELBOW CIRCUMFERENCE.** Measure the circumference of your arm either just above or just below your elbow, depending on where you'd like the cuff of an elbow-length sleeve to be.

- **ADDITIONAL SLEEVE LENGTHS.** Take additional sleeve lengths for short, elbow-length, and/or three-quarter sleeves the same way you did for long sleeves.

This may seem like a daunting list and an intimidating subject. But don't stress out too much! In terms of precision, as long as you're accurate to within an inch (2.5 cm) for circumferences and ½" (1.5 cm) for lengths, you'll be just fine. (Truly.)

## BASICS: FROM MEASUREMENTS TO SWEATER DIMENSIONS: DRAFTING YOUR PERSONAL SCHEMATIC (EXCEPT THE SHOULDERS)

Before you can write (or modify!) a sweater pattern, you'll need to be able to take your measurements and turn them into a set of garment dimensions. While each individual sweater you make (or modify) might be a little different and constructions can change things a little, too, it's worth getting a basic sense of your general garment ranges up front.

*Lengths should be used as is.* If you just found you need a total sweater length of 26" (66 cm) from hem to shoulder with an 8" (20.5 cm) armhole, the sweaters you make should match those lengths exactly.

*Circumferences require ease.* "Ease" is the difference between what your body measures, somewhere on your body, and what a garment measures at the same point. "Negative ease" means the garment is smaller than you are at that spot; "positive ease" means the garment is larger than you are at that spot.

For example: A garment that measures 40" (101.5 cm) in the hips has 2" (5 cm) of *positive ease* when worn by someone with 38" (96.5 cm) hips. It has 2" (5 cm) of *negative ease* when worn by someone with 42" (106.5 cm) hips. It has *zero ease* when worn by someone with 40" (101.5 cm) hips.

Generally speaking, hand-knit sweaters require less ease than woven-fabric clothing, or even some machine-knits, because hand-knit fabric has a tremendous amount of inherent stretch. Let's break down how much ease you need at different points on your torso and arms.

- **BUST/CHEST:** *Ease range -2" (-5 cm) to as large as you like.* For proper fit, you'll want the bust/chest measurement of your sweater to be no more than 2" (5 cm) smaller than your bust. Beyond that, you can pretty much do as you like. Wearing a sweater with 2" (5 cm) of negative ease will give the visual impression that your bust (or pecs) are "filling out" the fabric, making the chest look larger. Substantial positive ease will give the opposite impression, minimizing the size of your bust/chest compared to other parts of your body. A sweater with 0–2" (0–5 cm) of positive ease in the bust is fairly neutral for adult women; 2–4" (5–10 cm) of positive ease in the chest is an "average" range for adult men or children. Relaxed or oversize garments should have more ease.

- **WAIST:** *Ease range at least 3" (7.5 cm), preferably more.* Many people get uncomfortable when the waist of a garment is "too tight," and this feeling seems to occur once the fabric is within 3" (7.5 cm) of the body wearing it. I've observed, in classes and by working with knitters, that 4–6" (10–15 cm) of positive ease in the waist seems to be a comfortable, "average" range for adult women. For adult men and kids, 2–4" (5–10 cm) seems to be a comfortable, "average" range. Again, relaxed or oversize garments should have more ease.

- **HIPS (FOR SHORTER, FITTED SWEATERS):** *Ease range -2" (-5 cm) to 1" (2.5 cm).* If you're making a shorter, fitted garment with set-in sleeves, you'll need the sweater to be snug enough in your hips to anchor the hem through your body's movement. (Otherwise, every time you raise your arms, you'll bare your midriff.) This amount of negative ease won't look "tight," I promise! (You can see on page 130 an example of what -2" [-5 cm] of ease through the hips looks like.) In fact, -2" (-5 cm) of ease on a 40" (101.5 cm) hip is only 5 percent stretch—which is nothing for a hand-knit. But that amount of friction *will* keep a garment in place as you move, which is what you want.

- **HIPS (FOR SHORTER AND AVERAGE-LENGTH SWEATERS, LESS-FITTED CONSTRUCTIONS):** *Ease range -2" (-5 cm) to as much ease as you'd like.* As with other parts of the sweater, you'll begin to have fit problems if you make the garment more than 2" (5 cm) smaller in the hips than you are. But depending on the style of the garment, substantial positive ease might be appropriate—as with an oversize, cropped, drop-shoulder sweater. In this case, it's up to you.

- **HIPS (FOR LONGER AND TUNIC-LENGTH SWEATERS):** *Ease range at least 2" (5 cm) of positive ease for long, at least 6" (15 cm) of positive ease for tunic, can go over 12" (30.5 cm) of positive ease for A-line tunics.* Longer sweaters generally need more room through the hips. If the front of your sweater is brushing the tops of your legs, or the garment is tunic-length and reaches past the curve of your bum, you'll probably want to make sure the garment isn't close to your body.

It's a good idea to take your measurements and these guidelines, and create a few personal goal schematics for yourself for different kinds of sweaters. You can download a blank set of schematics from my website.

*BREAKING UP YOUR CIRCUMFERENCES OVER THE FRONT AND BACK OF YOUR SWEATER.*
For men, kids, and some women, you can take the circumferences from the previous step and split them in half to form the front and back of your garment. For busty women, however, doing so will result in a garment that's too loose in the back and too snug in the front—because a decent amount of their bust circumference is located only in the front.

If you're busty, to create a personal schematic that works perfectly for you, start by tallying the back bust width as if your **upper torso** is your full bust measurement, and split things evenly. **After you've done so, take your full bust measurement and add/subtract ease to get your target garment bust.** To determine the front bust, subtract the back bust you calculated based on your upper torso from your total target—the remainder is your front bust.

If this approach doesn't make sense yet, check out my examples for the constructions that follow—it's how I need to approach my own sweaters.

# Master Shaping Formula and Centering Stitch Patterns

Some math is so helpful you use it over and over again in sweater design. Here's a handy reference for it, to be used throughout the rest of the book.

### Spacing shaping with the Master Shaping Formula (simple).

In sweaters, you often want to know how to get from one stitch count to another over a certain vertical distance. Think waist and bust shaping, sleeve shaping, V-neckline shaping, etc.

In these examples, a few "work straight" rows on either end of the shaping segment are no big deal, so the formula is pretty simple:

$$rate\ of\ shaping* = \frac{total\ number\ of\ rows}{number\ of\ shaping\ rows}$$

*rounded down to the nearest whole (even) number.

For example, let's say we're working at a gauge of 4 stitches and 6 rows to the inch (2.5 cm), and you need to add 20 stitches between a sleeve's wrist and biceps. We know the number of shaping rows—10, since you add 2 stitches each time you work an increase row.

To find the total number of rows available, we need to take the entire sleeve length and then subtract the ribbing and "work straight" sections at the top. Let's assume the sleeve is 18" (45.5 cm) long from wrist to cap, with 3½" (9 cm) of ribbing. Leave 1" (2.5 cm) of straight knitting even before the cap, you've got 18" (45.5 cm) - 4½" (11.5 cm) = 13½" (34.5 cm) in which to shape; multiply by 6 rows per inch (cm) = 81 total rows for shaping.

The rate of shaping is then 81/10 = 8.1, which we round down to 8. After the ribbing, work an increase row every 8 rows, 10 times total.

### Centering a Stitch Pattern

Stitch patterns are typically written in terms of repeats—usually described as "a multiple of $x$ sts, plus $y$." This means that each time you repeat the stitch pattern, you're using $x$ stitches and then you need $y$ stitches to start/end up a row. The King Charles Brocade I used for the Dockhouse Pullover on page 131, for example, has a multiple of 8 stitches, plus 1.

When working an allover pattern, in a perfect world you've got a stitch count that is a multiple of $x$ sts plus $y$.

Unfortunately, that's often not the case—either because the cast-on math just won't work out perfectly for fit or because you're juggling another stitch pattern, or whatever.

No sweat! In these cases, you just need to *center* that pattern repeat on your stitches. The basic idea is to incorporate as many stitch pattern repeats as you can, and choose an unobtrusive stitch for any "remainder" stitches. Here's how:

First, take your total stitch count and divide by the main repeat number, rounding down the result to a whole number. This tells you how many whole repeats you'll be able to fit into your stitches. (For example, if I have 123 stitches on the front of my pullover and I'm using the King Charles Brocade, I can fit 123 / 8 = 15 repeats in evenly, rounded down to nearest whole number.)

Multiply the number of even repeats by the number of stitches, in each repeat (15 × 8 = 120), then subtract the resulting number from your total number of stitches. The result is how many remainder stitches you'll have left to deal with. (Continuing with the example, 123 sts - 120 in the main repeat = 3 left over. One of those will be used in the stitch pattern itself, leaving 2 stitches truly "left over.")

Divide this remainder by 2. This is the number of stitches you'll have on each side, outside of the stitch repeat. (For our example, that's just 1 stitch on each side.) If you've only got a few remainder stitches, work them in Stockinette, reverse Stockinette, Garter, or whatever other plain stitch pattern looks best. If this is a larger number, investigate (and maybe swatch!) to see whether it's possible to work a *partial repeat* on the sides. If it's an odd number, you'll have one stitch more at the beginning or end of your row. Don't worry—it will look just fine. (Or worry, and adjust your stitch count up or down by one!)

# 2

............................................

# Drop-Shoulder Sweaters

Many of the most famous sweaters—Arans, steeked Fair Isle pullovers, Ganseys—are made from this fundamentally rectangular construction. Since the 1980s, they've been mostly out of favor—my own childhood memories of drop-shoulder garments are of bulky and uncomfortable sweaters. But they've enjoyed a resurgence recently thanks to thin, drapey fabrics and updated silhouette variations, and if you've been holding out, I'd encourage you to give knitting them a try. Drop-shoulder garments have some distinct advantages: Thanks to their inherently oversize fit, they work well on many different bodies without alteration; they're simple to alter when needed; and the lack of curved shaping on most parts of the garment makes it easier to incorporate lots of different stitch patterning.

When a drop shoulder fits you well, there should be no straining in the shoulder area even through exaggerated movement. This tends to translate into a very roomy fit in the body as well—making drop shoulders the perfect choice for that super-luxe, drapey yarn you've been coveting.

## WHAT MAKES A DROP SHOULDER A DROP SHOULDER?

Drop-shoulder sweaters come in a number of variations, but all have a sleeve/body join that's primarily a straight line from hem to shoulder.

Traditionally, they're either knit in pieces from the bottom up and seamed, or in the round from the bottom up (body and sleeves separately) and then steeked and seamed:

(x2)                                    (x1)

Flat, in pieces                          In the round

Several common variations exist—from a **modified drop shoulder**, which is worked flat in pieces, but with a small notch at the armholes on the body (I find these easier to seam and have used this variation on the patterns in this book) to an **all-in-one construction** worked either side-to-side or hem-to-hem. (These typically include some dolman or curved shaping to the underarms.) Traditionally, armhole depths and biceps widths for drop shoulders have been very generous; another more recent variation pairs an exaggeratedly oversize body with slimmer sleeves.

Unlike with some of the other constructions, there's no clear advantage to one of these variations over another. They have slightly different implications for fit, stitch patterning, and fabric, but all make great sweaters for pretty much any body.

This chapter will focus primarily on drafting drop-shoulder patterns in pieces; I'll discuss creating other variations from that starting point.

## DESIGN AND FABRIC CONSIDERATIONS FOR DROP-SHOULDER SWEATERS

The seams inherent in nearly every drop-shoulder variation make this construction fairly structured— those seams act as a bony skeleton, if you will, for the garment. That structure gives you a lot of leeway in choosing which fabrics you'd like to wear in a drop-shoulder sweater.

Personally, I feel the oversize fit and relatively large amount of fabric in a drop-shoulder sweater work best with a fluid, somewhat heavy fabric that offers good drape. (Wool-silk blends are my favorite, but see more choices in chapter 10.) One of the things that turned me off to drop-shoulder sweaters in the past was the feeling of having bulky fabric under the arm; thinner, drapier fabrics minimize this feeling. That said, a drop-shoulder sweater can handle pretty much anything you throw at it, so wear what you like!

For the drop-shoulder garments later in this book, I chose one bulkier, lighter-than-air fabric with a simple eyelet pattern for the Baxter Turtleneck (page 151), a worsted-weight-and-yet-slinky wool for the Sunburst Cardigan (page 139), and a lovely fingering-weight wool-silk blend for the Fiddler's Reach Cardigan (page 155).

These drop-shoulder patterns span the most popular shapes—nothing too close to the body, nothing too figure-conscious. Some waist shaping on the back, along princess lines, can help keep a sweater from feeling boxy, but I wouldn't recommend anything more severe. Straight-sided (like the basics in this chapter), A-line, or even tapered may feel like a better match.

## Drafting a drop-shoulder pattern.

The only hard-and-fast rule about drop-shoulder sweaters is that the armhole depth of the finished garment will be equal to half the biceps circumference:

9" (23 cm)    18" (46 cm)

Beginning with either of these two numbers is a great place to start drafting your own drop-shoulder pattern—you can start with your desired armhole depth (and determine the biceps from there), or with your desired biceps measurement (in which case, the armhole depth will be half of what you choose).

Why does it matter? The seam where the sleeve and body attaches is straight, unlike your own shoulder joint, and limits your range of motion if it circles your shoulder joint too tightly. If the seam of the drop-shoulder sleeve is too snug, you'll tear it when you move your arms too far away from your torso.

Traditionally, drop-shoulder patterns begin with an armhole depth that's 1–2" (2.5–5 cm) longer than a set-in-sleeve armhole depth. This allows the body of the drop-shoulder sweater to sit closer to your body, without restricting movement in the armhole. The seam sits just a couple of inches (5 cm or so) off the corner of your shoulder, and attaches far enough below your actual armpit to allow both lift and rotation in the arms.

**Here's an example using my numbers:** My preferred set-in-sleeve armhole depth is 8" (20.5 cm); so I would typically start with a drop-shoulder armhole depth of 10" (25 cm). This translates into a biceps measurement of 20" (51 cm).

This gives an insight as to why you might want to start with the biceps measurement instead—my actual biceps measurement is 12½" (32 cm), so beginning with the armhole results in a tremendous amount of ease in the arm!

Starting with the biceps measurement allows you to craft a drop-shoulder pattern with slimmer arms, a popular style at the time of this writing. For a snug-armed look, you'll likely want between 1–4" (2.5–10 cm) of positive ease in the biceps. The armhole depth is then half your garment's biceps measurement.

**Again, using my numbers:** I might want a 14" (35.5 cm) biceps for my snugger-armed drop-shoulder garment. This will result in an armhole depth on the garment of just 7" (18 cm). The sleeve is now stylishly skimming my arm, but the armhole depth is shorter than my body's armhole. That means I'll need to push the attachment point well away from my body's armhole, farther down on my arm—resulting in a sweater with a foot (30.5 cm) or more of ease in my bust.

Neither way is right or wrong; it is all about what you want to wear.

Here's a blank schematic you can fill in for the rest of your drop-shoulder sweater:

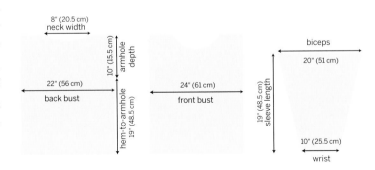

8" (20.5 cm) neck width
10" (15.5 cm) armhole depth
22" (56 cm) back bust
hem-to-armhole 19" (48.5 cm)
24" (61 cm) front bust
biceps 20" (51 cm)
19" (48.5 cm) sleeve length
10" (25.5 cm) wrist

**For the bust:** If your armhole depth is deep enough not to restrict movement, you can make the body circumference fairly snug to your torso—within 4-8" (10-20.5 cm) of your torso circumference—without problems. (It can also be larger, if you like.)

Once you decide on a total bust/chest circumference, you can either break it in half equally, front and back, or unevenly (this is appropriate if you've got a larger bust). For the latter, add your desired ease to your upper torso, then divide by 2—this is the back bust measurement. Then take your desired total circumference and subtract the back bust—this is your front bust measurement.

Here's an example with my measurements: My upper torso is 38" (96.5 cm), and my desired ease in a drop-shoulder garment is 6" (15 cm); 44" (112 cm). Divide by 2, and my back bust is 22" (56 cm). If I want 4" (10 cm) of ease at the fullest part of my bust, which is 42" (106.5 cm), that means I want a total garment bust circumference of 46" (117 cm); subtracting my back bust of 22" (56 cm), I have a front bust of 24" (61 cm).

If your armhole depth *isn't* deep enough to allow for full movement, you'll need to make the body circumference of the sweater large enough to move the sleeve/body attachment point onto your arm.

My recommendation for finding your circumference is to enlist a friend's quick help. Hold your arms straight out to your sides and have your friend place the zero point of the measuring tape at the spot on your arm where you want the sleeves to attach—ideally at least 4" (10 cm) away from the shoulder joint. Have your friend measure straight across your arms and body to the mirror-image point on the

other side of your shoulder joint—this is the width of the front and back of your garment.

Here's a quick illustration:

In this case, there shouldn't be any need to distribute the width differently across the front and back, no matter who you are—there will be enough ease that you'll be significantly smaller than the sweater all around.

The **sleeve length** and **hem-to-armhole length** can be determined from your measurements; the **wrist** should probably have at least a few inches of ease in a traditional drop-shoulder pattern, just so the sleeve shape isn't excessively exaggerated.

This just leaves the **neck width** of your sweater. Typical neck widths range between 6" (15 cm) on the narrow end and 12" (30.5 cm) on the wider end. You can hold a measuring tape up to your own neck, or measure the neck width of a favorite top, to get a sense of whether you're on the right track. (Just remember that any trim you add to the neckline will narrow it from this number!)

### Once you've filled in your schematic, you're ready to draft your pattern.

Let's follow this process with an example—an average-width crew-neck pullover, without waist shaping, for my measurements. (For this example, I'll stick with a traditional, roomy-armed drop-shoulder sweater, worked in pieces from the bottom up.)

Here's my personal schematic for this sweater:

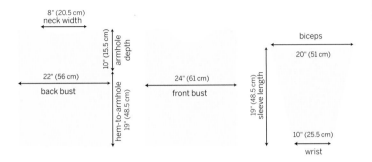

Next, turn the measurements into stitch and row counts based on your gauge. Let's assume I'm working at a fairly typical gauge of 5 stitches and 7 rows to 1" (2.5 cm):

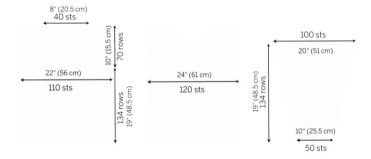

The body pieces of my sweater are extremely simple, aside from neck shaping (which you can read about on page 120): I cast on the appropriate number of stitches and work straight to the neck shaping. There are no further construction-specific calculations to be made.

For the sleeves, I'll need to use the Master Shaping Formula from page 19. I need to go from 50 sts at the cast-on to 100 sts at the top of the sleeve—adding a total of 50 stitches.

Since each increase row will add 2 stitches, I need to work 25 increase rows in my sleeve.

The sleeve is a total of 134 rows long, but I'll need some straight rows—a couple of inches (5 cm or so) of ribbing at the bottom, and 1" (2.5 cm) of straight at the top—leaving me with around 112 rows in which to work my shaping.

Using the Master Shaping Formula, 112 / 25 = 4.48, which rounds down to 4.

Turning that into instructions, I'll cast on 50 stitches, work my ribbing and then a few rows straight in Stockinette, then work an increase row every 4 rows, 25 times. After I reach 100 sts, I'll work straight until my sleeve measures the desired 19" (48 cm) and then bind off all stitches.

### FURTHER THINKING: STRANGER SHAPES

Now that we've tackled a basic, traditional drop shoulder, it's worth exploring some variations. If I wanted to create a slimmer-sleeved version for myself, the approach I outline above would result in me drafting a pattern that measures 26" (66 cm) across the body, for a total body circumference of 52" (132 cm)—which is a lot of ease for my frame!

Personally, that kind of garment sounds fairly appealing, but assume for a moment that I'd like to have my cake and eat it, too—a closer-to-the-body garment with slimmer sleeves. If I'm willing to play with the shape of my drop-shoulder sweater, I can probably make it work. I've got three main options:

- Arguably, the easiest approach is to work the garment in one piece, without shoulder seams. If there's no seam to tear, as in the "all-in-one" sketch below, you can make the sweater's armhole closer to your body without worry. There's a limit to this approach—you probably can't make the armhole any shallower than your set-in-sleeve-armhole depth—and you should curve the underarm a bit, but for many people this is a nice sweet spot.

- Another approach is to increase the width of the body of the garment at the top, curving the "armholes" of the sweater away from your shoulder joint. Adding a few inches of width over the course of the "armhole" is feasible here, and lets you remove the corresponding number of inches from the bust circumference of the sweater. Note that this will also create something of a dolman-sleeve structure, though it won't be nearly as exaggerated as in the all-in-one case, since the sharpest curve will lie at the shoulder rather than underarm.

- Finally, you could use a hybrid approach: Leave all the seams in place (sometimes desirable, both from a structural standpoint and a visual standpoint) and make the body somewhat of a T shape. This approach will need to stay fairly generously sized, but again, it is probably safe to make it a bit more snug than you otherwise could.

Below is a quick comparison of how these options will look as they come off your needles:

They'll all make lovely sweaters, if you're excited about the resulting shape. I encourage you to pull a few garments out of your closet, or go to a local shop, and really look at the way the armholes are shaped to begin to get a sense of what you love.

I've written the following basic, straight-sided sweaters in three gauges and twelve sizes, so if you'd prefer not to draft your own drop-shoulder patterns, you've got a great starting point. (They are all modified drop-shoulder patterns with traditional-size armholes.) I've shown these with recommended yarns, but I encourage you to experiment, too! Just keep the fabric recommendations on pages 125–126 in mind as you plan your garment. If you'd like a worksheet to help you tame the numbers as you knit, you can download one from my website.

All in one          Widening body          Slimmer-armed

# Basic Pullover: Drop-Shoulder Construction

A great crew-neck drop-shoulder pullover is one of the simplest, and loveliest, sweaters around. I like to keep things light and airy with this style, so I've chosen to work this one in a luxurious silk-mohair mix. I've also swatched a drapey hemp blend and a lusciously lightweight alpaca to give you a similar feel across the gauges.

This unisex garment is worked in pieces from the bottom up, and then seamed for stability. No waist shaping is included in any of the basic patterns, but should you choose to add some, please see pages 113–115 for details.

## FINISHED MEASUREMENTS

**SPORT:** 36½ (39½, 40½, 43½, 44½, 47½, 48½, 51½, 54, 56½, 60½, 64½)" [92.5 (100.5, 103, 110.5, 113, 120.5, 123, 131, 137, 143.5, 153.5, 164) cm] chest

**WORSTED:** 37½ (39, 41, 42½, 45½, 47, 49, 50½, 53½, 57, 61½, 65)" [95.5 (99, 104, 108, 115.5, 119.5, 124.5, 128.5, 136, 145, 156, 165) cm] chest

**ARAN:** 37 (39, 41, 43, 45, 47, 49, 51, 53, 57, 61, 65)" [94 (99, 104, 109, 114.5, 119.5, 124.5, 129.5, 134.5, 145, 155, 165) cm] chest

*Note: Sweater is intended to be worn with 4–8" (10–20.5 cm) ease in the bust; shown in worsted weight yarn and size 41" (104 cm).*

## YARN

**SPORT:** Elsebeth Lavold Hempathy [40% hemp / 40% cotton / 20% modal; 153 yards (140 meters) / 50 grams]: 9 (10, 10, 11, 12, 12, 13, 13, 14, 15, 16, 16) balls #059 Spring Grass

**WORSTED:** *(Note: Worsted weight is worked throughout with 1 strand each of A and B held together.)* Shibui Maai [70% superbaby alpaca / 30% fine merino; 175 yards (160 meters) / 50 grams]: 7 (7, 7, 7, 8, 8, 9, 9, 9, 10, 11, 11) hanks #2032 Field (A); Shibui Silk Cloud [60% kid mohair / 40% silk; 330 yards (300 meters) / 25 grams]: 4 (4, 4, 4, 4, 5, 5, 5, 5, 6, 6) hanks #2032 Field (B)

**ARAN:** Lana Grossa Alta Moda Alpaca [90% baby alpaca / 5% merino / 5% polyamide; 155 yards (141 meters) / 50 grams]: 8 (9, 10, 10, 11, 12, 12, 12, 13, 14, 15, 16) balls #49 Loden Mottled

## NEEDLES

**SPORT:** One pair straight needles and one 24" (60 cm) long circular needle (for Neckband) size US 4 (3.5 mm)

**WORSTED:** One pair straight needles and one 24" (60 cm) long circular needle (for Neckband) size US 8 (5 mm)

**ARAN:** One pair straight needles and one 24" (60 cm) long circular needle (for Neckband) size US 9 (5.5 mm)

Change needle size if necessary to obtain correct gauge.

## NOTIONS

Stitch markers

## GAUGE

**SPORT:** 24 sts and 36 rows = 4" (10 cm) in St st

**WORSTED:** 20 sts and 28 rows = 4" (10 cm) in St st with 1 strand each of A and B held together

**ARAN:** 16 sts and 24 rows = 4" (10 cm) in St st

## NOTES

If your size gives the number 0 for a particular instruction, skip that instruction and proceed to the next instruction.

Unless otherwise specified, decreases should be worked to match the slant of the edge being shaped, as follows: For left-slanting edges: On RS rows, k2, ssk, knit to end; on WS rows, p2, p2tog, purl to end. For right-slanting edges: On RS rows, knit to last 4 sts, k2tog, k2; on WS rows, purl to last 4 sts, ssp, p2. Increases should also be worked to match the slant of the edge being shaped, as follows: For right-slanting edges: On RS rows, k1, M1R, knit to end; on WS rows, p1, M1PR, purl to end. For left-slanting edges: On RS rows, knit to last st, M1L, k1; on WS rows, p1, M1PL, purl to end.

# BACK

*Note: For worsted weight, work with 1 strand each of A and B held together.*

CO

| | | | | | | | | | | | | |
|---|---|---|---|---|---|---|---|---|---|---|---|---|
| SPORT | 110 | 118 | 122 | 130 | 134 | 142 | 146 | 154 | 162 | 170 | 182 | 194 |
| WORSTED | 94 | 98 | 102 | 106 | 114 | 118 | 122 | 126 | 134 | 142 | 154 | 162 |
| ARAN | 74 | 78 | 82 | 86 | 90 | 94 | 98 | 102 | 106 | 114 | 122 | 130 |

sts.

Begin 2x2 Rib Flat; work even until piece measures 2¼" (5.5 cm), ending with a WS row.

Change to St st; work even until piece measures 16 (16, 16, 16½, 16½, 16¾, 16½, 16¾, 16½, 16, 16, 16)" [40.5 (40.5, 40.5, 42, 42, 42.5, 42, 42.5, 42, 40.5, 40.5, 40.5) cm] from the beginning, ending with a WS row.

## SHAPE ARMHOLES

BO

| | |
|---|---|
| SPORT | 6 |
| WORSTED | 4 |
| ARAN | 3 |

sts at the beginning of the next 2 rows.

| | | | | | | | | | | | | |
|---|---|---|---|---|---|---|---|---|---|---|---|---|
| SPORT | 98 | 106 | 110 | 118 | 122 | 130 | 134 | 142 | 150 | 158 | 170 | 182 |
| WORSTED | 86 | 90 | 94 | 98 | 106 | 110 | 114 | 118 | 126 | 134 | 146 | 154 |
| ARAN | 68 | 72 | 76 | 80 | 84 | 88 | 92 | 96 | 100 | 108 | 116 | 124 |

sts remain.

Work even until armholes measure 7½ (8, 8½, 9, 9½, 9½, 10, 10, 10½, 11, 11½, 11½)" [19 (20.5, 21.5, 23, 24, 24, 25.5, 25.5, 26.5, 28, 29, 29) cm], ending with a WS row.

## SHAPE NECK

**NEXT ROW (RS):** Knit

| | | | | | | | | | | | | |
|---|---|---|---|---|---|---|---|---|---|---|---|---|
| SPORT | 30 | 34 | 35 | 38 | 39 | 43 | 44 | 46 | 50 | 54 | 60 | 65 |
| WORSTED | 28 | 29 | 30 | 32 | 35 | 37 | 38 | 39 | 43 | 46 | 52 | 55 |
| ARAN | 22 | 24 | 25 | 27 | 28 | 30 | 31 | 32 | 34 | 38 | 42 | 45 |

sts, join a second ball of yarn, BO center

| | | | | | | | | | | | | |
|---|---|---|---|---|---|---|---|---|---|---|---|---|
| SPORT | 38 | 38 | 40 | 42 | 44 | 44 | 46 | 50 | 50 | 50 | 50 | 52 |
| WORSTED | 30 | 32 | 34 | 34 | 36 | 36 | 38 | 40 | 40 | 42 | 42 | 44 |
| ARAN | 24 | 24 | 26 | 26 | 28 | 28 | 30 | 32 | 32 | 32 | 32 | 34 |

sts, knit to end.

Working both sides at the same time, decrease 1 st at each neck edge every RS row twice.

| | | | | | | | | | | | | |
|---|---|---|---|---|---|---|---|---|---|---|---|---|
| SPORT | 28 | 32 | 33 | 36 | 37 | 41 | 42 | 44 | 48 | 52 | 58 | 63 |
| WORSTED | 26 | 27 | 28 | 30 | 33 | 35 | 36 | 37 | 41 | 44 | 50 | 53 |
| ARAN | 20 | 22 | 23 | 25 | 26 | 28 | 29 | 30 | 32 | 36 | 40 | 43 |

sts remain.

Work even until armholes measure 8½ (9, 9½, 10, 10½, 10½, 11, 11, 11½, 12, 12½, 12½)" [21.5 (23, 24, 25.5, 26.5, 26.5, 28, 28, 29, 30.5, 32, 32) cm], ending with a WS row.

## SHAPE SHOULDERS

BO

| | | | | | | | | | | | | |
|---|---|---|---|---|---|---|---|---|---|---|---|---|
| SPORT | 14 | 16 | 17 | 18 | 19 | 21 | 21 | 22 | 24 | 26 | 29 | 32 |
| WORSTED | 13 | 14 | 14 | 15 | 17 | 18 | 18 | 19 | 21 | 22 | 25 | 27 |
| ARAN | 10 | 11 | 12 | 13 | 13 | 14 | 15 | 15 | 16 | 18 | 20 | 22 |

sts at each armhole edge once, then BO

| | | | | | | | | | | | |
|---|---|---|---|---|---|---|---|---|---|---|---|
| SPORT | 14 | 16 | 16 | 18 | 18 | 20 | 21 | 22 | 24 | 26 | 29 | 31 |
| WORSTED | 13 | 13 | 14 | 15 | 16 | 17 | 18 | 18 | 20 | 22 | 25 | 26 |
| ARAN | 10 | 11 | 11 | 12 | 13 | 14 | 14 | 15 | 16 | 18 | 20 | 21 |

sts once.

## FRONT

Work as for Back until armholes measure 5¾ (6¼, 6¾, 7¼, 7¾, 7¾, 8¼, 8¼, 8¾, 9¼, 9¾, 9¾)" [14.5 (16, 17, 18.5, 19.5, 19.5, 21, 21, 22, 23.5, 25, 25) cm], ending with a WS row.

| | | | | | | | | | | | |
|---|---|---|---|---|---|---|---|---|---|---|---|
| SPORT | 98 | 106 | 110 | 118 | 122 | 130 | 134 | 142 | 150 | 158 | 170 | 182 |
| WORSTED | 86 | 90 | 94 | 98 | 106 | 110 | 114 | 118 | 126 | 134 | 146 | 154 |
| ARAN | 68 | 72 | 76 | 80 | 84 | 88 | 92 | 96 | 100 | 108 | 116 | 124 |

sts remain after armhole shaping is complete.

### SHAPE NECK
**NEXT ROW (RS):** Knit

| | | | | | | | | | | | |
|---|---|---|---|---|---|---|---|---|---|---|---|
| SPORT | 39 | 43 | 45 | 48 | 50 | 54 | 55 | 58 | 62 | 66 | 72 | 78 |
| WORSTED | 35 | 36 | 38 | 40 | 44 | 46 | 47 | 49 | 53 | 56 | 62 | 66 |
| ARAN | 27 | 29 | 31 | 33 | 34 | 36 | 38 | 39 | 41 | 45 | 49 | 53 |

sts, join a second ball of yarn, BO center

| | | | | | | | | | | | |
|---|---|---|---|---|---|---|---|---|---|---|---|
| SPORT | 20 | 20 | 20 | 22 | 22 | 22 | 24 | 26 | 26 | 26 | 26 | 26 |
| WORSTED | 16 | 18 | 18 | 18 | 18 | 18 | 20 | 20 | 20 | 22 | 22 | 22 |
| ARAN | 14 | 14 | 14 | 14 | 16 | 16 | 16 | 18 | 18 | 18 | 18 | 18 |

sts, knit to end.

Working both sides at the same time, decrease 1 st at each neck edge every row

| | | | | | | | | | | | |
|---|---|---|---|---|---|---|---|---|---|---|---|
| SPORT | 7 | 7 | 8 | 8 | 8 | 8 | 8 | 9 | 9 | 9 | 9 | 9 |
| WORSTED | 6 | 6 | 6 | 6 | 7 | 7 | 7 | 8 | 8 | 8 | 8 | 8 |
| ARAN | 5 | 5 | 5 | 5 | 5 | 5 | 6 | 6 | 6 | 6 | 6 | 6 |

times, then every RS row

| | | | | | | | | | | | |
|---|---|---|---|---|---|---|---|---|---|---|---|
| SPORT | 4 | 4 | 4 | 4 | 5 | 5 | 5 | 5 | 5 | 5 | 5 | 6 |
| WORSTED | 3 | 3 | 4 | 4 | 4 | 4 | 4 | 4 | 4 | 4 | 4 | 5 |
| ARAN | 2 | 2 | 3 | 3 | 3 | 3 | 3 | 3 | 3 | 3 | 3 | 4 |

times.

| | | | | | | | | | | | |
|---|---|---|---|---|---|---|---|---|---|---|---|
| SPORT | 28 | 32 | 33 | 36 | 37 | 41 | 42 | 44 | 48 | 52 | 58 | 63 |
| WORSTED | 26 | 27 | 28 | 30 | 33 | 35 | 36 | 37 | 41 | 44 | 50 | 53 |
| ARAN | 20 | 22 | 23 | 25 | 26 | 28 | 29 | 30 | 32 | 36 | 40 | 43 |

sts remain each shoulder.

Work even until armholes measure 8½ (9, 9½, 10, 10½, 10½, 11, 11, 11½, 12, 12½, 12½)" [21.5 (23, 24, 25.5, 26.5, 26.5, 28, 28, 29, 30.5, 32, 32) cm], ending with a WS row.

### SHAPE SHOULDERS
BO

| | | | | | | | | | | | |
|---|---|---|---|---|---|---|---|---|---|---|---|
| SPORT | 14 | 16 | 17 | 18 | 19 | 21 | 21 | 22 | 24 | 26 | 29 | 32 |
| WORSTED | 13 | 14 | 14 | 15 | 17 | 18 | 18 | 19 | 21 | 22 | 25 | 27 |
| ARAN | 10 | 11 | 12 | 13 | 13 | 14 | 15 | 15 | 16 | 18 | 20 | 22 |

sts at each armhole edge once, then BO

| | | | | | | | | | | | |
|---|---|---|---|---|---|---|---|---|---|---|---|
| SPORT | 14 | 16 | 16 | 18 | 18 | 20 | 21 | 22 | 24 | 26 | 29 | 31 |
| WORSTED | 13 | 13 | 14 | 15 | 16 | 17 | 18 | 18 | 20 | 22 | 25 | 26 |
| ARAN | 10 | 11 | 11 | 12 | 13 | 14 | 14 | 15 | 16 | 18 | 20 | 21 |

sts once.

## SLEEVES

*Note: For worsted weight, work with 1 strand each of A and B held together.*

CO

| | | | | | | | | | | | | |
|---|---|---|---|---|---|---|---|---|---|---|---|---|
| SPORT | 50 | 54 | 54 | 54 | 54 | 58 | 58 | 58 | 62 | 66 | 70 | 70 |
| WORSTED | 42 | 46 | 46 | 46 | 46 | 46 | 50 | 50 | 54 | 54 | 58 | 58 |
| ARAN | 34 | 38 | 38 | 38 | 38 | 38 | 38 | 42 | 42 | 46 | 46 | 50 |

sts. Begin 2x2 Rib Flat; work even until piece measures 3" (7.5 cm), ending with a WS row.

Change to St st; work 2 rows even.

### SHAPE SLEEVE

Beginning on the next RS row, increase 1 st each side every

| | | | | | | | | | | | | |
|---|---|---|---|---|---|---|---|---|---|---|---|---|
| SPORT | 4 | 4 | 4 | 3 | 3 | 3 | 3 | 3 | 3 | 3 | 3 | 3 |
| WORSTED | 4 | 4 | 4 | 3 | 3 | 3 | 3 | 3 | 3 | 3 | 3 | 3 |
| ARAN | 4 | 4 | 4 | 4 | 3 | 3 | 3 | 3 | 3 | 3 | 3 | 3 |

rows a total of

| | | | | | | | | | | | | |
|---|---|---|---|---|---|---|---|---|---|---|---|---|
| SPORT | 26 | 27 | 30 | 33 | 36 | 34 | 37 | 37 | 38 | 39 | 40 | 40 |
| WORSTED | 22 | 22 | 25 | 27 | 30 | 30 | 30 | 30 | 31 | 33 | 34 | 34 |
| ARAN | 17 | 17 | 19 | 21 | 23 | 23 | 25 | 23 | 25 | 25 | 27 | 25 |

times.

| | | | | | | | | | | | | |
|---|---|---|---|---|---|---|---|---|---|---|---|---|
| SPORT | 102 | 108 | 114 | 120 | 126 | 126 | 132 | 132 | 138 | 144 | 150 | 150 |
| WORSTED | 86 | 90 | 96 | 100 | 106 | 106 | 110 | 110 | 116 | 120 | 126 | 126 |
| ARAN | 68 | 72 | 76 | 80 | 84 | 84 | 88 | 88 | 92 | 96 | 100 | 100 |

sts.

Work even until piece measures 17½ (18, 18, 18, 18½, 18½, 18½, 18½, 18½, 19, 19¼, 19¼)" [44.5 (45.5, 45.5, 45.5, 47, 47, 47, 47, 47, 48.5, 49, 49) cm] from the beginning, ending with a WS row. BO all sts.

## FINISHING

Block pieces as desired. Sew shoulder seams. Sew in Sleeves, sewing BO edge at top of Sleeve to straight edge of armhole and upper side edges of Sleeve to BO edges of armhole; sew side and Sleeve seams.

### NECKBAND

With RS facing, using circular needle and beginning at right shoulder, pick up and knit approximately 1 st in each BO st, 2 sts for every 3 rows along vertical edges, and 3 sts for every 4 rows along diagonal edges. You will pick up approximately

| | | | | | | | | | | | | |
|---|---|---|---|---|---|---|---|---|---|---|---|---|
| SPORT | 112 | 112 | 116 | 120 | 120 | 120 | 124 | 132 | 132 | 132 | 132 | 136 |
| WORSTED | 92 | 96 | 100 | 100 | 100 | 100 | 104 | 108 | 108 | 112 | 112 | 116 |
| ARAN | 80 | 80 | 80 | 80 | 84 | 84 | 88 | 92 | 92 | 92 | 92 | 96 |

sts. *Note: Exact st count is not essential, but be sure to end with a multiple of 4 sts for ribbing to work out evenly.* Join for working in the rnd; pm for beginning of rnd. Begin 2x2 Rib in the Rnd; work even for ¾" (2 cm). BO all sts in pattern.

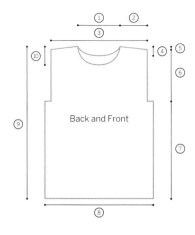

1   6¾ (7¼, 7½, 7½, 8, 8, 8½, 8¾, 8¾, 9¼, 9¼, 9½)"
    17 (18.5, 19, 19, 20.5, 20.5, 21.5, 22, 22, 23.5, 23.5, 24) cm

2   5¼ (5½, 5½, 6, 6½, 7, 7¼, 7½, 8¼, 8¾, 10, 10½)"
    13.5 (14, 14, 15, 16.5, 18, 18.5, 19, 21, 22, 25.5, 26.5) cm

3   17¼ (18, 18¾, 19½, 21¼, 22, 22¾, 23½, 25¼, 26¾, 29¼, 30¾)"
    44 (45.5, 47.5, 49.5, 54, 56, 58, 59.5, 64, 68, 74.5, 78) cm

4   1½"
    4 cm

5   ½"
    1.5 cm

6   8½ (9, 9½, 10, 10½, 10½, 11, 11, 11½, 12, 12½, 12½)"
    21.5 (23, 24, 25.5, 26.5, 26.5, 28, 28, 29, 30.5, 32, 32) cm

7   16 (16, 16, 16½, 16½, 16¾, 16½, 16¾, 16½, 16, 16, 16)"
    40.5 (40.5, 40.5, 42, 42, 42.5, 42, 42.5, 42, 40.5, 40.5, 40.5) cm

8   18¾ (19½, 20½, 21¼, 22¾, 23½, 24½, 25¼, 26¾, 28½, 30¾, 32½)"
    47.5 (49.5, 52, 54, 58, 59.5, 62, 64, 68, 72.5, 78, 82.5) cm

9   25 (25½, 26, 27, 27½, 27¾, 28, 28¼, 28½, 28½, 29, 29)"
    63.5 (65, 66, 68.5, 70, 70.5, 71, 72, 72.5, 72.5, 73.5, 73.5) cm

10  3¼"
    8.5 cm

11  17¼ (18, 19¼, 20, 21¼, 21¼, 22, 22, 23¼, 24, 25¼, 25¼)"
    44 (45.5, 49, 51, 54, 54, 56, 56, 59, 61, 64, 64) cm

12  17½ (18, 18, 18, 18½, 18½, 18½, 18½, 18½, 19, 19¼, 19¼)"
    44.5 (45.5, 45.5, 45.5, 47, 47, 47, 47, 47, 48.5, 49, 49) cm

13  8½ (9¼, 9¼, 9¼, 9¼, 9¼, 10, 10, 10¾, 10¾, 11½, 11½)"
    21.5 (23.5, 23.5, 23.5, 23.5, 23.5, 25.5, 25.5, 27.5, 27.5, 29, 29) cm

1   7 (7, 7½, 7½, 8, 8, 8½, 9, 9, 9, 9, 9½)"
    18 (18, 19, 19, 20.5, 20.5, 21.5, 23, 23, 23, 23, 24) cm

2   5 (5½, 5¾, 6¼, 6½, 7, 7¼, 7½, 8, 9, 10, 10¾)"
    12.5 (14, 14.5, 16, 16.5, 18, 18.5, 19, 20.5, 23, 25.5, 27.5) cm

3   17¼ (18, 18¾, 19½, 21¼, 22, 22¾, 23½, 25¼, 26¾, 29¼, 30¾)"
    44 (45.5, 47.5, 49.5, 54, 56, 58, 59.5, 64, 68, 74.5, 78) cm

4   1½"
    4 cm

5   ½"
    1.5 cm

6   8½ (9, 9½, 10, 10½, 10½, 11, 11, 11½, 12, 12½, 12½)"
    21.5 (23, 24, 25.5, 26.5, 26.5, 28, 28, 29, 30.5, 32, 32) cm

7   16 (16, 16, 16½, 16½, 16¾, 16½, 16¾, 16½, 16, 16, 16)"
    40.5 (40.5, 40.5, 42, 42, 42.5, 42, 42.5, 42, 40.5, 40.5, 40.5) cm

8   18¼ (19¾, 20¼, 21¾, 22¼, 23¾, 24¼, 25¾, 26¼, 28¼, 30¼, 32¼)"
    46.5 (50, 51.5, 55, 56.5, 60.5, 61.5, 65.5, 66.5, 72, 77, 82) cm

9   25 (25½, 26, 27, 27½, 27¾, 28, 28¼, 28½, 28½, 29, 29)"
    63.5 (65, 66, 68.5, 70, 70.5, 71, 72, 72.5, 72.5, 73.5, 73.5) cm

10  3¼"
    8.5 cm

11  17 (18, 19, 20, 21, 21, 22, 22, 23, 24, 25, 25)"
    43 (45.5, 48.5, 51, 53.5, 53.5, 56, 56, 58.5, 61, 63.5, 63.5) cm

12  17½ (18, 18, 18, 18½, 18½, 18½, 18½, 18½, 19, 19¼, 19¼)"
    44.5 (45.5, 45.5, 45.5, 47, 47, 47, 47, 47, 48.5, 49, 49) cm

13  8¼ (9, 9, 9, 9, 9¾, 9¾, 9¾, 10¼, 11, 11¾, 11¾)"
    21 (23, 23, 23, 23, 25, 25, 25, 26, 28, 30, 30) cm

1   7 (7, 7½, 7½, 8, 8, 8½, 9, 9, 9, 9, 9½)"
    18 (18, 19, 19, 20.5, 20.5, 21.5, 23, 23, 23, 23, 24) cm

2   5 (5½, 5¾, 6¼, 6½, 7, 7¼, 7½, 8, 9, 10, 10¾)"
    12.5 (14, 14.5, 16, 16.5, 18, 18.5, 19, 20.5, 23, 25.5, 27.5) cm

3   17 (18, 19, 20, 21, 22, 23, 24, 25, 27, 29, 31)"
    43 (45.5, 48.5, 51, 53.5, 56, 58.5, 61, 63.5, 68.5, 73.5, 78.5) cm

4   1½"
    4 cm

5   ½"
    1.5 cm

6   8½ (9, 9½, 10, 10½, 10½, 11, 11, 11½, 12, 12½, 12½)"
    21.5 (23, 24, 25.5, 26.5, 26.5, 28, 28, 29, 30.5, 32, 32) cm

7   16 (16, 16, 16½, 16½, 16¾, 16½, 16¾, 16½, 16, 16, 16)"
    40.5 (40.5, 40.5, 42, 42, 42.5, 42, 42.5, 42, 40.5, 40.5, 40.5) cm

8   18½ (19½, 20½, 21½, 22½, 23½, 24½, 25½, 26½, 28½, 30½, 32½)"
    47 (49.5, 52, 54.5, 57, 59.5, 62, 65, 67.5, 72.5, 77.5, 82.5) cm

9   25 (25½, 26, 27, 27½, 27¾, 28, 28¼, 28½, 28½, 29, 29)"
    63.5 (65, 66, 68.5, 70, 70.5, 71, 72, 72.5, 72.5, 73.5, 73.5) cm

10  3¼"
    8.5 cm

11  17 (18, 19, 20, 21, 21, 22, 22, 23, 24, 25, 25)"
    43 (45.5, 48.5, 51, 53.5, 53.5, 56, 56, 58.5, 61, 63.5, 63.5) cm

12  17½ (18, 18, 18, 18½, 18½, 18½, 18½, 18½, 19, 19¼, 19¼)"
    44.5 (45.5, 45.5, 45.5, 47, 47, 47, 47, 47, 48.5, 49, 49) cm

13  8½ (9½, 9½, 9½, 9½, 9½, 9½, 10½, 10½, 11½, 11½, 12½)"
    21.5 (24, 24, 24, 24, 24, 24, 26.5, 26.5, 29, 29, 32) cm

# Basic Cardigan: Drop-Shoulder Construction

What could be more versatile than a deep-V-neck cardigan? Drop-shoulder cardigans still need drape, in my opinion, but they can handle a slightly stiffer fabric than a pullover. In addition to the light silk-wool yarn shown in the sample, I've chosen a dense wool-silk fingering yarn and an obscenely soft superwash hand-dyed yarn for this pattern.

This unisex garment is worked in pieces from the bottom up, and then seamed for stability. The Front Bands/Collar is then picked up and worked in one piece. No waist shaping is included in any of the basic patterns, but should you choose to add some, please see pages 113–115 for details.

### FINISHED MEASUREMENTS

**FINGERING:** 37¾ (39¾, 41¾, 43¾, 45¾, 47¾, 49¾, 51¾, 53¾, 57¾, 61¾, 65¾)" [96 (101, 106, 111, 116, 121.5, 126.5, 131.5, 136.5, 146.5, 157, 167) cm] chest, buttoned

**DK:** 37 (39¼, 41½, 43, 45¼, 48¼, 50¼, 53¼, 54, 57, 61¾, 65¼)" [94 (99.5, 105.5, 109, 115, 122.5, 127.5, 135.5, 137, 145, 157, 165.5) cm] chest, buttoned

**WORSTED:** 36½ (39¼, 41, 43¼, 45½, 47, 49½, 51¾, 55¼, 58½, 61½, 65½)" [92.5 (99.5, 104, 110, 115.5, 119.5, 125.5, 131.5, 140.5, 148.5, 156, 166.5) cm] chest, buttoned

*Note: Sweater is intended to be worn with 4–8" (10–20.5 cm) ease in the bust; shown in DK weight yarn and size 41½" (105.5 cm).*

### YARN

**FINGERING:** Quince and Co. Tern [75% American wool / 25% silk; 221 yards (202 meters) / 50 grams]: 9 (9, 10, 11, 11, 12, 12, 13, 13, 14, 16, 16) hanks Seaweed

**DK:** Elsebeth Lavold Silky Wool [45% wool / 35% silk / 20% nylon; 192 yards (175 meters) / 50 grams]: 7 (8, 8, 9, 9, 10, 10, 10, 11, 12, 13, 13) hanks #83 Sapling Green

**WORSTED:** indigodragonfly MerGoat Worsted [80% superwash merino / 10% cashmere / 10% nylon; 190 yards (174 meters) / 115 grams]: 7 (8, 8, 9, 9, 10, 10, 10, 11, 12, 13, 13) hanks Sage Fright

### NEEDLES

**FINGERING:** One pair straight needles and one 40" (100 cm) long circular needle (for Front Bands/Collar) size US 2 (2.75 mm)

**DK:** One pair straight needles and one 40" (100 cm) long circular needle (for Front Bands/Collar) size US 6 (4 mm)

**WORSTED:** One pair straight needles and one 40" (100 cm) long circular needle (for Front Bands/Collar) size US 7 (4.5 mm)

Change needle size if necessary to obtain correct gauge.

### NOTIONS

Stitch markers, seven ¾-inch (19-mm) buttons

### GAUGE

**FINGERING:** 32 sts and 40 rows = 4" (10 cm) in St st

**DK:** 22 sts and 31 rows = 4" (10 cm) in St st

**WORSTED:** 20 sts and 29 rows = 4" (10 cm) in St st

### NOTES

If your size gives the number 0 for a particular instruction, skip that instruction and proceed to the next instruction.

Unless otherwise specified, decreases should be worked to match the slant of the edge being shaped, as follows: For left-slanting edges: On RS rows, k2, ssk, knit to end; on WS rows, p2, p2tog, purl to end. For right-slanting edges: On RS rows, knit to last 4 sts, k2tog, k2; on WS rows, purl to last 4 sts, ssp, p2. Increases should also be worked to match the slant of the edge being shaped, as follows: For right-slanting edges: On RS rows, k1, M1R, knit to end; on WS rows, p1, M1PR, purl to end. For left-slanting edges: On RS rows, knit to last st, M1L, k1; on WS rows, p1, M1PL, purl to end.

# BACK

CO

| | | | | | | | | | | | | |
|---|---|---|---|---|---|---|---|---|---|---|---|---|
| **FINGERING** | 146 | 154 | 162 | 170 | 178 | 186 | 194 | 202 | 210 | 226 | 242 | 258 |
| **DK** | 102 | 106 | 110 | 118 | 122 | 130 | 134 | 142 | 146 | 154 | 166 | 178 |
| **WORSTED** | 90 | 94 | 102 | 106 | 110 | 118 | 122 | 126 | 134 | 142 | 150 | 162 |

sts.

Begin 2x2 Rib Flat; work even until piece measures 2¼" (5.5 cm), ending with a WS row.

Change to St st; work even until piece measures 16 (16, 16½, 16½, 17, 17, 17, 17½, 17½, 17½, 17½, 18)" [40.5 (40.5, 42, 42, 43, 43, 43, 44.5, 44.5, 44.5, 44.5, 45.5) cm] from the beginning, ending with a WS row.

## SHAPE ARMHOLES

BO

| | |
|---|---|
| **FINGERING** | 6 |
| **DK** | 4 |
| **WORSTED** | 4 |

sts at the beginning of the next 2 rows.

| | | | | | | | | | | | | |
|---|---|---|---|---|---|---|---|---|---|---|---|---|
| **FINGERING** | 134 | 142 | 150 | 158 | 166 | 174 | 182 | 190 | 198 | 214 | 230 | 246 |
| **DK** | 94 | 98 | 102 | 110 | 114 | 122 | 126 | 134 | 138 | 146 | 158 | 170 |
| **WORSTED** | 82 | 86 | 94 | 98 | 102 | 110 | 114 | 118 | 126 | 134 | 142 | 154 |

sts remain.

Work even until armholes measure 7½ (8, 8½, 9, 9½, 9½, 10, 10, 10½, 11, 11½, 11½)" [19 (20.5, 21.5, 23, 24, 24, 25.5, 25.5, 26.5, 28, 29, 29) cm], ending with a WS row.

## SHAPE NECK

**NEXT ROW (RS):** Knit

| | | | | | | | | | | | | |
|---|---|---|---|---|---|---|---|---|---|---|---|---|
| **FINGERING** | 42 | 45 | 48 | 51 | 54 | 57 | 60 | 62 | 66 | 73 | 81 | 88 |
| **DK** | 30 | 31 | 33 | 36 | 37 | 41 | 42 | 44 | 46 | 50 | 56 | 61 |
| **WORSTED** | 26 | 27 | 30 | 32 | 33 | 37 | 38 | 39 | 43 | 46 | 50 | 55 |

sts, join a second ball of yarn, BO center

| | | | | | | | | | | | | |
|---|---|---|---|---|---|---|---|---|---|---|---|---|
| **FINGERING** | 50 | 52 | 54 | 56 | 58 | 60 | 62 | 66 | 66 | 68 | 68 | 70 |
| **DK** | 34 | 36 | 36 | 38 | 40 | 40 | 42 | 46 | 46 | 46 | 46 | 48 |
| **WORSTED** | 30 | 32 | 34 | 34 | 36 | 36 | 38 | 40 | 40 | 42 | 42 | 44 |

sts, knit to end.

Working both sides at the same time, decrease 1 st at each neck edge every RS row twice.

| | | | | | | | | | | | | |
|---|---|---|---|---|---|---|---|---|---|---|---|---|
| **FINGERING** | 40 | 43 | 46 | 49 | 52 | 55 | 58 | 60 | 64 | 71 | 79 | 86 |
| **DK** | 28 | 29 | 31 | 34 | 35 | 39 | 40 | 42 | 44 | 48 | 54 | 59 |
| **WORSTED** | 24 | 25 | 28 | 30 | 31 | 35 | 36 | 37 | 41 | 44 | 48 | 53 |

sts for shoulder.

Work even until armholes measure 8½ (9, 9½, 10, 10½, 10½, 11, 11, 11½, 12, 12½, 12½)" [21.5 (23, 24, 25.5, 26.5, 26.5, 28, 28, 29, 30.5, 32, 32) cm], ending with a WS row.

## SHAPE SHOULDERS

BO

| | | | | | | | | | | | | |
|---|---|---|---|---|---|---|---|---|---|---|---|---|
| **FINGERING** | 20 | 22 | 23 | 25 | 26 | 28 | 29 | 30 | 32 | 36 | 40 | 43 |
| **DK** | 14 | 15 | 16 | 17 | 18 | 20 | 20 | 21 | 22 | 24 | 27 | 30 |
| **WORSTED** | 12 | 13 | 14 | 15 | 16 | 18 | 18 | 19 | 21 | 22 | 24 | 27 |

sts at each armhole edge once, then

| | | | | | | | | | | | | |
|---|---|---|---|---|---|---|---|---|---|---|---|---|
| FINGERING | 20 | 21 | 23 | 24 | 26 | 27 | 29 | 30 | 32 | 35 | 39 | 43 |
| DK | 14 | 14 | 15 | 17 | 17 | 19 | 20 | 21 | 22 | 24 | 27 | 29 |
| WORSTED | 12 | 12 | 14 | 15 | 15 | 17 | 18 | 18 | 20 | 22 | 24 | 26 |

sts once.

## LEFT AND RIGHT FRONTS

CO

| | | | | | | | | | | | | |
|---|---|---|---|---|---|---|---|---|---|---|---|---|
| FINGERING | 71 | 75 | 79 | 83 | 87 | 91 | 95 | 99 | 103 | 111 | 119 | 127 |
| DK | 47 | 51 | 55 | 55 | 59 | 63 | 67 | 71 | 71 | 75 | 83 | 87 |
| WORSTED | 43 | 47 | 47 | 51 | 55 | 55 | 59 | 63 | 67 | 71 | 75 | 79 |

sts.

### LEFT FRONT:

**ROW 1 (RS):** *K2, p2; repeat from * to last 3 sts, k3.
**ROW 2:** P3, *k2, p2; repeat from * to end.

### RIGHT FRONT:

**ROW 1 (RS):** K3, *p2, k2; repeat from * to end.
**ROW 2:** *P2, k2; repeat from * to last 3 sts, p3.

### BOTH FRONTS:

Work even until piece measures 2¼" (5.5 cm), ending with a WS row.

Change to St st; work even until piece measures 16 (16, 16½, 16½, 17, 17, 17, 17½, 17½, 17½, 17½, 18)" [40.5 (40.5, 42, 42, 43, 43, 43, 44.5, 44.5, 44.5, 44.5, 45.5) cm] from the beginning, ending at the armhole edge.

### SHAPE ARMHOLE

BO

| | |
|---|---|
| FINGERING | 7 |
| DK | 5 |
| WORSTED | 5 |

sts at armhole edge once.

| | | | | | | | | | | | | |
|---|---|---|---|---|---|---|---|---|---|---|---|---|
| FINGERING | 64 | 68 | 72 | 76 | 80 | 84 | 88 | 92 | 96 | 104 | 112 | 120 |
| DK | 42 | 46 | 50 | 50 | 54 | 58 | 62 | 66 | 66 | 70 | 78 | 82 |
| WORSTED | 38 | 42 | 42 | 46 | 50 | 50 | 54 | 58 | 62 | 66 | 70 | 74 |

sts.

### LEFT FRONT:

Work 3 rows even.

### RIGHT FRONT:

Work 2 rows even.

### BOTH FRONTS:

Beginning on the next RS row, decrease 1 st at neck edge every

| | | | | | | | | | | | | |
|---|---|---|---|---|---|---|---|---|---|---|---|---|
| FINGERING | 3 | 3 | 3 | 3 | 3 | 3 | 3 | 3 | 3 | 3 | 3 | 3 |
| DK | 4 | 3 | 3 | 4 | 4 | 4 | 3 | 3 | 3 | 4 | 3 | 4 |
| WORSTED | 4 | 3 | 4 | 4 | 3 | 4 | 4 | 3 | 3 | 3 | 3 | 4 |

rows a total of

| | | | | | | | | | | | | |
|---|---|---|---|---|---|---|---|---|---|---|---|---|
| FINGERING | 24 | 25 | 26 | 27 | 28 | 29 | 30 | 32 | 32 | 33 | 33 | 34 |
| DK | 14 | 17 | 19 | 16 | 19 | 19 | 22 | 24 | 22 | 22 | 24 | 23 |
| WORSTED | 14 | 17 | 14 | 16 | 19 | 15 | 18 | 21 | 21 | 22 | 22 | 21 |

times.

| | | | | | | | | | | | | |
|---|---|---|---|---|---|---|---|---|---|---|---|---|
| FINGERING | 40 | 43 | 46 | 49 | 52 | 55 | 58 | 60 | 64 | 71 | 79 | 86 |
| DK | 28 | 29 | 31 | 34 | 35 | 39 | 40 | 42 | 44 | 48 | 54 | 59 |
| WORSTED | 24 | 25 | 28 | 30 | 31 | 35 | 36 | 37 | 41 | 44 | 48 | 53 |

sts remain.

Work even until armhole measures 8½ (9, 9½, 10, 10½, 10½, 11, 11, 11½, 12, 12½, 12½)" [21.5 (23, 24, 25.5, 26.5, 26.5, 28, 28, 29, 30.5, 32, 32) cm], ending at the armhole edge.

### SHAPE SHOULDER

BO

| | | | | | | | | | | | | |
|---|---|---|---|---|---|---|---|---|---|---|---|---|
| FINGERING | 20 | 22 | 23 | 25 | 26 | 28 | 29 | 30 | 32 | 36 | 40 | 43 |
| DK | 14 | 15 | 16 | 17 | 18 | 20 | 20 | 21 | 22 | 24 | 27 | 30 |
| WORSTED | 12 | 13 | 14 | 15 | 16 | 18 | 18 | 19 | 21 | 22 | 24 | 26 |

sts at armhole edge once, then

| | | | | | | | | | | | | |
|---|---|---|---|---|---|---|---|---|---|---|---|---|
| FINGERING | 20 | 21 | 23 | 24 | 26 | 27 | 29 | 30 | 32 | 35 | 39 | 43 |
| DK | 14 | 14 | 15 | 17 | 17 | 19 | 20 | 21 | 22 | 24 | 27 | 29 |
| WORSTED | 12 | 12 | 14 | 15 | 15 | 17 | 18 | 18 | 20 | 22 | 24 | 26 |

sts once.

## SLEEVES

CO

| | | | | | | | | | | | | |
|---|---|---|---|---|---|---|---|---|---|---|---|---|
| FINGERING | 66 | 70 | 70 | 74 | 74 | 74 | 78 | 78 | 82 | 86 | 94 | 94 |
| DK | 46 | 50 | 50 | 50 | 50 | 50 | 54 | 54 | 58 | 58 | 62 | 66 |
| WORSTED | 42 | 46 | 46 | 46 | 46 | 46 | 50 | 50 | 54 | 54 | 58 | 58 |

sts.

Begin 2x2 Rib Flat; work even until piece measures 3" (7.5 cm), ending with a WS row.

Change to St st; work 2 rows even.

### SHAPE SLEEVE

Beginning on the next RS row, increase 1 st each side every

| | | | | | | | | | | | | |
|---|---|---|---|---|---|---|---|---|---|---|---|---|
| FINGERING | 3 | 3 | 4 | 3 | 3 | 3 | 2 | 2 | 2 | 2 | 2 | 2 |
| DK | 4 | 4 | 4 | 3 | 3 | 3 | 3 | 3 | 3 | 3 | 3 | 3 |
| WORSTED | 4 | 4 | 4 | 3 | 3 | 3 | 3 | 3 | 3 | 3 | 3 | 3 |

rows a total of

| | | | | | | | | | | | | |
|---|---|---|---|---|---|---|---|---|---|---|---|---|
| FINGERING | 35 | 37 | 41 | 43 | 47 | 47 | 49 | 49 | 51 | 53 | 53 | 53 |
| DK | 24 | 25 | 28 | 30 | 33 | 33 | 34 | 34 | 35 | 37 | 38 | 36 |
| WORSTED | 22 | 22 | 25 | 27 | 30 | 30 | 30 | 30 | 31 | 33 | 34 | 34 |

times.

| | | | | | | | | | | | | |
|---|---|---|---|---|---|---|---|---|---|---|---|---|
| FINGERING | 136 | 144 | 152 | 160 | 168 | 168 | 176 | 176 | 184 | 192 | 200 | 200 |
| DK | 94 | 100 | 106 | 110 | 116 | 116 | 122 | 122 | 128 | 132 | 138 | 138 |
| WORSTED | 86 | 90 | 96 | 100 | 106 | 106 | 110 | 110 | 116 | 120 | 126 | 126 |

sts.

Work even until piece measures 17½ (18, 18, 18, 18½, 18½, 18½, 18½, 18½, 19, 19¼, 19¼)" [44.5 (45.5, 45.5, 45.5, 47, 47, 47, 47, 47, 48.5, 49, 49) cm] from the beginning, ending with a WS row.

BO all sts.

## FINISHING

Block pieces as desired. Sew shoulder seams. Sew in Sleeves, sewing BO edge at top of Sleeve to straight edge of armhole and upper side edges of Sleeve to BO edges of armhole; sew side and Sleeve seams.

## FRONT BANDS/COLLAR

With RS facing, using circular needle, beginning at lower Right Front edge and ending at lower Left Front edge, pick up and knit approximately 1 st in each BO st, 2 sts for every 3 rows along vertical edges, and 3 sts for every 4 rows along diagonal edges. You will pick up approximately

| | | | | | | | | | | | | |
|---|---|---|---|---|---|---|---|---|---|---|---|---|
| FINGERING | 132 | 132 | 132 | 136 | 136 | 138 | 136 | 138 | 136 | 132 | 132 | 132 |
| DK | 91 | 91 | 91 | 94 | 94 | 95 | 94 | 95 | 94 | 91 | 91 | 91 |
| WORSTED | 83 | 83 | 83 | 85 | 85 | 87 | 85 | 87 | 85 | 83 | 83 | 83 |

sts along the straight edges of the Fronts,

| | | | | | | | | | | | | |
|---|---|---|---|---|---|---|---|---|---|---|---|---|
| FINGERING | 68 | 72 | 76 | 80 | 84 | 85 | 89 | 89 | 93 | 97 | 101 | 101 |
| DK | 46 | 49 | 53 | 54 | 58 | 58 | 61 | 62 | 64 | 66 | 70 | 69 |
| WORSTED | 42 | 45 | 47 | 50 | 53 | 52 | 55 | 56 | 58 | 61 | 63 | 63 |

sts along each shaped neck edge and

| | | | | | | | | | | | | |
|---|---|---|---|---|---|---|---|---|---|---|---|---|
| FINGERING | 74 | 74 | 78 | 78 | 82 | 84 | 84 | 88 | 88 | 92 | 92 | 92 |
| DK | 52 | 54 | 54 | 54 | 58 | 56 | 60 | 64 | 62 | 64 | 64 | 66 |
| WORSTED | 44 | 46 | 50 | 48 | 50 | 52 | 54 | 56 | 56 | 58 | 58 | 58 |

sts along Back neck. You will have approximately

| | | | | | | | | | | | | |
|---|---|---|---|---|---|---|---|---|---|---|---|---|
| FINGERING | 474 | 482 | 494 | 510 | 522 | 530 | 534 | 542 | 546 | 550 | 558 | 558 |
| DK | 326 | 334 | 342 | 350 | 362 | 362 | 370 | 378 | 378 | 378 | 386 | 386 |
| WORSTED | 294 | 302 | 310 | 318 | 326 | 330 | 334 | 342 | 342 | 346 | 350 | 350 |

sts. *Note: Exact st count is not essential, but be sure to end with a multiple of 4 sts + 2 for ribbing to work out evenly.* Begin 2x2 Rib Flat; work even for

| | |
|---|---|
| FINGERING | 7 |
| DK | 5 |
| WORSTED | 5 |

rows.

**BUTTONHOLE ROW (RS):** Work

| | |
|---|---|
| FINGERING | 10 |
| DK | 6 |
| WORSTED | 4 |

sts, [BO 2 sts, work

| | |
|---|---|
| FINGERING | 19 |
| DK | 12 |
| WORSTED | 11 |

sts] 7 times, work to end.

Work

| | |
|---|---|
| FINGERING | 8 |
| DK | 6 |
| WORSTED | 5 |

rows even, CO 2 sts over BO sts on first row using Backward Loop CO (see Special Techniques, page 188). BO all sts in pattern.

Sew buttons opposite buttonholes.

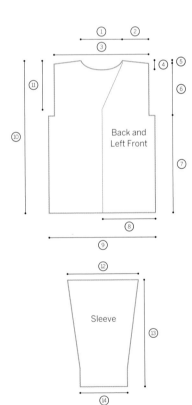

**FINGERING WEIGHT**

1  6¾ (7, 7¼, 7½, 7¾, 8, 8¼, 8¾, 8¾, 9, 9, 9¼)"
   17 (18, 18.5, 19, 19.5, 20.5, 21, 22, 22, 23, 23, 23.5) cm

2  5 (5½, 5¾, 6¼, 6½, 7, 7¼, 7½, 8, 9, 10, 10¾)"
   12.5 (14, 14.5, 16, 16.5, 18, 18.5, 19, 20.5, 23, 25.5, 27.5) cm

3  16¾ (17¾, 18¾, 19¾, 20¾, 21¾, 22¾, 23¾, 24¾, 26¾, 28¾, 30¾)"
   42.5 (45, 47.5, 50, 52.5, 55, 58, 60.5, 63, 68, 73, 78) cm

4  1½"
   4 cm

5  ½"
   1.5 cm

6  8½ (9, 9½, 10, 10½, 10½, 11, 11, 11½, 12, 12½, 12½)"
   21.5 (23, 24, 25.5, 26.5, 26.5, 28, 28, 29, 30.5, 32, 32) cm

7  16 (16, 16½, 16½, 17, 17, 17, 17½, 17½, 17½, 17½, 18)"
   40.5 (40.5, 42, 42, 43, 43, 43, 44.5, 44.5, 44.5, 44.5, 45.5) cm

8  9 (9½, 10, 10½, 11, 11½, 12, 12½, 13, 14, 15, 16)"
   23 (24, 25.5, 26.5, 28, 29, 30.5, 32, 33, 35.5, 38, 40.5) cm

9  18¼ (19¼, 20¼, 21¼, 22¼, 23¼, 24¼, 25¼, 26¼, 28¼, 30¼, 32¼)"
   46.5 (49, 51.5, 54, 56.5, 59, 61.5, 64, 66.5, 72, 77, 82) cm

10  25 (25½, 26½, 27, 28, 28, 28½, 29, 29½, 30, 30½, 31)"
    63.5 (65, 67.5, 68.5, 71, 71, 72.5, 73.5, 75, 76, 77.5, 78.5) cm

11  8½ (9, 9½, 10, 10½, 10½, 11, 11, 11½, 12, 12½, 12½)"
    21.5 (23, 24, 25.5, 26.5, 26.5, 28, 28, 29, 30.5, 32, 32) cm

12  17 (18, 19, 20, 21, 21, 22, 22, 23, 24, 25, 25)"
    43 (45.5, 48.5, 51, 53.5, 53.5, 56, 56, 58.5, 61, 63.5, 63.5) cm

13  17½ (18, 18, 18, 18½, 18½, 18½, 18½, 18½, 19, 19¼, 19¼)"
    44.5 (45.5, 45.5, 45.5, 47, 47, 47, 47, 47, 48.5, 49, 49) cm

14  8¼ (8¾, 8¾, 9¼, 9¼, 9¼, 9¾, 9¾, 10¼, 10¾, 11¾, 11¾)"
    21 (22, 22, 23.5, 23.5, 23.5, 25, 25, 26, 27.5, 30, 30) cm

## DK WEIGHT

1    7 (7¼, 7¼, 7¾, 8, 8, 8¼, 9, 9, 9, 9, 9½)"
      18 (18.5, 18.5, 19.5, 20.5, 20.5, 21, 23, 23, 23, 23, 24) cm

2    5 (5¼, 5¾, 6¼, 6¼, 7, 7¼, 7¾, 8, 8¾, 9¾, 10¾)"
      12.5 (13.5, 14.5, 16, 16, 18, 18.5, 19.5, 20.5, 22, 25, 27.5) cm

3    17 (17¾, 18½, 20, 20¾, 22¼, 23, 24¼, 25, 26½, 28¾, 31)"
      43 (45, 47, 51, 52.5, 56.5, 58.5, 61.5, 63.5, 67.5, 73, 78.5) cm

4    1½"
      4 cm

5    ½"
      1.5 cm

6    8½ (9, 9½, 10, 10½, 10½, 11, 11, 11½, 12, 12½, 12½)"
      21.5 (23, 24, 25.5, 26.5, 26.5, 28, 28, 29, 30.5, 32, 32) cm

7    16 (16, 16½, 16½, 17, 17, 17, 17½, 17½, 17½, 17½, 18)"
      40.5 (40.5, 42, 42, 43, 43, 43, 44.5, 44.5, 44.5, 44.5, 45.5) cm

8    8½ (9¼, 10, 10, 10¾, 11½, 12¼, 13, 13, 13¾, 15, 15¾)"
      21.5 (23.5, 25.5, 25.5, 27.5, 29, 31, 33, 33, 35, 38, 40) cm

9    18½ (19¼, 20, 21½, 22¼, 23¾, 24¼, 25¾, 26½, 28, 30¼, 32¼)"
      47 (49, 51, 54.5, 56.5, 60.5, 61.5, 65.5, 67.5, 71, 77, 82) cm

10   25 (25½, 26½, 27, 28, 28, 28½, 29, 29½, 30, 30½, 31)"
      63.5 (65, 67.5, 68.5, 71, 71, 72.5, 73.5, 75, 76, 77.5, 78.5) cm

11   8½ (9, 9½, 10, 10½, 10½, 11, 11, 11½, 12, 12½, 12½)"
      21.5 (23, 24, 25.5, 26.5, 26.5, 28, 28, 29, 30.5, 32, 32) cm

12   17 (18¼, 19¼, 20, 21, 21, 22¼, 22¼, 23¼, 24, 25, 25)"
      43 (46.5, 49, 51, 53.5, 53.5, 56.5, 56.5, 59, 61, 63.5, 63.5) cm

13   17½ (18, 18, 18½, 18½, 18½, 18½, 18½ 19, 19¼, 19¼)"
      44.5 (45.5, 45.5, 45.5, 47, 47, 47, 47, 47, 48.5, 49, 49) cm

14   8¼ (9, 9, 9, 9, 9, 9¾, 9¾, 10½, 10½, 11¼, 12)"
      21 (23, 23, 23, 23, 23, 25, 25, 26.5, 26.5, 28.5, 30.5) cm

## WORSTED WEIGHT

1    6¾ (7¼, 7½, 7½, 8, 8, 8½, 8¾, 8¾, 9¼, 9¼, 9½)"
      17 (18.5, 19, 19, 20.5, 20.5, 21.5, 22, 22, 23.5, 23.5, 24) cm

2    4¾ (5, 5½, 6, 6¼, 7, 7¼, 7½, 8¼, 8¾, 9½, 10½)"
      12 (12.5, 14, 15, 16, 18, 18.5, 19, 21, 22, 24, 26.5) cm

3    16½ (17¼, 18¾, 19½, 20½, 22, 22¾, 23½, 25¼, 26¾, 28½, 30¾)"
      42 (44, 47.5, 49.5, 52, 56, 58, 59.5, 64, 68, 72.5, 78) cm

4    1½"
      4 cm

5    ½"
      1.5 cm

6    8½ (9, 9½, 10, 10½, 10½, 11, 11, 11½, 12, 12½, 12½)"
      21.5 (23, 24, 25.5, 26.5, 26.5, 28, 28, 29, 30.5, 32, 32) cm

7    16 (16, 16½, 16½, 17, 17, 17, 17½, 17½, 17½, 17½, 18)"
      40.5 (40.5, 42, 42, 43, 43, 43, 44.5, 44.5, 44.5, 44.5, 45.5) cm

8    8½ (9½, 9½, 10¼, 11, 11, 11¾, 12½, 13½, 14¼, 15, 15¾)"
      21.5 (24, 24, 26, 28, 28, 30, 32, 34.5, 36, 38, 40) cm

9    18 (18¾, 20½, 21¼, 22, 23½, 24½, 25¼, 26¾, 28½, 30, 32½)"
      45.5 (47.5, 52, 54, 56, 59.5, 62, 64, 68, 72.5, 76, 82.5) cm

10   25 (25½, 26½, 27, 28, 28, 28½, 29, 29½, 30, 30½, 31)"
      63.5 (65, 67.5, 68.5, 71, 71, 72.5, 73.5, 75, 76, 77.5, 78.5) cm

11   8½ (9, 9½, 10, 10½, 10½, 11, 11, 11½, 12, 12½, 12½)"
      21.5 (23, 24, 25.5, 26.5, 26.5, 28, 28, 29, 30.5, 32, 32) cm

12   17¼ (18, 19¼, 20, 21¼, 21¼, 22, 22, 23¼, 24, 25¼, 25¼)"
      44 (45.5, 49, 51, 54, 54, 56, 56, 59, 61, 64, 64) cm

13   17½ (18, 18, 18½, 18½, 18½, 18½, 18½ 19, 19¼, 19¼)"
      44.5 (45.5, 45.5, 45.5, 47, 47, 47, 47, 47, 48.5, 49, 49) cm

14   8½ (9¼, 9¼, 9¼, 9¼, 9¼, 10, 10, 10¾, 10¾, 11½, 11½)"
      21.5 (23.5, 23.5, 23.5, 23.5, 23.5, 25.5, 25.5, 27.5, 27.5, 29, 29) cm

# 3

······································································

# Raglan Sweaters

Legend has it that raglans came about in response to a lord tearing his shirts open after losing his arm in a war. Raglans made it into sportswear design following their use in baseball jerseys here in the US.

Whatever their origin, raglans are *sportswear*—they're designed to allow for a roomy fit through the shoulders, *without* a giant fit through the body and arms. When a raglan fits you well, the sleeves attach to the body relatively far away from the actual bend of your armpit, and you can move your arms in exaggeratedly wide circles without causing the shoulder area to stretch.

## WHAT MAKES A RAGLAN A RAGLAN?

Raglan sweaters have two major characteristics:

- The sleeve and body have the same number of rows between armhole shaping and neck edge.
- The shaping between the armhole and neck edge happens along four distinct lines, two each on the front and back.

They can be knit in one piece with faux seams, or four pieces and then seamed together, starting either at the neck of the sweater and working top down, or at the hem of the sweater and working bottom up in either case.

In pieces                        All in one

In the simplest form of a raglan, the shaping lines are perfectly straight. A *compound* raglan adjusts the rate of shaping in the raglan lines to more closely match the curvature of the shoulder joint in something of an "S" shape. You can further adjust the shaping on the tops of the sleeves to make the back armhole depth deeper than the front armhole depth:

Standard

Asymmetric

For adult women, I *strongly* prefer seamed raglans. First, for stability; since the weight-bearing points of a raglan sweater rest in the middle of your knitwear rather than at a seamed edge. Second, for fit: Working the garment in pieces and seaming the edges lets you adjust the shaping rates on front, back, and sleeves independently, without causing any puckering or biasing of fabric in the shoulder region.

This chapter will focus on drafting raglan patterns in pieces; to create an all-in-one pattern, calculate it in pieces and then combine the stitch counts together.

## DESIGN AND FABRIC CONSIDERATIONS FOR RAGLANS

Even with seams, raglans are one of the least structured sweater constructions—they don't work well in an extremely drapey, fluid fabric. Given that:

- Seamed raglans are more structured than all-in-one raglans.

- Pullovers are more structured than cardigans.

- Shallow necklines are more structured than deep necklines.

So a high-necked pullover, like the Meadowbrook Cowl on page 159, can handle the drape inherent in the silk-linen-wool blend—whereas an all-in-one open cardigan with a deep-V neckline will need fabric that can practically walk on its own.

When deciding what shape you'd like the body of your raglan sweater to be, consider that the shoulder area is going to be looser and more casual than with other constructions. I personally think raglans look best without too much waist shaping—either an A-line style, like the Meadowbrook Cowl (page 159), or where waist shaping is worked on the back of the sweater only.

The basic designs in this chapter, as well as the Dockhouse Pullover (page 131) and Jump Shot Hoodie (page 165), lack any waist shaping at all.

### *Drafting a raglan pattern.*

To draft your own raglan pattern, start by filling in a personal schematic for the front, back, and sleeves of your sweater. Fill in the arrows labeled here:

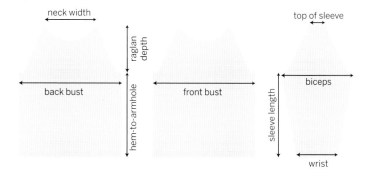

There are a few measurements we talked about in the previous section, and a few we have not. You can fill in the following by copying them from your personal schematic in chapter 1:

- The **wrist**, **biceps**, front and back **bust** (and waist, and hip, if you're not making a straight sweater).

- The **raglan depth**, which should be equal to your set-in-sleeve armhole depth.

- The **sleeve length** and **hem-to-armhole length**.

You'll need to determine the following:

- The **neck width** of the raglan. This should be the same on the front and back. Typical neck widths range between 6" (15 cm) on the narrow end and 12" (25 cm) on the wider end. Narrower necks will cause the raglan lines to be more angled, and wider necks cause them to be more vertical:

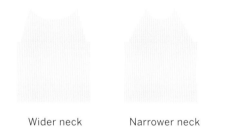

Wider neck          Narrower neck

The choice is up to you, and you can sanity-check this measurement by holding a measuring tape up to your upper chest/shoulders.

- The **width of the top of the sleeve** will sit directly on top of your shoulder, forming part of the neck edge. It will add half its width to the overall armhole depth of the sweater.

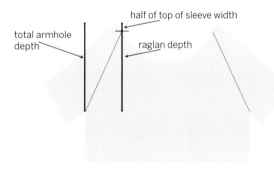

Again, this width is up to you. But it's generally in the 1–4" (2.5–10 cm) range. The bottom end of the range makes sense for smaller sizes, or especially wide necklines; the top of the range is more typical for especially narrow necklines or at the larger end of the size range. If you're not sure, 2½–3" (6.5–7.5 cm) is a great place to start.

***Once you've filled in your schematic, you're ready to draft your pattern.***

Let's follow this process with an example—a fairly wide crew-neck pullover, without waist shaping, for my measurements. Here's my personal schematic for this sweater:

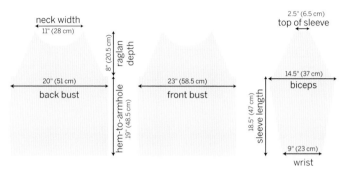

Next, turn the measurements into stitch and row counts based on your gauge. Let's assume I'm working at a fairly typical gauge of 5 stitches and 7 rows to 1" (2.5 cm):

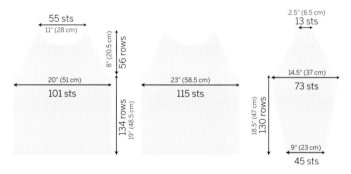

The body of my sweater is pretty simple—I cast on the appropriate number of stitches and work to the raglan shaping. So for this section of the book, let's focus on **drafting the instructions for the raglan shaping** on the back, front, and sleeves.

- First, approximately 1" (2.5 cm) of stitches gets bound off at the start of the raglan shaping on both the sleeves and the body. The same number of stitches should be bound off on all pieces.

- Then, calculate shaping for raglans (see box at right).

- On the back of my sweater, I need to get from 91 stitches (after bind-offs) to 55 stitches, removing 36 stitches over the 56 rows in my raglan shaping. (Rate of 3, with 2 rows left over.)

- On the front of my sweater, I need to get from 105 stitches (after bind-offs) to the 55 stitches for my neck, removing 50 stitches over the same 56 rows. (Rate of 2, with 6 rows left over.)

- On the sleeves of my sweater, I need to get from 63 stitches (after bind-offs) to 13 stitches, again removing 50 stitches.* (If I wanted a wider-sleeved top, this could also be different from the front!)

As you can see, it would be difficult for me to properly fit myself with an all-in-one raglan construction—the shaping I need on my back versus my arms and front is too different.

On the other hand, if you get an identical shaping rate on all your pieces, the all-in-one construction might work just fine! You'll lose the structure of the seams, but there will be no biasing or fabric distortion to worry about.

### FURTHER THINKING: COMPOUND RAGLANS

Compound raglans let you vary the line of the raglan to be less straight and more S-like. This produces a fit that more closely matches the body. To make one, work some every-fourth-row shaping in the center of your raglan section, whether or not you have "remainders" initially.

#### ADJUSTING THE FRONT AND BACK OF THE RAGLAN DEPTH SEPARATELY.

On real people, back armhole depths and front armhole depths are different. In most sweater designs, adjusting for this is more trouble than it's worth—but raglans make it simple. Make the back raglan shaping

---

* Again, a rate of 2, with 6 rows left over.

# Calculate Shaping for Raglans

To calculate the rate of shaping on a simple, single raglan edge:

- Calculate the **number of stitches to be removed along the raglan edge** by subtracting the stitch count at the top of your piece from the stitch count just after the bind-offs, dividing by 2.

- Calculate the **number of rows in the shaping portion of the raglan** by subtracting the two bind-off rows from your raglan depth.

- Use the **Master Shaping Formula** to calculate the simplest possible rate. If there are no remainders, you're done!

- If there are **remainders**, calculate the number of "work even" rows you need to have by multiplying your rate by the number of shaping rows and subtracting the result from the total rows in the raglan.

- Distribute those "work even" rows back into your raglan instructions, either evenly throughout (for a simple raglan) or in the center of the raglan only (for a compound raglan).

2 to 4 rows longer than the front. At the tops of your sleeves, work stepped bind-offs to match.

I've written the following basic, straight-sided sweaters in three gauges and twelve sizes, so if you'd prefer not to draft your own raglan patterns, you've got a great starting point. I've shown these with recommended yarns, but I encourage you to experiment, too! Just keep in mind that the fabric should be strong, and structured, as described on page 12. If you'd like a worksheet to help you tame the numbers as you knit, you can download one from my website.

# Basic Pullover: Raglan Construction

A crew-neck raglan pullover is the hand-knit equivalent of the perfect sweatshirt. I love light fabrics, so I've chosen a fingering-weight wool with a touch of mohair for the sample. I've also recommended a soft worsted-weight wool, and a light, woolen-spun bulky for a sweater that can handle even the coldest days.

This unisex garment is worked in pieces from the bottom up, and then seamed for stability. No waist shaping is included in any of the basic patterns, but should you choose to add some, please see pages 113–115 for details.

## FINISHED MEASUREMENTS

**FINGERING:** 32½ (35, 37, 38½, 40½, 43, 45, 46½, 48½, 53, 56½, 61)" [82.5 (89, 94, 98, 103, 109, 114.5, 118, 123, 134.5, 143.5, 155) cm] chest

**WORSTED:** 32½ (34, 37, 38½, 40, 43, 44½, 47½, 50, 53, 56, 60½)" [82.5 (86.5, 94, 98, 101.5, 109, 113, 120.5, 127, 134.5, 142, 153.5) cm] chest

**BULKY:** 30½ (33½, 36, 38½, 41½, 44, 46½, 49½, 52, 54½, 57½, 60)" [77.5 (85, 91.5, 98, 105.5, 112, 118, 125.5, 132, 138.5, 146, 152.5) cm] chest

*Note: Sweater is intended to be worn with 3–6" (7.5–15 cm) ease in the bust; shown in fingering weight yarn and size 37" (94 cm). Bulky yarns require more ease than lighter-weight.*

## YARN

**FINGERING:** The Fibre Company Cumbria Fingering [60% merino wool / 30% masham wool / 10% mohair; 328 yards (300 meters) / 100 grams]: 4 (5, 5, 5, 6, 6, 7, 7, 7, 8, 8, 9) hanks Derwentwater

**WORSTED:** Quince and Co. Lark [100% American wool; 134 yards (123 meters) / 50 grams]: 8 (9, 10, 11, 12, 12, 13, 14, 14, 15, 16, 18) hanks Fjord

**BULKY:** Harrisville Designs Turbine [100% virgin wool; 110 yards (100 meters) / 100 grams]: 5 (6, 7, 7, 8, 8, 9, 10, 10, 11, 11, 12) hanks Aquifer

## NEEDLES

**FINGERING:** One pair straight needles and one 24" (60 cm) long circular needle (for Neckband) size US 2 (2.75 mm)

**WORSTED:** One pair straight needles and one 24" (60 cm) long circular needle (for Neckband) size US 7 (4.5 mm)

**BULKY:** One pair straight needles and one 24" (60 cm) long circular needle (for Neckband) size US 10.5 (6.5 mm)

Change needle size if necessary to obtain correct gauge.

## NOTIONS

Stitch markers

## GAUGE

**FINGERING:** 28 sts and 36 rows = 4" (10 cm) in St st

**WORSTED:** 22 sts and 32 rows = 4" (10 cm) in St st

**BULKY:** 12 sts and 22 rows = 4" (10 cm) in St st

## NOTES

If your size gives the number 0 for a particular instruction, skip that instruction and proceed to the next instruction.

Unless otherwise specified, decreases should be worked to match the slant of the edge being shaped, as follows: For left-slanting edges, k2, ssk, knit to end; for right-slanting edges, knit to last 4 sts, k2tog, k2. Increases should also be worked to match the slant of the edge being shaped, as follows: For right-slanting edges: On RS rows, k1, M1R, knit to end; on WS rows, p1, M1PR, purl to end. For left-slanting edges: On RS rows, knit to last st, M1L, k1; on WS rows, p1, M1PL, purl to end.

# BACK
## CO

| | | | | | | | | | | | | |
|---|---|---|---|---|---|---|---|---|---|---|---|---|
| FINGERING | 114 | 122 | 130 | 134 | 142 | 150 | 158 | 162 | 170 | 186 | 198 | 214 |
| WORSTED | 90 | 94 | 102 | 106 | 110 | 118 | 122 | 130 | 138 | 146 | 154 | 166 |
| BULKY | 46 | 50 | 54 | 58 | 62 | 66 | 70 | 74 | 78 | 82 | 86 | 90 |

sts.

Begin 2x2 Rib Flat; work even until piece measures 2¼" (5.5 cm), ending with a WS row.

Change to St st; work even until piece measures 15¼ (15¼, 15½, 15½, 16, 16, 16, 16¼, 16½, 15½, 16¾, 16¾)" [38.5 (38.5, 39.5, 39.5, 40.5, 40.5, 40.5, 41.5, 42, 39.5, 42.5, 42.5) cm] from the beginning, ending with a WS row.

## SHAPE RAGLAN ARMHOLES
### BO

| | | | | | | | | | | | | |
|---|---|---|---|---|---|---|---|---|---|---|---|---|
| FINGERING | 9 | 9 | 9 | 9 | 9 | 9 | 9 | 9 | 11 | 11 | 11 | 14 |
| WORSTED | 7 | 7 | 7 | 7 | 7 | 7 | 7 | 7 | 9 | 9 | 9 | 11 |
| BULKY | 3 | 3 | 3 | 3 | 3 | 3 | 4 | 4 | 5 | 5 | 5 | 6 |

sts at the beginning of the next 2 rows.

Decrease 1 st each side every RS row

| | | | | | | | | | | | | |
|---|---|---|---|---|---|---|---|---|---|---|---|---|
| FINGERING | 8 | 9 | 12 | 12 | 13 | 15 | 15 | 15 | 15 | 20 | 23 | 26 |
| WORSTED | 5 | 5 | 8 | 8 | 8 | 10 | 9 | 11 | 12 | 13 | 15 | 17 |
| BULKY | 1 | 1 | 2 | 3 | 4 | 4 | 3 | 5 | 5 | 5 | 5 | 6 |

time(s), then every other RS row

| | | | | | | | | | | | | |
|---|---|---|---|---|---|---|---|---|---|---|---|---|
| FINGERING | 8 | 7 | 5 | 6 | 6 | 5 | 6 | 7 | 7 | 4 | 2 | 0 |
| WORSTED | 9 | 9 | 7 | 8 | 9 | 8 | 10 | 9 | 8 | 8 | 7 | 6 |
| BULKY | 9 | 9 | 8 | 8 | 8 | 8 | 10 | 9 | 9 | 9 | 10 | 10 |

times, then every RS row

| | | | | | | | | | | | | |
|---|---|---|---|---|---|---|---|---|---|---|---|---|
| FINGERING | 7 | 9 | 11 | 11 | 13 | 15 | 15 | 15 | 15 | 19 | 22 | 25 |
| WORSTED | 4 | 5 | 7 | 7 | 7 | 9 | 8 | 10 | 11 | 12 | 14 | 16 |
| BULKY | 0 | 0 | 2 | 2 | 3 | 4 | 3 | 4 | 4 | 5 | 5 | 5 |

times.

| | | | | | | | | | | | | |
|---|---|---|---|---|---|---|---|---|---|---|---|---|
| FINGERING | 50 | 54 | 56 | 58 | 60 | 62 | 68 | 70 | 74 | 78 | 82 | 84 |
| WORSTED | 40 | 42 | 44 | 46 | 48 | 50 | 54 | 56 | 58 | 62 | 64 | 66 |
| BULKY | 20 | 24 | 24 | 26 | 26 | 28 | 30 | 30 | 32 | 34 | 36 | 36 |

sts remain. Work 1 WS row even.

Armholes measure approximately 7¼ (7¼, 7½, 8, 8¾, 9, 9½, 10, 10, 10½, 11, 11½)" [18.5 (18.5, 19, 20.5, 22, 23, 24, 25.5, 25.5, 26.5, 28, 29) cm].
BO all sts.

# FRONT

Work as for Back until you have worked

| | | | | | | | | | | | | |
|---|---|---|---|---|---|---|---|---|---|---|---|---|
| FINGERING | 38 | 40 | 42 | 46 | 52 | 56 | 60 | 64 | 64 | 70 | 74 | 78 |
| WORSTED | 34 | 36 | 38 | 42 | 46 | 50 | 54 | 58 | 58 | 62 | 66 | 70 |
| BULKY | 24 | 24 | 26 | 28 | 32 | 34 | 38 | 40 | 40 | 42 | 46 | 48 |

rows from beginning of Raglan shaping. Place marker on either side of center

| | | | | | | | | | | | | |
|---|---|---|---|---|---|---|---|---|---|---|---|---|
| FINGERING | 26 | 30 | 32 | 34 | 36 | 38 | 44 | 46 | 50 | 54 | 58 | 60 |
| WORSTED | 18 | 20 | 22 | 24 | 26 | 28 | 32 | 34 | 36 | 40 | 42 | 44 |
| BULKY | 2 | 6 | 6 | 8 | 8 | 10 | 12 | 12 | 14 | 16 | 18 | 18 |

sts.

## SHAPE RAGLAN ARMHOLES AND NECK

*Note: Remaining armhole shaping and neck shaping are worked at the same time; please read entire section through before beginning.*

**NEXT ROW (RS):** Continuing to work armhole shaping as established, work to marker, join a second ball of yarn, BO center

| | | | | | | | | | | | | |
|---|---|---|---|---|---|---|---|---|---|---|---|---|
| FINGERING | 26 | 30 | 32 | 34 | 36 | 38 | 44 | 46 | 50 | 54 | 58 | 60 |
| WORSTED | 18 | 20 | 22 | 24 | 26 | 28 | 32 | 34 | 36 | 40 | 42 | 44 |
| BULKY | 2 | 6 | 6 | 8 | 8 | 10 | 12 | 12 | 14 | 16 | 18 | 18 |

sts, work to end.

Working both sides at the same time, decrease 1 st at each neck edge every RS row

| | |
|---|---|
| FINGERING | 4 |
| WORSTED | 4 |
| BULKY | 3 |

times, then every other RS row

| | |
|---|---|
| FINGERING | 4 |
| WORSTED | 3 |
| BULKY | 2 |

times.

When all armhole and neck shaping is complete, 4 sts remain each shoulder. Work 1 WS row even. Armholes measure same as for Back. BO all sts.

## SLEEVES

CO

| | | | | | | | | | | | | |
|---|---|---|---|---|---|---|---|---|---|---|---|---|
| FINGERING | 58 | 62 | 66 | 70 | 74 | 74 | 74 | 74 | 74 | 78 | 78 | 82 |
| WORSTED | 46 | 50 | 50 | 54 | 58 | 58 | 58 | 58 | 58 | 62 | 62 | 66 |
| BULKY | 26 | 26 | 30 | 30 | 34 | 34 | 34 | 34 | 34 | 34 | 34 | 38 |

sts.

Begin 2x2 Rib Flat; work even until piece measures 3" (7.5 cm), ending with a WS row.

Change to St st; work 2 rows even.

## SHAPE SLEEVE

Increase 1 st each side every

| | | | | | | | | | | | | |
|---|---|---|---|---|---|---|---|---|---|---|---|---|
| FINGERING | 11 | 10 | 9 | 9 | 7 | 6 | 5 | 4 | 4 | 3 | 3 | 3 |
| WORSTED | 13 | 13 | 9 | 9 | 8 | 7 | 6 | 5 | 4 | 4 | 3 | 3 |
| BULKY | 14 | 10 | 12 | 11 | 12 | 11 | 8 | 7 | 6 | 5 | 4 | 4 |

rows a total of

| | | | | | | | | | | | | |
|---|---|---|---|---|---|---|---|---|---|---|---|---|
| FINGERING | 10 | 11 | 13 | 14 | 16 | 19 | 23 | 26 | 30 | 31 | 35 | 36 |
| WORSTED | 8 | 8 | 11 | 12 | 13 | 15 | 18 | 21 | 24 | 24 | 27 | 28 |
| BULKY | 5 | 7 | 6 | 7 | 6 | 7 | 9 | 10 | 12 | 13 | 15 | 14 |

times.

| | | | | | | | | | | | | |
|---|---|---|---|---|---|---|---|---|---|---|---|---|
| FINGERING | 78 | 84 | 92 | 98 | 106 | 112 | 120 | 126 | 134 | 140 | 148 | 154 |
| WORSTED | 62 | 66 | 72 | 78 | 84 | 88 | 94 | 100 | 106 | 110 | 116 | 122 |
| BULKY | 36 | 40 | 42 | 44 | 46 | 48 | 52 | 54 | 58 | 60 | 64 | 66 |

sts.

Work even until piece measures 17 (17, 17, 18, 18, 18, 18, 18, 18, 17½, 17, 16½)" [43 (43, 43, 45.5, 45.5, 45.5, 45.5, 45.5, 45.5, 44.5, 43, 42) cm] from the beginning, ending with a WS row.

**SHAPE RAGLAN CAP**

BO

| | | | | | | | | | | | |
|---|---|---|---|---|---|---|---|---|---|---|---|
| FINGERING | 9 | 9 | 9 | 9 | 9 | 9 | 9 | 9 | 11 | 11 | 11 | 14 |
| WORSTED | 7 | 7 | 7 | 7 | 7 | 7 | 7 | 7 | 9 | 9 | 9 | 11 |
| BULKY | 3 | 3 | 3 | 3 | 3 | 3 | 4 | 4 | 5 | 5 | 5 | 6 |

sts at the beginning of the next 2 rows.

Decrease 1 st each side every RS row

| | | | | | | | | | | | |
|---|---|---|---|---|---|---|---|---|---|---|---|
| FINGERING | 8 | 9 | 12 | 12 | 13 | 15 | 15 | 15 | 15 | 20 | 23 | 26 |
| WORSTED | 5 | 5 | 8 | 8 | 8 | 10 | 9 | 11 | 10 | 13 | 15 | 17 |
| BULKY | 1 | 1 | 2 | 3 | 4 | 4 | 3 | 5 | 5 | 5 | 5 | 6 |

time(s), then every other RS row

| | | | | | | | | | | | |
|---|---|---|---|---|---|---|---|---|---|---|---|
| FINGERING | 11 | 9 | 6 | 5 | 6 | 5 | 3 | 2 | 1 | 1 | 0 | 2 |
| WORSTED | 11 | 10 | 8 | 7 | 7 | 7 | 6 | 5 | 5 | 5 | 5 | 6 |
| BULKY | 9 | 7 | 7 | 7 | 8 | 8 | 9 | 9 | 9 | 9 | 9 | 10 |

time(s), then every RS row

| | | | | | | | | | | | |
|---|---|---|---|---|---|---|---|---|---|---|---|
| FINGERING | 1 | 5 | 9 | 13 | 13 | 15 | 21 | 25 | 27 | 25 | 26 | 21 |
| WORSTED | 0 | 3 | 5 | 9 | 11 | 11 | 16 | 18 | 19 | 18 | 18 | 16 |
| BULKY | 0 | 4 | 4 | 4 | 3 | 4 | 5 | 4 | 4 | 5 | 7 | 5 |

times.

| | | | | | | | | | | | |
|---|---|---|---|---|---|---|---|---|---|---|---|
| FINGERING | 20 | 20 | 20 | 20 | 24 | 24 | 24 | 24 | 26 | 26 | 28 | 28 |
| WORSTED | 16 | 16 | 16 | 16 | 18 | 18 | 18 | 18 | 20 | 20 | 22 | 22 |
| BULKY | 10 | 10 | 10 | 10 | 10 | 10 | 10 | 10 | 12 | 12 | 12 | 12 |

sts remain.

Work 1 WS even. Cap measures same as for Back armholes.

BO all sts.

# FINISHING

Block pieces as desired. Sew raglan seams. Sew side and Sleeve seams.

**NECKBAND**

With RS facing, using circular needle and beginning at right back shoulder, pick up and knit approximately 1 st in each BO st, 2 sts for every 3 rows along vertical edges, and 3 sts for every 4 rows along diagonal edges. You will pick up approximately

| | | | | | | | | | | | |
|---|---|---|---|---|---|---|---|---|---|---|---|
| FINGERING | 160 | 168 | 172 | 176 | 188 | 192 | 204 | 208 | 220 | 228 | 240 | 244 |
| WORSTED | 124 | 128 | 132 | 136 | 144 | 148 | 156 | 160 | 168 | 176 | 184 | 188 |
| BULKY | 64 | 72 | 72 | 76 | 76 | 80 | 84 | 84 | 92 | 96 | 100 | 100 |

sts. *Note: Exact st count is not essential, but be sure to end with a multiple of 4 sts for ribbing to work out evenly.* Join for working in the rnd; pm for beginning of rnd. Begin 2x2 Rib in the Rnd; work even for ¾" (2 cm). BO all sts in pattern.

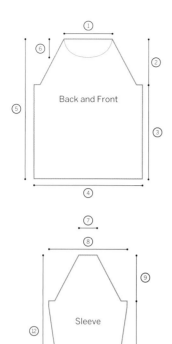

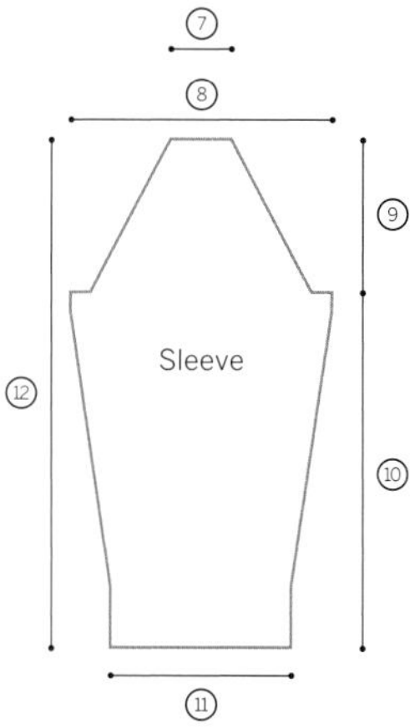

Back and Front

Sleeve

## WORSTED WEIGHT

1   7¼ (7¾, 8, 8¼, 8¾, 9, 9¾, 10¼, 10½, 11¼, 11¾, 12)"
    18.5 (19.5, 20.5, 21, 22, 23, 25, 26, 26.5, 28.5, 30, 30.5) cm

2   7¼ (7¼, 7½, 8, 8¾, 9, 9½, 10, 10, 10½, 11, 11½)"
    18.5 (18.5, 19, 20.5, 22, 23, 24, 25.5, 25.5, 26.5, 28, 29) cm

3   15¼ (15¼, 15½, 15½, 16, 16, 16, 16¼, 16½, 15½, 16¾, 16¾)"
    38.5 (38.5, 39.5, 39.5, 40.5, 40.5, 40.5, 41.5, 42, 39.5, 42.5, 42.5) cm

4   16¼ (17, 18½, 19¼, 20, 21½, 22¼, 23¾, 25, 26½, 28, 30¼)"
    41.5 (43, 47, 49, 51, 54.5, 56.5, 60.5, 63.5, 67.5, 71, 77) cm

5   22½ (22½, 23, 23½, 24¾, 25, 25½, 26¼, 26½, 26, 27¾, 28¼)"
    57 (57, 58.5, 59.5, 63, 63.5, 65, 66.5, 67.5, 66, 70.5, 72) cm

6   3 (2¾, 2¾, 2¾, 3, 2¾, 2¾, 2¾, 2¾, 2¾, 2¾, 2¾)"
    7.5 (7, 7, 7, 7.5, 7, 7, 7, 7, 7, 7, 7) cm

7   3 (3, 3, 3, 3¼, 3¼, 3¼, 3¼, 3¾, 3¾, 4, 4)"
    7.5 (7.5, 7.5, 7.5, 8.5, 8.5, 8.5, 8.5, 9.5, 9.5, 10, 10) cm

8   11¼ (12, 13, 14¼, 15¼, 16, 17, 18¼, 19¼, 20, 21, 22¼)"
    28.5 (30.5, 33, 36, 38.5, 40.5, 43, 46.5, 49, 51, 53.5, 56.5) cm

9   7¼ (7¼, 7½, 8, 8¾, 9, 9½, 10, 10, 10½, 11, 11½)"
    18.5 (18.5, 19, 20.5, 22, 23, 24, 25.5, 25.5, 26.5, 28, 29) cm

10  17 (17, 17, 18, 18, 18, 18, 18, 18, 17½, 17, 16½)"
    43 (43, 43, 45.5, 45.5, 45.5, 45.5, 45.5, 45.5, 44.5, 43, 42) cm

11  8¼ (9, 9, 9¾, 10½, 10½, 10½, 10½, 10½, 11¼, 11¼, 12)"
    21 (23, 23, 25, 26.5, 26.5, 26.5, 26.5, 26.5, 28.5, 28.5, 30.5) cm

12  24¼ (24¼, 24.5, 26, 26¾, 27, 27½, 28, 28, 28, 28, 28)"
    61.5 (61.5, 62, 66, 68, 68.5, 70, 71, 71, 71, 71, 71) cm

## BULKY WEIGHT

1   6¾ (8, 8, 8¾, 8¾, 9¼, 10, 10, 10¾, 11¼, 12, 12)"
    17 (20.5, 20.5, 22, 22, 23.5, 25.5, 25.5, 27.5, 28.5, 30.5, 30.5) cm

2   7¼ (7¼, 7½, 8, 8¾, 9, 9½, 10, 10, 10½, 11, 11½)"
    18.5 (18.5, 19, 20.5, 22, 23, 24, 25.5, 25.5, 26.5, 28, 29) cm

3   15¼ (15¼, 15½, 15½, 16, 16, 16, 16¼, 16½, 15½, 16¾, 16¾)"
    38.5 (38.5, 39.5, 39.5, 40.5, 40.5, 40.5, 41.5, 42, 39.5, 42.5, 42.5) cm

4   15¼ (16¾, 18, 19¼, 20¾, 22, 23¼, 24¾, 26, 27¼, 28¾, 30)"
    38.5 (42.5, 45.5, 49, 52.5, 56, 59, 63, 66, 69, 73, 76) cm

5   22½ (22½, 23, 23½, 24¾, 25, 25½, 26¼, 26½, 26, 27¾, 28¼)"
    57 (57, 58.5, 59.5, 63, 63.5, 65, 66.5, 67.5, 66, 70.5, 72) cm

6   3 (3, 2¾, 3, 3, 2¾, 2½, 2¾, 2¾, 2¾, 2¾, 2¾)"
    7.5 (7.5, 7, 7.5, 7.5, 7, 6.5, 7, 7, 7, 7, 7) cm

7   3¼ (3¼, 3¼, 3¼, 3¼, 3¼, 3¼, 3¼, 4, 4, 4, 4)"
    8.5 (8.5, 8.5, 8.5, 8.5, 8.5, 8.5, 8.5, 10, 10, 10, 10) cm

8   12 (13¼, 14, 14¾, 15¼, 16, 17¼, 18, 19¼, 20, 21¼, 22)"
    30.5 (33.5, 35.5, 37.5, 38.5, 40.5, 44, 45.5, 49, 51, 54, 56) cm

9   7¼ (7¼, 7½, 8, 8¾, 9, 9½, 10, 10, 10½, 11, 11½)"
    18.5 (18.5, 19, 20.5, 22, 23, 24, 25.5, 25.5, 26.5, 28, 29) cm

10  17 (17, 17, 18, 18, 18, 18, 18, 18, 17½, 17, 16½)"
    43 (43, 43, 45.5, 45.5, 45.5, 45.5, 45.5, 45.5, 44.5, 43, 42) cm

11  8¾ (8¾, 10, 10, 11¼, 11¼, 11¼, 11¼, 11¼, 11¼, 11¼, 12¾)"
    22 (22, 25.5, 25.5, 28.5, 28.5, 28.5, 28.5, 28.5, 28.5, 28.5, 32.5) cm

12  24¼ (24¼, 24½, 26, 26¾, 27, 27½, 28, 28, 28, 28, 28)"
    61.5 (61.5, 62, 66, 68, 68.5, 70, 71, 71, 71, 71, 71) cm

## FINGERING WEIGHT

1   7¼ (7¾, 8, 8¼, 8¾, 9, 9¾, 10¼, 10½, 11¼, 11¾, 12)"
    18.5 (19.5, 20.5, 21, 22, 23, 25, 26, 26.5, 28.5, 30, 30.5) cm

2   7¼ (7¼, 7½, 8, 8¾, 9, 9½, 10, 10, 10½, 11, 11½)"
    18.5 (18.5, 19, 20.5, 22, 23, 24, 25.5, 25.5, 26.5, 28, 29) cm

3   15¼ (15¼, 15½, 15½, 16, 16, 16, 16¼, 16½, 15½, 16¾, 16¾)"
    38.5 (38.5, 39.5, 39.5, 40.5, 40.5, 40.5, 41.5, 42, 39.5, 42.5, 42.5) cm

4   16¼ (17, 18½, 19¼, 20, 21½, 22¼, 23¾, 25, 26½, 28, 30¼)"
    41.5 (43, 47, 49, 51, 54.5, 56.5, 60.5, 63.5, 67.5, 71, 77) cm

5   22½ (22½, 23, 23½, 24¾, 25, 25½, 26¼, 26½, 26, 27¾, 28¼)"
    57 (57, 58.5, 59.5, 63, 63.5, 65, 66.5, 67.5, 66, 70.5, 72) cm

6   3 (2¾, 2¾, 2¾, 3, 2¾, 2¾, 2¾, 2¾, 2¾, 2¾, 2¾)"
    7.5 (7, 7, 7, 7.5, 7, 7, 7, 7, 7, 7, 7) cm

7   3 (3, 3, 3, 3¼, 3¼, 3¼, 3¼, 3¾, 3¾, 4, 4)"
    7.5 (7.5, 7.5, 7.5, 8.5, 8.5, 8.5, 8.5, 9.5, 9.5, 10, 10) cm

8   11¼ (12, 13, 14¼, 15¼, 16, 17, 18¼, 19¼, 20, 21, 22¼)"
    28.5 (30.5, 33, 36, 38.5, 40.5, 43, 46.5, 49, 51, 53.5, 56.5) cm

9   7¼ (7¼, 7½, 8, 8¾, 9, 9½, 10, 10, 10½, 11, 11½)"
    18.5 (18.5, 19, 20.5, 22, 23, 24, 25.5, 25.5, 26.5, 28, 29) cm

10  17 (17, 17, 18, 18, 18, 18, 18, 18, 17½, 17, 16½)"
    43 (43, 43, 45.5, 45.5, 45.5, 45.5, 45.5, 45.5, 44.5, 43, 42) cm

11  8¼ (9, 9, 9¾, 10½, 10½, 10½, 10½, 10½, 11¼, 11¼, 12)"
    21 (23, 23, 25, 26.5, 26.5, 26.5, 26.5, 26.5, 28.5, 28.5, 30.5) cm

12  24¼ (24¼, 24.5, 26, 26¾, 27, 27½, 28, 28, 28, 28, 28)"
    61.5 (61.5, 62, 66, 68, 68.5, 70, 71, 71, 71, 71, 71) cm

# Basic Cardigan: Raglan Construction

Raglan cardigans are the least structured sweaters around, so I've chosen yarns that are up to the challenge. Brooklyn Tweed's Shelter is a lovely, larger-gauge woolen-spun that's still light as a feather. For the alternate gauges, I've selected a soft, 100 percent sport-weight wool made on the coast of Maine (where they really know how to sweater), and a luxurious but sturdy wool-silk blend.

This unisex garment is worked in pieces from the bottom up, and then seamed for stability. The button band is then picked up and worked in one piece. No waist shaping is included in any of the basic patterns, but should you choose to add some, please see pages 113–115 for details.

FINISHED MEASUREMENTS

**SPORT:** 33¼ (35½, 36¾, 39, 41¼, 43½, 44¾, 47, 49¼, 52¾, 57¼, 60¾)" [84.5 (90, 93.5, 99, 105, 110.5, 113.5, 119.5, 125, 134, 145.5, 154.5) cm] chest, buttoned

**DK:** 33¼ (35½, 37, 39¼, 41½, 43, 45¼, 48¼, 51, 54, 57, 61¾)" [84.5 (90, 94, 99.5, 105.5, 109, 115, 122.5, 129.5, 137, 145, 157) cm] chest, buttoned

**ARAN:** 33 (34¾, 36¾, 38½, 40, 42¾, 45¾, 47, 49, 52¾, 56, 61¾)" [84 (88.5, 93.5, 98, 101.5, 108.5, 116, 119.5, 124.5, 134, 142, 157) cm] chest, buttoned

*Note: Sweater is intended to be worn with 3–6" (7.5–15 cm) ease in the bust; shown in Aran weight yarn and size 36¾" (93.5 cm).*

YARN

**SPORT:** Quince & Co. Chickadee [100% American wool; 181 yards (166 meters) / 50 grams]: 6 (7, 7, 8, 9, 9, 9, 10, 11, 11, 12, 13) hanks Bird's Egg

**DK:** Eden Cottage Yarns Titus DK [75% merino wool / 25% mulberry silk; 245 yards (225 meters) / 100 grams]: 5 (5, 6, 6, 7, 7, 8, 8, 8, 9, 10, 11) hanks Midnight

**ARAN:** Brooklyn Tweed Shelter [100% Targhee-Columbia wool; 140 yards (128 meters) / 50 grams]: 6 (7, 7, 8, 8, 9, 10, 10, 11, 11, 12, 13) hanks Faded Quilt

NEEDLES

**SPORT:** One pair straight needles and one 40" (100 cm) long circular needle (for Front Bands/Collar) size US 5 (3.75 mm)

**DK:** One pair straight needles and one 40" (100 cm) long circular needle (for Front Bands/Collar) size US 6 (4 mm)

**ARAN:** One pair straight needles and one 40" (100 cm) long circular needle (for Front Bands/Collar) size US 8 (5 mm)

Change needle size if necessary to obtain correct gauge.

NOTIONS

Stitch markers, seven ¾-inch (19-mm) buttons

GAUGE

**SPORT:** 24 sts and 32 rows = 4" (10 cm) in St st
**DK:** 22 sts and 32 rows = 4" (10 cm) in St st
**ARAN:** 18 sts and 26 rows = 4" (10 cm) in St st

NOTES

If your size gives the number 0 for a particular instruction, skip that instruction and proceed to the next instruction.

Unless otherwise specified, decreases should be worked to match the slant of the edge being shaped, as follows: For left-slanting edges: On RS rows, k2, ssk, knit to end; on WS rows, p2, p2tog, purl to end. For right-slanting edges: On RS rows, knit to last 4 sts, k2tog, k2; on WS rows, purl to last 4 sts, ssp, p2. Increases should also be worked to match the slant of the edge being shaped, as follows: For right-slanting edges: On RS rows, k1, M1R, knit to end; on WS rows, p1, M1PR, purl to end. For left-slanting edges: On RS rows, knit to last st, M1L, k1; on WS rows, p1, M1PL, purl to end.

## BACK

### CO

| | | | | | | | | | | | | |
|---|---|---|---|---|---|---|---|---|---|---|---|---|
| SPORT | 98 | 102 | 110 | 114 | 122 | 126 | 134 | 138 | 146 | 158 | 170 | 182 |
| DK | 90 | 94 | 102 | 106 | 110 | 118 | 122 | 130 | 138 | 146 | 154 | 166 |
| ARAN | 74 | 78 | 82 | 86 | 90 | 98 | 102 | 106 | 110 | 118 | 126 | 138 |

sts.

Begin 2x2 Rib Flat; work even until piece measures 2¼" (5.5 cm), ending with a WS row.

Change to St st; work even until piece measures 15¼ (15¼, 15½, 15½, 16, 16, 16, 16¼, 16½, 15½, 16¾, 16¾)" [38.5 (38.5, 39.5, 39.5, 40.5, 40.5, 40.5, 41.5, 42, 39.5, 42.5, 42.5) cm] from the beginning, ending with a WS row.

### SHAPE RAGLAN ARMHOLES

BO

| | | | | | | | | | | | | |
|---|---|---|---|---|---|---|---|---|---|---|---|---|
| SPORT | 8 | 8 | 8 | 8 | 8 | 8 | 8 | 8 | 9 | 9 | 9 | 12 |
| DK | 7 | 7 | 7 | 7 | 7 | 7 | 7 | 7 | 9 | 9 | 9 | 11 |
| ARAN | 6 | 6 | 6 | 6 | 6 | 6 | 6 | 6 | 7 | 7 | 7 | 9 |

sts at the beginning of the next 2 rows.

Decrease 1 st each side every RS row

| | | | | | | | | | | | | |
|---|---|---|---|---|---|---|---|---|---|---|---|---|
| SPORT | 7 | 6 | 9 | 9 | 11 | 11 | 12 | 12 | 13 | 17 | 20 | 21 |
| DK | 5 | 5 | 8 | 8 | 8 | 10 | 9 | 11 | 12 | 13 | 15 | 17 |
| ARAN | 4 | 5 | 5 | 6 | 6 | 9 | 8 | 8 | 8 | 10 | 13 | 15 |

times, then every other RS row

| | | | | | | | | | | | | |
|---|---|---|---|---|---|---|---|---|---|---|---|---|
| SPORT | 7 | 8 | 6 | 7 | 6 | 7 | 7 | 8 | 7 | 4 | 2 | 2 |
| DK | 9 | 9 | 7 | 8 | 9 | 8 | 10 | 9 | 8 | 8 | 7 | 6 |
| ARAN | 7 | 7 | 7 | 7 | 8 | 6 | 7 | 8 | 8 | 7 | 5 | 4 |

times, then every RS row

| | | | | | | | | | | | | |
|---|---|---|---|---|---|---|---|---|---|---|---|---|
| SPORT | 6 | 6 | 8 | 8 | 10 | 10 | 11 | 11 | 12 | 16 | 19 | 20 |
| DK | 4 | 5 | 7 | 7 | 7 | 9 | 8 | 10 | 11 | 12 | 14 | 16 |
| ARAN | 4 | 4 | 5 | 5 | 5 | 8 | 8 | 8 | 8 | 10 | 12 | 14 |

times.

| | | | | | | | | | | | | |
|---|---|---|---|---|---|---|---|---|---|---|---|---|
| SPORT | 42 | 46 | 48 | 50 | 52 | 54 | 58 | 60 | 64 | 66 | 70 | 72 |
| DK | 40 | 42 | 44 | 46 | 48 | 50 | 54 | 56 | 58 | 62 | 64 | 66 |
| ARAN | 32 | 34 | 36 | 38 | 40 | 40 | 44 | 46 | 48 | 50 | 52 | 54 |

sts remain. Work 1 RS row even.

Armholes measure approximately 7 (7¼, 7½, 8, 8½, 9, 9½, 10, 10, 10½, 11, 11½)" [18 (18.5, 19, 20.5, 21.5, 23, 24, 25.5, 25.5, 26.5, 28, 29) cm].
BO all sts.

## LEFT AND RIGHT FRONTS

### CO

| | | | | | | | | | | | | |
|---|---|---|---|---|---|---|---|---|---|---|---|---|
| SPORT | 47 | 51 | 51 | 55 | 59 | 63 | 63 | 67 | 71 | 75 | 83 | 87 |
| DK | 43 | 47 | 47 | 51 | 55 | 55 | 59 | 63 | 67 | 71 | 75 | 83 |
| ARAN | 35 | 39 | 39 | 43 | 43 | 47 | 51 | 51 | 55 | 59 | 63 | 67 |

sts.

### LEFT FRONT:

**ROW 1 (RS):** *K2, p2; repeat from * to last 3 sts, k3.
**ROW 2:** P3, *k2, p2; repeat from * to end.

### RIGHT FRONT:

**ROW 1 (RS):** K3, *p2, k2; repeat from * to end.
**ROW 2:** *P2, k2; repeat from * to last 3 sts, p3.

***BOTH FRONTS:***

Work even until piece measures 2¼" (5.5 cm), ending with a WS row.

Change to St st.

***ARAN GAUGE ONLY:***

Knit 1 row, decreasing

| ARAN | 1 | 3 | 1 | 3 | 1 | 3 | 3 | 1 | 3 | 3 | 3 | 1 |
|---|---|---|---|---|---|---|---|---|---|---|---|---|

st(s) evenly spaced across.

| ARAN | 34 | 36 | 38 | 40 | 42 | 44 | 48 | 50 | 52 | 56 | 60 | 66 |
|---|---|---|---|---|---|---|---|---|---|---|---|---|

sts remain.

***ALL GAUGES:***

Work even until piece measures 14¼ (14¼, 14½, 14½, 15, 15, 15, 15¼, 14¾, 13½, 15¼, 15¾)" [36 (36, 37, 37, 38, 38, 38, 38.5, 37.5, 34.5, 38.5, 40) cm] from the beginning, ending with a WS row.

### SHAPE NECK AND RAGLAN ARMHOLE

*Note: Neck and armhole shaping are worked at the same time; please read entire section through before beginning.*

Beginning on the next RS row, decrease 1 st at neck edge every

| SPORT | 4 | 3 | 4 | 3 | 3 | 3 | 4 | 3 | 3 | 4 | 3 | 3 |
|---|---|---|---|---|---|---|---|---|---|---|---|---|
| DK | 4 | 3 | 4 | 4 | 3 | 4 | 4 | 4 | 4 | 4 | 3 | 3 |
| ARAN | 5 | 4 | 4 | 3 | 4 | 4 | 3 | 4 | 3 | 3 | 3 | 3 |

rows a total of

| SPORT | 15 | 19 | 16 | 19 | 20 | 23 | 21 | 24 | 26 | 25 | 29 | 28 |
|---|---|---|---|---|---|---|---|---|---|---|---|---|
| DK | 14 | 17 | 14 | 17 | 20 | 17 | 21 | 22 | 23 | 25 | 26 | 29 |
| ARAN | 10 | 13 | 12 | 15 | 14 | 14 | 18 | 17 | 20 | 21 | 22 | 21 |

times.

AT THE SAME TIME, when piece measures 15¼ (15¼, 15½, 15½, 16, 16, 16, 16¼, 16½, 15½, 16¾, 16¾)" [38.5 (38.5, 39.5, 39.5, 40.5, 40.5, 40.5, 41.5, 42, 39.5, 42.5, 42.5) cm] from the beginning, ending at the armhole edge, shape armhole as follows:

Continuing to work neck shaping as established, BO

| SPORT | 8 | 8 | 8 | 8 | 8 | 8 | 8 | 8 | 9 | 9 | 9 | 12 |
|---|---|---|---|---|---|---|---|---|---|---|---|---|
| DK | 7 | 7 | 7 | 7 | 7 | 7 | 7 | 7 | 9 | 9 | 9 | 11 |
| ARAN | 6 | 6 | 6 | 6 | 6 | 6 | 6 | 6 | 7 | 7 | 7 | 9 |

sts at armhole edge once.

Decrease 1 st at armhole edge every RS row

| SPORT | 7 | 6 | 9 | 9 | 11 | 11 | 12 | 12 | 13 | 17 | 20 | 21 |
|---|---|---|---|---|---|---|---|---|---|---|---|---|
| DK | 5 | 5 | 8 | 8 | 8 | 10 | 9 | 11 | 12 | 13 | 15 | 17 |
| ARAN | 4 | 5 | 5 | 6 | 6 | 9 | 8 | 8 | 8 | 10 | 13 | 15 |

times, then every other RS row

| SPORT | 7 | 8 | 6 | 7 | 6 | 7 | 7 | 8 | 7 | 4 | 2 | 2 |
|---|---|---|---|---|---|---|---|---|---|---|---|---|
| DK | 9 | 9 | 7 | 8 | 9 | 8 | 10 | 9 | 8 | 8 | 7 | 6 |
| ARAN | 7 | 7 | 7 | 7 | 8 | 6 | 7 | 8 | 8 | 7 | 5 | 4 |

times, then every RS row

| SPORT | 6 | 6 | 8 | 8 | 10 | 10 | 11 | 11 | 12 | 16 | 19 | 20 |
|---|---|---|---|---|---|---|---|---|---|---|---|---|
| DK | 4 | 5 | 7 | 7 | 7 | 9 | 8 | 10 | 11 | 12 | 14 | 16 |
| ARAN | 4 | 4 | 5 | 5 | 5 | 8 | 8 | 8 | 8 | 10 | 12 | 14 |

times.

When all shaping is complete, 4 sts remain. Work 1 WS row even. Armhole measures same as for Back.

BO all sts.

# SLEEVES

CO

| | | | | | | | | | | | | |
|---|---|---|---|---|---|---|---|---|---|---|---|---|
| SPORT | 50 | 54 | 58 | 58 | 62 | 62 | 62 | 66 | 66 | 70 | 70 | 70 |
| DK | 46 | 50 | 50 | 54 | 58 | 58 | 58 | 58 | 58 | 62 | 62 | 66 |
| ARAN | 38 | 42 | 42 | 46 | 46 | 46 | 46 | 50 | 50 | 50 | 50 | 54 |

sts.

Begin 2x2 Rib Flat; work even until piece measures 3" (7.5 cm), ending with a WS row.

Change to St st; work 2 rows even.

## SHAPE SLEEVE

Beginning on the next RS row, increase 1 st each side every

| | | | | | | | | | | | | |
|---|---|---|---|---|---|---|---|---|---|---|---|---|
| SPORT | 13 | 11 | 10 | 8 | 8 | 6 | 5 | 5 | 4 | 4 | 3 | 3 |
| DK | 13 | 13 | 9 | 9 | 8 | 7 | 6 | 5 | 4 | 4 | 3 | 3 |
| ARAN | 14 | 14 | 9 | 10 | 8 | 7 | 5 | 5 | 5 | 4 | 3 | 3 |

rows a total of

| | | | | | | | | | | | | |
|---|---|---|---|---|---|---|---|---|---|---|---|---|
| SPORT | 8 | 9 | 10 | 13 | 14 | 17 | 20 | 21 | 24 | 25 | 28 | 31 |
| DK | 8 | 8 | 11 | 12 | 13 | 15 | 18 | 21 | 24 | 24 | 27 | 28 |
| ARAN | 6 | 6 | 9 | 9 | 11 | 13 | 16 | 16 | 18 | 20 | 23 | 23 |

times.

| | | | | | | | | | | | | |
|---|---|---|---|---|---|---|---|---|---|---|---|---|
| SPORT | 66 | 72 | 78 | 84 | 90 | 96 | 102 | 108 | 114 | 120 | 126 | 132 |
| DK | 62 | 66 | 72 | 78 | 84 | 88 | 94 | 100 | 106 | 110 | 116 | 122 |
| ARAN | 50 | 54 | 60 | 64 | 68 | 72 | 78 | 82 | 86 | 90 | 96 | 100 |

sts.

Work even until piece measures 17 (17, 17, 18, 18, 18, 18, 18, 18, 17½, 17, 16½)" [43 (43, 43, 45.5, 45.5, 45.5, 45.5, 45.5, 45.5, 44.5, 43, 42) cm] from the beginning, ending with a WS row.

## SHAPE RAGLAN CAP

BO

| | | | | | | | | | | | | |
|---|---|---|---|---|---|---|---|---|---|---|---|---|
| SPORT | 8 | 8 | 8 | 8 | 8 | 8 | 8 | 8 | 9 | 9 | 9 | 12 |
| DK | 7 | 7 | 7 | 7 | 7 | 7 | 7 | 7 | 9 | 9 | 9 | 11 |
| ARAN | 6 | 6 | 6 | 6 | 6 | 6 | 6 | 6 | 7 | 7 | 7 | 9 |

sts at the beginning of the next 2 rows.

Decrease 1 st each side every RS row

| | | | | | | | | | | | | |
|---|---|---|---|---|---|---|---|---|---|---|---|---|
| SPORT | 2 | 6 | 9 | 9 | 11 | 11 | 12 | 12 | 13 | 17 | 20 | 21 |
| DK | 2 | 5 | 8 | 8 | 8 | 10 | 9 | 11 | 10 | 13 | 15 | 17 |
| ARAN | 2 | 5 | 5 | 6 | 6 | 9 | 8 | 8 | 8 | 10 | 13 | 15 |

times, then every other RS row

| | | | | | | | | | | | | |
|---|---|---|---|---|---|---|---|---|---|---|---|---|
| SPORT | 11 | 9 | 7 | 6 | 6 | 5 | 4 | 3 | 2 | 1 | 1 | 3 |
| DK | 11 | 10 | 8 | 7 | 7 | 7 | 6 | 5 | 5 | 5 | 5 | 6 |
| ARAN | 10 | 9 | 7 | 6 | 7 | 7 | 5 | 5 | 4 | 4 | 3 | 5 |

time(s), then every RS row

| | | | | | | | | | | | | |
|---|---|---|---|---|---|---|---|---|---|---|---|---|
| SPORT | 3 | 4 | 6 | 10 | 10 | 14 | 17 | 21 | 22 | 22 | 21 | 18 |
| DK | 3 | 3 | 5 | 9 | 11 | 11 | 16 | 18 | 19 | 18 | 18 | 16 |
| ARAN | 0 | 0 | 5 | 7 | 7 | 6 | 12 | 14 | 16 | 16 | 16 | 12 |

times.

| | | | | | | | | | | | | |
|---|---|---|---|---|---|---|---|---|---|---|---|---|
| SPORT | 18 | 18 | 18 | 18 | 20 | 20 | 20 | 20 | 22 | 22 | 24 | 24 |
| DK | 16 | 16 | 16 | 16 | 18 | 18 | 18 | 18 | 20 | 20 | 22 | 22 |
| ARAN | 14 | 14 | 14 | 14 | 16 | 16 | 16 | 16 | 16 | 16 | 18 | 18 |

sts remain. Work 1 WS row even. Cap measures same as for Back armholes.

BO all sts.

## FINISHING

Block pieces as desired. Sew raglan seams. Sew side and Sleeve seams.

### FRONT BANDS/COLLAR

With RS facing, using circular needle, beginning at lower Right Front edge and ending at lower Left Front edge, pick up and knit approximately 1 st in each BO st, 2 sts for every 3 rows along vertical edges, and 3 sts for every 4 rows along diagonal edges. You will pick up approximately

| | | | | | | | | | | | | |
|---|---|---|---|---|---|---|---|---|---|---|---|---|
| SPORT | 86 | 86 | 88 | 88 | 91 | 91 | 90 | 92 | 89 | 82 | 92 | 94 |
| DK | 78 | 78 | 79 | 80 | 82 | 83 | 83 | 83 | 81 | 74 | 84 | 86 |
| ARAN | 64 | 65 | 66 | 66 | 67 | 67 | 67 | 68 | 67 | 61 | 69 | 71 |

sts along the straight edges of the Fronts,

| | | | | | | | | | | | | |
|---|---|---|---|---|---|---|---|---|---|---|---|---|
| SPORT | 50 | 52 | 53 | 56 | 60 | 63 | 66 | 69 | 74 | 78 | 80 | 79 |
| DK | 45 | 48 | 48 | 52 | 55 | 57 | 61 | 64 | 67 | 72 | 73 | 74 |
| ARAN | 37 | 39 | 39 | 42 | 44 | 46 | 50 | 52 | 56 | 59 | 60 | 59 |

sts along each shaped neck edge, and

| | | | | | | | | | | | | |
|---|---|---|---|---|---|---|---|---|---|---|---|---|
| SPORT | 42 | 46 | 48 | 50 | 52 | 54 | 58 | 60 | 64 | 66 | 70 | 72 |
| DK | 40 | 42 | 44 | 46 | 48 | 50 | 54 | 56 | 58 | 62 | 64 | 66 |
| ARAN | 32 | 34 | 36 | 38 | 40 | 40 | 44 | 46 | 48 | 50 | 52 | 54 |

sts along Back neck. You will have approximately

| | | | | | | | | | | | | |
|---|---|---|---|---|---|---|---|---|---|---|---|---|
| SPORT | 350 | 358 | 366 | 374 | 394 | 402 | 410 | 422 | 434 | 430 | 462 | 466 |
| DK | 318 | 326 | 330 | 342 | 358 | 366 | 378 | 386 | 394 | 394 | 422 | 430 |
| ARAN | 262 | 270 | 274 | 282 | 294 | 298 | 310 | 318 | 326 | 322 | 346 | 350 |

sts. *Note: Exact st count is not essential, but be sure to end with a multiple of 4 sts + 2 for ribbing to work out evenly.* Begin 2x2 Rib; work

| | |
|---|---|
| SPORT | 5 |
| DK | 5 |
| ARAN | 5 |

rows even.

**BUTTONHOLE ROW (RS):** Work

| | |
|---|---|
| SPORT | 10 |
| DK | 8 |
| ARAN | 6 |

sts, [BO 2 sts, work

| | | | | | | | | | | | | |
|---|---|---|---|---|---|---|---|---|---|---|---|---|
| SPORT | 12 | 12 | 12 | 12 | 13 | 13 | 13 | 13 | 12 | 11 | 13 | 13 |
| DK | 11 | 11 | 11 | 11 | 11 | 11 | 11 | 11 | 11 | 10 | 11 | 12 |
| ARAN | 8 | 8 | 8 | 8 | 9 | 9 | 9 | 9 | 9 | 8 | 9 | 9 |

sts] 7 times, work to end.

Work

| | |
|---|---|
| SPORT | 5 |
| DK | 5 |
| ARAN | 4 |

rows even, CO 2 sts over BO sts on first row using Backward Loop CO (see Special Techniques, page 188). BO all sts in pattern.

Sew buttons opposite buttonholes.

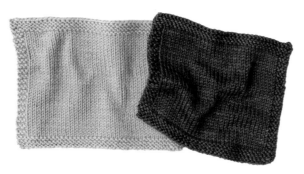

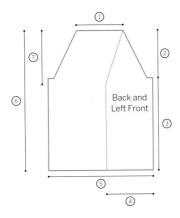

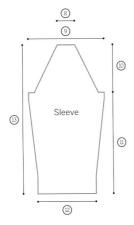

1   7¼ (7¾, 8, 8¼, 8¾, 9, 9¾, 10¼, 10½, 11¼, 11¾, 12)"
    18.5 (19.5, 20.5, 21, 22, 23, 25, 26, 26.5, 28.5, 30, 30.5) cm

2   7 (7¼, 7½, 8, 8½, 9, 9½, 10, 10, 10½, 11, 11½)"
    18 (18.5, 19, 20.5, 21.5, 23, 24, 25.5, 25.5, 26.5, 28, 29) cm

3   15¼ (15¼, 15½, 15½, 16, 16, 16, 16¼, 16½ 15½, 16¾, 16¾)"
    38.5 (38.5, 39.5, 39.5, 40.5, 40.5, 40.5, 41.5, 42, 39.5, 42.5, 42.5) cm

4   7¾ (8½, 8½, 9¼, 10, 10, 10¾, 11½, 12¼, 13, 13¾, 15)"
    19.5 (21.5, 21.5, 23.5, 25.5, 25.5, 27.5, 29, 31, 33, 35, 38) cm

5   16¼ (17, 18½, 19¼, 20, 21½, 22¼, 23¾, 25, 26½, 28, 30¼)"
    41.5 (43, 47, 49, 51, 54.5, 56.5, 60.5, 63.5, 67.5, 71, 77) cm

6   22¼ (22½, 23, 23½, 24½, 25, 25½, 26¼, 26½, 26, 27¾, 28¼)"
    56.5 (57, 58.5, 59.5, 62, 63.5, 65, 66.5, 67.5, 66, 70.5, 72) cm

7   8 (8¼, 8½, 9, 9½, 10, 10½, 11, 11¾, 12½, 12½, 12½)"
    20.5 (21, 21.5, 23, 24, 25.5, 26.5, 28, 30, 32, 32, 32) cm

8   3 (3, 3, 3¼, 3¼, 3¼, 3¼, 3¾, 3¾, 4, 4)"
    7.5 (7.5, 7.5, 7.5, 8.5, 8.5, 8.5, 8.5, 9.5, 9.5, 10, 10) cm

9   11¼ (12, 13, 14¼, 15¼, 16, 17, 18¼, 19¼, 20, 21, 22¼)"
    28.5 (30.5, 33, 36, 38.5, 40.5, 43, 46.5, 49, 51, 53.5, 56.5) cm

10  7 (7¼, 7½, 8, 8½, 9, 9½, 10, 10, 10½, 11, 11½)"
    18 (18.5, 19, 20.5, 21.5, 23, 24, 25.5, 25.5, 26.5, 28, 29) cm

11  17 (17, 17, 18, 18, 18, 18, 18, 18, 17½, 17, 16½)"
    43 (43, 43, 45.5, 45.5, 45.5, 45.5, 45.5, 45.5, 44.5, 43, 42) cm

12  8¼ (9, 9, 9¾, 10½, 10½, 10½, 10½, 10½, 11¼, 11¼, 12)"
    21 (23, 23, 25, 26.5, 26.5, 26.5, 26.5, 26.5, 28.5, 28.5, 30.5) cm

13  24 (24¼, 24½, 26, 26½, 27, 27½, 28, 28, 28, 28, 28)"
    61 (61.5, 62, 66, 67.5, 68.5, 70, 71, 71, 71, 71, 71) cm

1   7 (7½, 8, 8½, 9, 9, 9¾, 10¼, 10¾, 11, 11½, 12)"
    18 (19, 20.5, 21.5, 23, 23, 25, 26, 27.5, 28, 29, 30.5) cm

2   7 (7¼, 7½, 8, 8½, 9, 9½, 10, 10, 10½, 11, 11½)"
    18 (18.5, 19, 20.5, 21.5, 23, 24, 25.5, 25.5, 26.5, 28, 29) cm

3   15¼ (15¼, 15½, 15½, 16, 16, 16, 16¼, 16½ 15½, 16¾, 16¾)"
    38.5 (38.5, 39.5, 39.5, 40.5, 40.5, 40.5, 41.5, 42, 39.5, 42.5, 42.5) cm

4   7½ (8, 8½, 9, 9¼, 9¾, 10¾, 11, 11½, 12½, 13¼, 14¾)"
    19 (20.5, 21.5, 23, 23.5, 25, 27.5, 28, 29, 32, 33.5, 37.5) cm

5   16½ (17¼, 18¼, 19, 20, 21¾, 22¾, 23½, 24½, 26¼, 28, 30¾)"
    42 (44, 46.5, 48.5, 51, 55, 58, 59.5, 62, 66.5, 71, 78) cm

6   22¼ (22½, 23, 23½, 24½, 25, 25½, 26¼, 26½, 26, 27¾, 28¼)"
    56.5 (57, 58.5, 59.5, 62, 63.5, 65, 66.5, 67.5, 66, 70.5, 72) cm

7   8 (8¼, 8½, 9, 9½, 10, 10½, 11, 11¾, 12½, 12½, 12½)"
    20.5 (21, 21.5, 23, 24, 25.5, 26.5, 28, 30, 32, 32, 32) cm

8   3 (3, 3, 3, 3½, 3½, 3½, 3½, 3½, 3½, 4, 4)"
    7.5 (7.5, 7.5, 7.5, 9, 9, 9, 9, 9, 9, 10, 10) cm

9   11 (12, 13¼, 14¼, 15, 16, 17¼, 18¼, 19, 20, 21¼, 22¼)"
    28 (30.5, 33.5, 36, 38, 40.5, 44, 46.5, 48.5, 51, 54, 56.5) cm

10  7 (7¼, 7½, 8, 8½, 9, 9½, 10, 10, 10½, 11, 11½)"
    18 (18.5, 19, 20.5, 21.5, 23, 24, 25.5, 25.5, 26.5, 28, 29) cm

11  17 (17, 17, 18, 18, 18, 18, 18, 18, 17½, 17, 16½)"
    43 (43, 43, 45.5, 45.5, 45.5, 45.5, 45.5, 45.5, 44.5, 43, 42) cm

12  8½ (9¼, 9¼, 10¼, 10¼, 10¼, 10¼, 11, 11, 11, 11, 12)"
    21.5 (23.5, 23.5, 26, 26, 26, 26, 28, 28, 28, 28, 30.5) cm

13  24 (24¼, 24½, 26, 26½, 27, 27½, 28, 28, 28, 28, 28)"
    61 (61.5, 62, 66, 67.5, 68.5, 70, 71, 71, 71, 71, 71) cm

1   7 (7¾, 8, 8¼, 8¾, 9, 9¾, 10, 10¾, 11, 11¾, 12)"
    18 (19.5, 20.5, 21, 22, 23, 25, 25.5, 27.5, 28, 30, 30.5) cm

2   7 (7¼, 7½, 8, 8½, 9, 9½, 10, 10, 10½, 11, 11½)"
    18 (18.5, 19, 20.5, 21.5, 23, 24, 25.5, 25.5, 26.5, 28, 29) cm

3   15¼ (15¼, 15½, 15½, 16, 16, 16, 16¼, 16½ 15½, 16¾, 16¾)"
    38.5 (38.5, 39.5, 39.5, 40.5, 40.5, 40.5, 41.5, 42, 39.5, 42.5, 42.5) cm

4   7¾ (8½, 8½, 9¼, 9¾, 10½, 10½, 11¼, 11¾, 12½, 13¾, 14½)"
    19.5 (21.5, 21.5, 23.5, 25, 26.5, 26.5, 28.5, 30, 32, 35, 37) cm

5   16¼ (17, 18¼, 19, 20¼, 21, 22¼, 23, 24¼, 26¼, 28¼, 30¼)"
    41.5 (43, 46.5, 48.5, 51.5, 53.5, 56.5, 58.5, 61.5, 66.5, 72, 77) cm

6   22¼ (22½, 23, 23½, 24½, 25, 25½, 26¼, 26½, 26, 27¾, 28¼)"
    56.5 (57, 58.5, 59.5, 62, 63.5, 65, 66.5, 67.5, 66, 70.5, 72) cm

7   8 (8¼, 8½, 9, 9½, 10, 10½, 11, 11¾, 12½, 12½, 12½)"
    20.5 (21, 21.5, 23, 24, 25.5, 26.5, 28, 30, 32, 32, 32) cm

8   3 (3, 3, 3, 3¼, 3¼, 3¼, 3¼, 3¾, 3¾, 4, 4)"
    7.5 (7.5, 7.5, 7.5, 8.5, 8.5, 8.5, 8.5, 9.5, 9.5, 10, 10) cm

9   11 (12, 13, 14, 15, 16, 17, 18, 19, 20, 21, 22)"
    28 (30.5, 33, 35.5, 38, 40.5, 43, 45.5, 48.5, 51, 53.5, 56) cm

10  7 (7¼, 7½, 8, 8½, 9, 9½, 10, 10, 10½, 11, 11½)"
    18 (18.5, 19, 20.5, 21.5, 23, 24, 25.5, 25.5, 26.5, 28, 29) cm

11  17 (17, 17, 18, 18, 18, 18, 18, 18, 17½, 17, 16½)"
    43 (43, 43, 45.5, 45.5, 45.5, 45.5, 45.5, 45.5, 44.5, 43, 42) cm

12  8¼ (9, 9¾, 9¾, 10¼, 10¼, 10¼, 11, 11, 11¾, 11¾, 11¾)"
    21 (23, 25, 25, 26, 26, 26, 28, 28, 30, 30, 30) cm

13  24 (24¼, 24½, 26, 26½, 27, 27½, 28, 28, 28, 28, 28)"
    61 (61.5, 62, 66, 67.5, 68.5, 70, 71, 71, 71, 71, 71) cm

CHAPTER

4

..........................................................

# Yoke Sweaters

Fashion-wise, the circular yoke sweater is a fairly recent construction, gaining prominence in the earlier part of the twentieth century. As a design silhouette, it provides an exciting canvas where colorwork, lace, cables, or texture can be worked without break across the entire top of the body of a garment. Traditionally, yoke sweaters were backdrops for stunning stranded colorwork and made exceptionally warm, keep-the-freezing-sea-off-you garments, but in recent years they've become a canvas for a much wider range of designs.

Fit considerations for a yoke depend on the depth of the yoke itself—how far down on your body the circular portion reaches. Since the circular portion is essentially a poncho, the yoke either needs to be quite short (in which case you can make the sweater as snug as you like), or you need enough room through the top of the sweater to raise your arms (lest you turn into a T. Rex).

## WHAT MAKES A YOKE A YOKE?

However a circular yoke sweater is knit, the circular portion at the top of the sweater:

- Is worked in one piece.

- Has the same number of rows on the body and sleeves of the sweater.

Aside from those constraints, you can work them from the neck down and then split for the sleeves and body, or from the bottom up, joining sleeves to body. The body and sleeves can be worked in the round, as with the yoke; or they can be worked flat (on a machine, for example), with the sides and sleeves being seamed before (or after) being joined at the yoke.

Fully in the round

- worked top down or bottom up

- sleeves separate from body before (or after) yoke complete

- body and sleeves can be worked flat (e.g., on a machine) and then joined into the round

Yoke shaping can come in a very few distinct horizontal bands, as in Elizabeth Zimmermann's Percentage System, or can be spread more evenly through the yoke itself, as in the sweaters in this book. Short rows can be used on the back of the sweater and sleeves in order to tilt the front neckline a bit deeper.

The choices you'll face have very little to do with the *fit* of your sweater, so I recommend **starting any yoke sweater with the stitch pattern you'll be working on the yoke**. This will give you a number of important bits of information, including:

■ What stitch-repeat multiples you'll need your yoke stitch count to be, both at the top and bottom (if you don't know this yet, I'd suggest 12 since it's an incredibly versatile number).

■ How deep a yoke your stitch pattern requires.

■ Whether it should be worked top down or bottom up.

■ Whether you can spread the yoke shaping out evenly along the top half of the yoke rows or must insert 3 rows of yoke shaping.

Once you've got a stitch pattern worked into a wedge like this one:

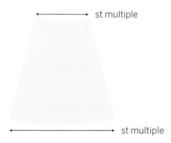

st multiple

st multiple

you're ready to start drafting.

### DESIGN AND FABRIC CONSIDERATIONS FOR CIRCULAR YOKES

With no seams, yoke sweaters don't have much of a skeleton to provide structure. They *do* balance their weight evenly across the wearer's body, and when worked with stranded colorwork, the yoke of the garment can get quite sturdy—making them more versatile in the yarn department than raglans.

Still, circular yokes aren't the best choice for an especially drapey or unstructured fabric. You'll want your fabric to have a good amount of integrity and memory to get a sweater you can wear for decades.

Two of the most common yarns for yoke sweaters, a sport-weight (or even lighter) woolen-spun yarn like Jamieson's Spindrift or the larger Icelandic Lopi yarn, are "sticky" enough to be worked at a fairly open gauge. This helps preserve some flexibility in the stranded fabric and makes the garment warmer (since the spaces between the stitches trap air).

If you're working with a slicker yarn, like superwash, you'll need to knit it quite firmly to get enough durability for a yoke sweater—and this goes doubly for any yoke where the stitch pattern doesn't provide structure (like straight Stockinette stitch or lace).

Design-wise, yoke sweaters don't have a ton of variation other than the stitch pattern. You can alter the length and shape of the body, like I've done with the Constellation Tunic on page 173; you can adjust the neck treatments, like in the Penobscot Pullover on page 147; and you can even add some asymmetry (especially if you're working a cardigan like the Quiet Moment Cardigan on page 169).

You can alter the shape and length of the sleeves similarly—but you'll always be working with a round neckline, unless you want to steek your sweater. This sets you up for trims like turtlenecks; *possibly* high cowls, if you use several short rows to drop the front necklines; picked-up collars; and hoods. But that's about it—the design of a yoke sweater is all about, and inherently tied to, that stitch pattern.

Unlike drop-shoulder and raglan sweaters, I think yoke sweaters can look gorgeous with hourglass-style waist shaping—so if that's what you like, go for it! They typically include a lot of plain Stockinette at the waist, so they make a great target for the dart-style waist shaping described on page 115 as well as more traditional "side seam" waist shaping. (That's in quotes because you're unlikely to be seaming these garments!)

The basic designs in this chapter, like the other construction chapters, lack any waist shaping at all.

### DRAFTING A CIRCULAR YOKE PATTERN

I recommend figuring out your yoke stitch pattern before you attempt to fill in the rest of your personal yoke schematic. This will give you a big leg up on the rest of your calculations.

Once you have a stitch pattern identified, start with the armholes. The first measurement to fill in is your **yoke depth**:

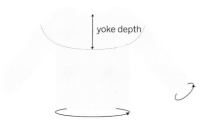

which is the vertical distance, in inches, between the neck edge of the sweater and the point at which the body and sleeves separate (or between the point at which they join and the neck edge, if you're working bottom up).

Some stitch patterns will be so intricate that you'll need a fairly deep yoke just to fit them in; other times, you'll have more discretion. The yoke depth shouldn't ever be shorter than your body's armhole depth; they tend to be most comfortable to wear when they're in the neighborhood of your set-in-sleeve armhole depth, up to 2" (5 cm) deeper.

Once you have the yoke depth settled, you're ready to fill in the rest of the labels in this personal schematic:

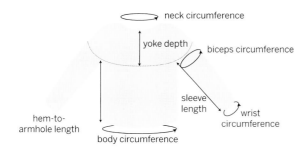

**Lengths** can be matched directly to your measurements—take your desired total sweater length, then subtract the yoke depth you've selected to determine your hem-to-armhole length. Likewise, the sleeve length can be adjusted from your set-in-sleeve lengths (if the yoke depth is deeper than your armhole, subtract length for your yoke sleeve, since the sleeve and body will attach farther down; if they're the same, leave the sleeve length as is).

**Circumferences**, as always, work in a fairly large range based on your ease preferences. If the yoke is on the shallower side (i.e., not much longer than your set-in-sleeve armhole depth), you can make the **body** of your yoke sweater fit however you'd like—be it oversize, skintight, or somewhere in between. Most of the hand-knitting industry considers 2–4" (5–10 cm) of ease through the chest a "standard" fit, but your preferences may definitely vary.

If your yoke is on the longer side, though, you'll want to build more ease into the body, since that's what will give you a good a range of motion. I'd recommend 4" (10 cm) or more, for very deep yokes.

Either way, I'd recommend at least 1" (2.5 cm) of ease in your **biceps**, even if you're looking for a very figure-conscious garment; 2" (5 cm) of ease in the biceps would represent more of a "standard" fit. If you're making the body of the sweater oversize, I'd recommend increasing the biceps ease to match the look of the body. In a long-sleeved sweater, 2–4" (5–10 cm) of ease for the **wrist** is a standard amount.

The **neck circumference** is a matter of personal preference—and I think the best way to draft a personal yoke sweater is to take a piece of string and tie it around your neck until you have a neck opening you like. Then cut the string, measure it, and—presto! You have a neck circumference that will make you perfectly happy. [If you'd like some general guidance, narrower-necked yoke sweaters tend to be in the 21–24" (53.5–61 cm) range; wider-necked sweaters tend to be in the 23½–27" (59.5–68.5 cm) range.]

One more little measurement that isn't listed on the schematic: At the underarms, on both the body and the sleeves, you'll need to bind off (or place on a holder, for later grafting) the underarm stitches. Exactly how many you bind off is again more a matter of personal preference than anything else, but a range of 2–4" (5–10 cm) is fairly typical.

ONCE YOU'VE FILLED IN YOUR SCHEMATIC, YOU'RE READY TO DRAFT YOUR PATTERN

Let's follow this process with an example—a fairly wide-necked yoke pullover, without waist shaping, for my measurements. (I tend to work my yoke sweaters from the bottom up for some reason—maybe I like the stitches to be pointing right-side up?!) Here's my personal schematic:

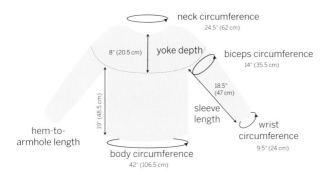

Next, turn the measurements into **preliminary** stitch and row counts based on your gauge. Let's assume I'm working at a fairly typical gauge of 5 stitches and 7 rows to 1" (2.5 cm):

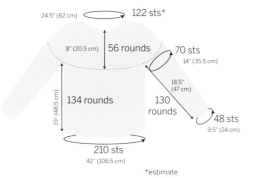

These counts are preliminary because there's still a little bit of work to do to get the counts you'll need in order to figure out your yoke shaping.

The body and sleeves of my sweater are pretty simple—I cast on 210 stitches for the hem of my sweater and work in the round as desired until the body is complete. I then **bind off 14 stitches for each armhole** and place the remaining 91 stitches each for the front and back on a holder while I knit the sleeves.

For the sleeves, I'll cast on 48 stitches and use the Master Shaping Formula (see page 19) to increase appropriately to 70 stitches. Once the sleeves are long enough, I'll again **bind off 14 stitches at the underarm** and put the remaining 56 stitches on a holder.

Before I can go further, I'll need to **figure out my yoke shaping**—and that means talking about stitch multiples. It's almost certain that I'm working my yoke sweater in a stitch pattern that has a *multiple* at the base of the yoke—for example, a 12-stitch, 10-row border. After you join your stitches together, it's helpful to work a single stitch-count-adjustment row to ensure your stitch pattern works out evenly. In this case, let's assume I've selected a stitch pattern that starts with 12 stitches at the bottom and ends with 5 stitches at the top.

For my sweater, in my joining row I'll have 56 + 91 + 56 + 91 = 294 stitches. To get to the nearest multiple of 12 stitches—288—I'll need to subtract 6 stitches in the first round after joining the held stitches together.

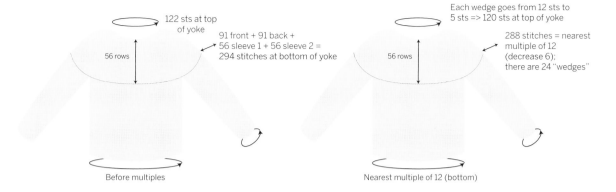

122 sts at top of yoke

56 rows

91 front + 91 back + 56 sleeve 1 + 56 sleeve 2 = 294 stitches at bottom of yoke

56 rows

Before multiples

Each wedge goes from 12 sts to 5 sts => 120 sts at top of yoke

288 stitches = nearest multiple of 12 (decrease 6); there are 24 "wedges"

Nearest multiple of 12 (bottom)

Once you've made this stitch count adjustment, **you've basically already drafted your yoke shaping pattern**, back at the beginning—you've got a wedge of stitch patterning that decreases at the top.

In my example, I've got 24 repeats of 12 stitches each; each repeat of 12 stitches goes down to 5 stitches at the top—which means that instead of ending with the 122 stitches I originally estimated, I'll have 24 x 5 = 120 stitches to bind off at the neck.

If you follow the advice laid out so far, you'll get a yoke sweater whose front neck depth and back neck depth are the same. This isn't the end of the world, but most of us prefer a front neck depth that's at least a little lower than the back. Short rows are the way to get a deeper front neckline.

You'll want your first (longest) short row to reach all the way toward the front of the sleeve; they can be placed either immediately after joining, or both immediately after joining and just before binding off (when working bottom up):

short rows can be placed immediately after joining, or at the top just before binding off (working bottom up)

How many short rows you insert depends on how far you'd like the neck to drop. You can typically get somewhere in the range of 2-3" (5-7.5 cm) of drop before it starts to look strange; I'd recommend inserting two wedges of 1-1½" (2.5-4 cm) rather than making a single large wedge.

When working the short rows, you'll want to keep each wrap ½-1" (1.5-2.5 cm) away from the next to ensure a smooth fabric.

I've found in my years of working with knitters that one of the best tricks for fit issues like a tummy or larger bust is to adjust the width of the front separately from the width of the back. Since your bust and/or tummy are only on your front, making the front wider than the back gives your body the fabric it needs without enlarging the fit everywhere.

Unfortunately, that approach gets trickier with a yoke sweater—there should be the same number of stitches in the front of the neck and the back of the neck, so the front "wedges" will need a different rate of decrease than back and sleeve "wedges" if you've started out with a front bust that's wider than the back bust.

That's not to say this is impossible! You'll likely want to swatch two versions of your yoke wedge, and spend some time massaging the neck numbers to match . . . but the result of your hard work will be a sweater that fits you properly everywhere.

I've written the following basic, straight-sided sweaters in three gauges and twelve sizes, so if you'd prefer not to draft your own yoke patterns, you've got a great starting point. I've shown these with recommended yarns, but I encourage you to experiment, too! Just keep in mind you'll need a fairly firm fabric since yoke sweaters are short on structure. If you'd like a worksheet to help you tame the numbers as you knit, you can download one from my website.

# Guidelines on Yoke Shaping

If your stitch pattern *doesn't* dictate the shaping by necessity, here are some basic ground rules.

### How many stitches to remove in each "wedge."

The precise way to figure this out is to add up the circumferences of the non-bound-off sleeve and body stitches and divide the neck circumference by that number. The result is a percentage of the stitches in each wedge you must remove.

For example, if I've started with 12-stitch wedges, have 57½" (146 cm) of stitches when I join the yoke, and want to end up with a wide neckline of 25" (63.5 cm), I need to remove 25 / 57½ = 43.4 percent of the stitches, or approximately 5 stitches, in each of my 12-stitch wedges

But if that made you shudder, I can give you some general guidelines for an "average-width" neckline:

- If you're in the middle of the size range, removing half (or a stitch or two more) of each wedge is a good place to start.

- If you're at the smaller end of the size range, you likely won't need to remove as many stitches—your full chest circumference will be closer to your desired neck circumference than in the middle of the range. See where removing 40 percent of the stitches will get you, circumference-wise, and go from there.

- If you're at the larger end of the size range, you likely will need to remove *more* than half the stitches—your full chest circumference will be further away from your desired neck circumference than in the middle of the range. See where removing 60 percent of the stitches takes you, and go from there.

### How to remove those stitches.

Here you have two fundamental choices. In all cases, you'll work your first decreases roughly halfway through the yoke (from the bottom up) and then aim to split the rest of the decreases between the top two quarters of the yoke.

You can try to group the decreases into a small number of massive decrease rows (if you have a fundamentally horizontal stitch pattern with a few bands of Stockinette stitch), or you can make each decrease row more gentle, and have more of them (this tends to work better with vertical panels of stitch patterning).

The choice is up to you; decreasing the stitches more gradually tends to produce a smoother fabric, while working all the decreases in just three (or four) decrease rounds tends to cause some rippling. I've definitely seen this rippling exaggerated into a lovely style element, though! (Or, if your garment has some negative ease through the bust, you may smooth out the fabric on your own.)

Whether in bands or more gradually, I personally favor removing 20-25 percent of the stitches in the bottom half of the yoke; 30-35 percent of the stitches in the third quarter of the yoke; and the remaining 40-50 percent of the stitches in the top quarter of the yoke.

None of these rules are hard-and-fast, though—there's no single right answer here, and your own preference is what matters most. I strongly recommend swatching a single "wedge" of your yoke until you're happy, and drafting the pattern from there.

# Basic Pullover: Yoke Construction

I usually think "yoke pullover" is synonymous with "have a field day with your colors," but I was really surprised at how lovely a basic one-color garment can be. In addition to the rustic (but soft!) woolen-spun I used for the sample, I've selected a soft sport-weight baby alpaca and a light, sturdy woolen-spun Aran yarn.

This unisex garment is worked in the round from the bottom up, and then worked in the round to the neckline. No waist shaping is included in any of the basic patterns, but should you choose to add some, please see pages 113–115 for details.

## FINISHED MEASUREMENTS

**SPORT:** 33¼ (36, 38, 40, 42, 44, 46, 48, 52, 56, 60, 64)" [84.5 (91.5, 96.5, 101.5, 106.5, 112, 117, 122, 132, 142, 152.5, 162.5) cm] chest

**WORSTED:** 33½ (36¾, 38½, 40, 41½, 44¾, 46½, 48, 52¾, 56, 60¾, 64)" [85 (93.5, 98, 101.5, 105.5, 113.5, 118, 122, 134, 142, 154.5, 162.5) cm] chest

**ARAN:** 33¾ (35½, 37¼, 41, 42¾, 44½, 46¼, 48, 51½, 57, 60½, 64)" [85.5 (90, 94.5, 104, 108.5, 113, 117.5, 122, 131, 145, 153.5, 162.5) cm] chest

*Note: Sweater is intended to be worn with 2–4" (5–10 cm) ease in the bust; shown in worsted weight yarn and size 38½" (98 cm).*

## YARN

**SPORT:** Blue Sky Fibers Baby Alpaca [100% baby alpaca; 110 yards (100 meters) / 50 grams]: 10 (11, 12, 12, 13, 14, 15, 15, 17, 18, 19, 21) hanks Natural Light Gray

**WORSTED:** Swans Island All-American Worsted [75% Rambouillet wool, 25% alpaca; 210 yards (192 meters) / 80 grams]: 5 (6, 6, 6, 7, 7, 8, 8, 9, 9, 10, 11) hanks Granite

**ARAN:** Harrisville Designs Watershed [100% pure virgin wool; 110 yards (100 meters) / 50 grams]: 9 (9, 10, 11, 11, 12, 12, 13, 14, 15, 16, 17) hanks Granite

## NEEDLES

**SPORT:** One circular needle 24" (60 cm) long or longer and one set of double-pointed needles, size US 4 (3.5 mm)

**WORSTED:** One circular needle 24" (60 cm) long or longer and one set of double-pointed needles, size US 7 (4.5 mm)

**ARAN:** One circular needle 24" (60 cm) long or longer and one set of double-pointed needles, size US 8 (5 mm)

Change needle size if necessary to obtain correct gauge.

## NOTIONS

Stitch markers (including 1 in unique color or style), stitch holders or waste yarn

## GAUGE

**SPORT:** 24 sts and 32 rows = 4" (10 cm) in St st
**WORSTED:** 20 sts and 28 rows = 4" (10 cm) in St st
**ARAN:** 18 sts and 26 rows = 4" (10 cm) in St st

## NOTES

If your size gives the number 0 for a particular instruction, skip that instruction and proceed to the next instruction.

## BODY

Using circular needle, CO

| | | | | | | | | | | | | |
|---|---|---|---|---|---|---|---|---|---|---|---|---|
| SPORT | 200 | 216 | 228 | 240 | 252 | 264 | 276 | 288 | 312 | 336 | 360 | 384 |
| WORSTED | 168 | 184 | 192 | 200 | 208 | 224 | 232 | 240 | 264 | 280 | 304 | 320 |
| ARAN | 152 | 160 | 168 | 184 | 192 | 200 | 208 | 216 | 232 | 256 | 272 | 288 |

sts. Join for working in the rnd, being careful not to twist sts; pm for beginning of rnd and after

| | | | | | | | | | | | | |
|---|---|---|---|---|---|---|---|---|---|---|---|---|
| SPORT | 100 | 108 | 114 | 120 | 126 | 132 | 138 | 144 | 156 | 168 | 180 | 192 |
| WORSTED | 84 | 92 | 96 | 100 | 104 | 112 | 116 | 120 | 132 | 140 | 152 | 160 |
| ARAN | 76 | 80 | 84 | 92 | 96 | 100 | 104 | 108 | 116 | 128 | 136 | 144 |

sts for side.

Begin 2x2 Rib in the Rnd; work even until piece measures 2¼" (5.5 cm).

Change to St st; work even until piece measures 16 (16, 16, 16.5, 16.5, 17, 17, 17, 17, 17, 17, 17)" [40.5 (40.5, 40.5, 42, 42, 43, 43, 43, 43, 43, 43) cm] from the beginning, ending with a WS row.

**DIVIDING RND:** BO

| | | | | | | | | | | | | |
|---|---|---|---|---|---|---|---|---|---|---|---|---|
| SPORT | 8 | 8 | 9 | 9 | 9 | 11 | 11 | 11 | 12 | 12 | 14 | 14 |
| WORSTED | 7 | 7 | 8 | 8 | 8 | 9 | 9 | 9 | 10 | 10 | 12 | 12 |
| ARAN | 6 | 6 | 7 | 7 | 7 | 8 | 8 | 8 | 9 | 9 | 11 | 11 |

sts, work to

| | | | | | | | | | | | | |
|---|---|---|---|---|---|---|---|---|---|---|---|---|
| SPORT | 8 | 8 | 9 | 9 | 9 | 11 | 11 | 11 | 12 | 12 | 14 | 14 |
| WORSTED | 7 | 7 | 8 | 8 | 8 | 9 | 9 | 9 | 10 | 10 | 12 | 12 |
| ARAN | 6 | 6 | 7 | 7 | 7 | 8 | 8 | 8 | 9 | 9 | 11 | 11 |

sts before side marker, BO

| | | | | | | | | | | | | |
|---|---|---|---|---|---|---|---|---|---|---|---|---|
| SPORT | 16 | 16 | 18 | 18 | 18 | 22 | 22 | 22 | 24 | 24 | 28 | 28 |
| WORSTED | 14 | 14 | 16 | 16 | 16 | 18 | 18 | 18 | 20 | 20 | 24 | 24 |
| ARAN | 12 | 12 | 14 | 14 | 14 | 16 | 16 | 16 | 18 | 18 | 22 | 22 |

sts, work to last

| | | | | | | | | | | | | |
|---|---|---|---|---|---|---|---|---|---|---|---|---|
| SPORT | 8 | 8 | 9 | 9 | 9 | 11 | 11 | 11 | 12 | 12 | 14 | 14 |
| WORSTED | 7 | 7 | 8 | 8 | 8 | 9 | 9 | 9 | 10 | 10 | 12 | 12 |
| ARAN | 6 | 6 | 7 | 7 | 7 | 8 | 8 | 8 | 9 | 9 | 11 | 11 |

sts, BO to end.

| | | | | | | | | | | | | |
|---|---|---|---|---|---|---|---|---|---|---|---|---|
| SPORT | 84 | 92 | 96 | 102 | 108 | 110 | 116 | 122 | 132 | 144 | 152 | 164 |
| WORSTED | 70 | 78 | 80 | 84 | 88 | 94 | 98 | 102 | 112 | 120 | 128 | 136 |
| ARAN | 64 | 68 | 70 | 78 | 82 | 84 | 88 | 92 | 98 | 110 | 114 | 122 |

remain each for Front and Back. Break yarn; transfer sts to holder or waste yarn.

## SLEEVES

CO

| | | | | | | | | | | | | |
|---|---|---|---|---|---|---|---|---|---|---|---|---|
| SPORT | 52 | 52 | 52 | 56 | 56 | 56 | 56 | 56 | 56 | 60 | 60 | 64 |
| WORSTED | 44 | 44 | 44 | 44 | 44 | 44 | 48 | 48 | 48 | 52 | 52 | 52 |
| ARAN | 40 | 40 | 40 | 40 | 40 | 40 | 44 | 44 | 44 | 44 | 44 | 48 |

sts. Join for working in the rnd, being careful not to twist sts; pm for beginning of rnd.

Begin 2x2 Rib in the Rnd; work even until piece measures 3" (7.5 cm).

Change to St st; work 2 rnds even.

**SHAPE SLEEVE**
Increase 2 sts every

| | | | | | | | | | | | | |
|---|---|---|---|---|---|---|---|---|---|---|---|---|
| SPORT | 12 | 11 | 9 | 10 | 8 | 7 | 6 | 5 | 4 | 4 | 3 | 3 |
| WORSTED | 14 | 12 | 10 | 9 | 8 | 6 | 6 | 5 | 4 | 4 | 4 | 3 |
| ARAN | 15 | 13 | 10 | 9 | 8 | 6 | 6 | 5 | 4 | 4 | 3 | 3 |

rnds a total of

| | | | | | | | | | | | | |
|---|---|---|---|---|---|---|---|---|---|---|---|---|
| SPORT | 9 | 10 | 12 | 11 | 14 | 17 | 20 | 23 | 26 | 27 | 30 | 34 |
| WORSTED | 7 | 8 | 10 | 11 | 13 | 16 | 16 | 19 | 21 | 22 | 24 | 29 |
| ARAN | 6 | 7 | 9 | 10 | 12 | 14 | 14 | 17 | 19 | 21 | 23 | 26 |

times, as follows: K1, M1R, knit to last st, M1L, k1.

| | | | | | | | | | | | | |
|---|---|---|---|---|---|---|---|---|---|---|---|---|
| SPORT | 70 | 72 | 76 | 78 | 84 | 90 | 96 | 102 | 108 | 114 | 120 | 132 |
| WORSTED | 58 | 60 | 64 | 66 | 70 | 76 | 80 | 86 | 90 | 96 | 100 | 110 |
| ARAN | 52 | 54 | 58 | 60 | 64 | 68 | 72 | 78 | 82 | 86 | 90 | 100 |

sts.

Work even until piece measures 18 (18, 18, 18½, 18½, 18½, 18½, 18½, 18, 18, 17½, 17)" [45.5 (45.5, 45.5, 47, 47, 47, 47, 47, 45.5, 45.5, 44.5, 43) cm] from the beginning.

**NEXT RND:** BO

| | | | | | | | | | | | | |
|---|---|---|---|---|---|---|---|---|---|---|---|---|
| SPORT | 8 | 8 | 9 | 9 | 9 | 11 | 11 | 11 | 12 | 12 | 14 | 14 |
| WORSTED | 7 | 7 | 8 | 8 | 8 | 9 | 9 | 9 | 10 | 10 | 12 | 12 |
| ARAN | 6 | 6 | 7 | 7 | 7 | 8 | 8 | 8 | 9 | 9 | 11 | 11 |

sts, work to last

| | | | | | | | | | | | | |
|---|---|---|---|---|---|---|---|---|---|---|---|---|
| SPORT | 8 | 8 | 9 | 9 | 9 | 11 | 11 | 11 | 12 | 12 | 14 | 14 |
| WORSTED | 7 | 7 | 8 | 8 | 8 | 9 | 9 | 9 | 10 | 10 | 12 | 12 |
| ARAN | 6 | 6 | 7 | 7 | 7 | 8 | 8 | 8 | 9 | 9 | 11 | 11 |

sts, BO to end.

| | | | | | | | | | | | | |
|---|---|---|---|---|---|---|---|---|---|---|---|---|
| SPORT | 54 | 56 | 58 | 60 | 66 | 68 | 74 | 80 | 84 | 90 | 92 | 104 |
| WORSTED | 44 | 46 | 48 | 50 | 54 | 58 | 62 | 68 | 70 | 76 | 76 | 86 |
| ARAN | 40 | 42 | 44 | 46 | 50 | 52 | 56 | 62 | 64 | 68 | 68 | 78 |

remain. Break yarn; transfer sts to holder or waste yarn.

## YOKE

**JOINING RND:** Using circular needle, knit across

| | | | | | | | | | | | | |
|---|---|---|---|---|---|---|---|---|---|---|---|---|
| SPORT | 42 | 46 | 48 | 51 | 54 | 55 | 58 | 61 | 66 | 72 | 76 | 82 |
| WORSTED | 35 | 39 | 40 | 42 | 44 | 47 | 49 | 51 | 56 | 60 | 64 | 68 |
| ARAN | 32 | 34 | 35 | 39 | 41 | 42 | 44 | 46 | 49 | 55 | 57 | 61 |

sts (first half of Back), pm in unique color or style for beginning of rnd and center Back, knit across

| | | | | | | | | | | | | |
|---|---|---|---|---|---|---|---|---|---|---|---|---|
| SPORT | 42 | 46 | 48 | 51 | 54 | 55 | 58 | 61 | 66 | 72 | 76 | 82 |
| WORSTED | 35 | 39 | 40 | 42 | 44 | 47 | 49 | 51 | 56 | 60 | 64 | 68 |
| ARAN | 32 | 34 | 35 | 39 | 41 | 42 | 44 | 46 | 49 | 55 | 57 | 61 |

sts (second half of Back), pm, knit across

| | | | | | | | | | | | | |
|---|---|---|---|---|---|---|---|---|---|---|---|---|
| SPORT | 54 | 56 | 58 | 60 | 66 | 68 | 74 | 80 | 84 | 90 | 92 | 104 |
| WORSTED | 44 | 46 | 48 | 50 | 54 | 58 | 62 | 68 | 70 | 76 | 76 | 86 |
| ARAN | 40 | 42 | 44 | 46 | 50 | 52 | 56 | 62 | 64 | 68 | 68 | 78 |

Left Sleeve sts, pm, knit across

| | | | | | | | | | | | | |
|---|---|---|---|---|---|---|---|---|---|---|---|---|
| SPORT | 84 | 92 | 96 | 102 | 108 | 110 | 116 | 122 | 132 | 144 | 152 | 164 |
| WORSTED | 70 | 78 | 80 | 84 | 88 | 94 | 98 | 102 | 112 | 120 | 128 | 136 |
| ARAN | 64 | 68 | 70 | 78 | 82 | 84 | 88 | 92 | 98 | 110 | 114 | 122 |

Front sts, pm, knit across

| | | | | | | | | | | | | |
|---|---|---|---|---|---|---|---|---|---|---|---|---|
| SPORT | 54 | 56 | 58 | 60 | 66 | 68 | 74 | 80 | 84 | 90 | 92 | 104 |
| WORSTED | 44 | 46 | 48 | 50 | 54 | 58 | 62 | 68 | 70 | 76 | 76 | 86 |
| ARAN | 40 | 42 | 44 | 46 | 50 | 52 | 56 | 62 | 64 | 68 | 68 | 78 |

Right Sleeve sts, pm, knit to beginning of rnd.

| | | | | | | | | | | | | |
|---|---|---|---|---|---|---|---|---|---|---|---|---|
| SPORT | 276 | 296 | 308 | 324 | 348 | 356 | 380 | 404 | 432 | 468 | 488 | 536 |
| WORSTED | 228 | 248 | 256 | 268 | 284 | 304 | 320 | 340 | 364 | 392 | 408 | 444 |
| ARAN | 208 | 220 | 228 | 248 | 264 | 272 | 288 | 308 | 324 | 356 | 364 | 400 |

sts.

**NEXT RND:** Knit 1 rnd, increasing or decreasing sts as indicated below. If the number is positive, work that many increases; if the number is negative, work that many decreases; if the number is 0, knit to end. Work the increases or decreases on the Back and/or Fronts, working at the markers between Body and Sleeves.

| | | | | | | | | | | | | |
|---|---|---|---|---|---|---|---|---|---|---|---|---|
| SPORT | 0 | 4 | 4 | 0 | 0 | 4 | 4 | 4 | 0 | 0 | 4 | 4 |
| WORSTED | 0 | 4 | -4 | -4 | 4 | -4 | 4 | -4 | -4 | 4 | 0 | 0 |
| ARAN | -4 | -4 | 0 | 4 | 0 | 4 | 0 | 4 | 0 | 4 | -4 | -4 |

| | | | | | | | | | | | | |
|---|---|---|---|---|---|---|---|---|---|---|---|---|
| SPORT | 276 | 300 | 312 | 324 | 348 | 360 | 384 | 408 | 432 | 468 | 492 | 540 |
| WORSTED | 228 | 252 | 252 | 264 | 288 | 300 | 324 | 336 | 360 | 396 | 408 | 444 |
| ARAN | 204 | 216 | 228 | 252 | 264 | 276 | 288 | 312 | 324 | 360 | 360 | 396 |

sts. Remove markers between Back and Left and Right Sleeves, leaving beginning-of-rnd marker and markers between Front and Left and Right Sleeves in place.

## SHAPE BACK NECK (OPTIONAL)

**SHORT ROW 1 (RS):** Knit to 1 st before Left Sleeve marker, w&t.

**SHORT ROW 2 (WS):** Purl to 1 st before Right Sleeve marker, w&t.

**SHORT ROW 3:** Knit to

| | |
|---|---|
| SPORT | 7 |
| WORSTED | 5 |
| ARAN | 4 |

sts before wrapped st from previous RS row, w&t.

**SHORT ROW 4:** Purl to

| | |
|---|---|
| SPORT | 7 |
| WORSTED | 5 |
| ARAN | 4 |

sts before wrapped st from previous WS row, w&t.

Repeat Short Rows 3 and 4

| | |
|---|---|
| SPORT | 5 |
| WORSTED | 4 |
| ARAN | 4 |

times.

Knit to end, working wraps together with wrapped sts as you come to them, and removing all markers except beginning-of-rnd marker.

Knit

| | | | | | | | | | | | | |
|---|---|---|---|---|---|---|---|---|---|---|---|---|
| SPORT | 18 | 20 | 22 | 23 | 25 | 26 | 27 | 29 | 30 | 32 | 34 | 36 |
| WORSTED | 15 | 16 | 18 | 19 | 21 | 22 | 22 | 24 | 25 | 27 | 29 | 30 |
| ARAN | 13 | 14 | 16 | 17 | 18 | 19 | 20 | 22 | 23 | 24 | 26 | 27 |

rnds, working remaining wraps together with wrapped sts as you come to them on first rnd.

**NEXT RND:** *K12, pm for shaping; repeat from * to last 12 sts, knit to end.

**YOKE DECREASE RND:** *K2tog, knit to marker, sm; repeat from * to end.

| | | | | | | | | | | | | |
|---|---|---|---|---|---|---|---|---|---|---|---|---|
| SPORT | 23 | 25 | 26 | 27 | 29 | 30 | 32 | 34 | 36 | 39 | 41 | 45 |
| WORSTED | 19 | 21 | 21 | 22 | 24 | 25 | 27 | 28 | 30 | 33 | 34 | 37 |
| ARAN | 17 | 18 | 19 | 21 | 22 | 23 | 24 | 26 | 27 | 30 | 30 | 33 |

sts decreased.

Work

| | | | | | | | | | | | | |
|---|---|---|---|---|---|---|---|---|---|---|---|---|
| SPORT | 5 | 6 | 6 | 7 | 5 | 5 | 5 | 5 | 5 | 6 | 6 | 6 |
| WORSTED | 5 | 5 | 6 | 6 | 4 | 4 | 4 | 5 | 5 | 5 | 5 | 6 |
| ARAN | 4 | 5 | 5 | 3 | 4 | 4 | 4 | 4 | 4 | 5 | 5 | 5 |

rnds even.

Repeat Yoke Decrease Rnd.

Work

|  | | | | | | | | | | | | |
|---|---|---|---|---|---|---|---|---|---|---|---|---|
| SPORT | 5 | 5 | 6 | 6 | 4 | 4 | 5 | 5 | 5 | 5 | 6 | 6 |
| WORSTED | 4 | 5 | 5 | 5 | 4 | 4 | 4 | 4 | 4 | 5 | 5 | 5 |
| ARAN | 4 | 4 | 5 | 3 | 3 | 4 | 4 | 4 | 4 | 4 | 5 | 5 |

rnds even.

Repeat Yoke Decrease Rnd.

**SELECTED SIZES ONLY (PROCEED TO *ALL SIZES* IF YOUR SIZE IS 0):**
Work

|  | | | | | | | | | | | | |
|---|---|---|---|---|---|---|---|---|---|---|---|---|
| SPORT | 0 | 0 | 0 | 0 | 4 | 4 | 4 | 5 | 5 | 5 | 5 | 6 |
| WORSTED | 0 | 0 | 0 | 0 | 3 | 3 | 4 | 4 | 4 | 4 | 5 | 5 |
| ARAN | 0 | 0 | 0 | 3 | 3 | 3 | 3 | 4 | 4 | 4 | 4 | 5 |

rnds even.

Repeat Yoke Decrease Rnd.

**ALL SIZES:**
Work

|  | | | | | | | | | | | | |
|---|---|---|---|---|---|---|---|---|---|---|---|---|
| SPORT | 3 | 4 | 4 | 4 | 4 | 5 | 5 | 5 | 4 | 4 | 4 | 5 |
| WORSTED | 3 | 3 | 3 | 3 | 4 | 4 | 4 | 4 | 3 | 3 | 4 | 4 |
| ARAN | 2 | 3 | 3 | 3 | 3 | 4 | 4 | 4 | 3 | 3 | 3 | 4 |

rnds even.

Repeat Yoke Decrease Rnd.

Work

|  | | | | | | | | | | | | |
|---|---|---|---|---|---|---|---|---|---|---|---|---|
| SPORT | 3 | 3 | 4 | 4 | 4 | 4 | 4 | 5 | 4 | 4 | 4 | 4 |
| WORSTED | 2 | 3 | 3 | 3 | 3 | 4 | 4 | 4 | 3 | 3 | 3 | 4 |
| ARAN | 2 | 2 | 3 | 3 | 3 | 3 | 3 | 4 | 3 | 3 | 3 | 3 |

rnds even.

Repeat Yoke Decrease Rnd.

Work

|  | | | | | | | | | | | | |
|---|---|---|---|---|---|---|---|---|---|---|---|---|
| SPORT | 3 | 3 | 3 | 3 | 4 | 4 | 4 | 4 | 3 | 4 | 4 | 4 |
| WORSTED | 2 | 2 | 3 | 3 | 3 | 3 | 3 | 4 | 3 | 3 | 3 | 3 |
| ARAN | 2 | 2 | 2 | 2 | 3 | 3 | 3 | 3 | 2 | 3 | 3 | 3 |

rnds even.

Repeat Yoke Decrease Rnd.

**SELECTED SIZES ONLY (PROCEED TO *ALL SIZES* IF YOUR SIZE IS 0):**
Work

|  | | | | | | | | | | | | |
|---|---|---|---|---|---|---|---|---|---|---|---|---|
| SPORT | 0 | 0 | 0 | 0 | 0 | 0 | 0 | 0 | 3 | 3 | 4 | 4 |
| WORSTED | 0 | 0 | 0 | 0 | 0 | 0 | 0 | 0 | 3 | 3 | 3 | 3 |
| ARAN | 0 | 0 | 0 | 0 | 0 | 0 | 0 | 0 | 2 | 2 | 3 | 3 |

rnds even.

Repeat Yoke Decrease Rnd.

**ALL SIZES:**

|  | | | | | | | | | | | | |
|---|---|---|---|---|---|---|---|---|---|---|---|---|
| SPORT | 138 | 150 | 156 | 162 | 145 | 150 | 160 | 170 | 144 | 156 | 164 | 180 |
| WORSTED | 114 | 126 | 126 | 132 | 120 | 125 | 135 | 140 | 120 | 132 | 136 | 148 |
| ARAN | 102 | 108 | 114 | 105 | 110 | 115 | 120 | 130 | 108 | 120 | 120 | 132 |

sts remain.

Knit 1 rnd, decreasing

| | | | | | | | | | | | | |
|---|---|---|---|---|---|---|---|---|---|---|---|---|
| SPORT | 6 | 18 | 20 | 22 | 5 | 10 | 20 | 26 | 0 | 8 | 12 | 28 |
| WORSTED | 6 | 14 | 14 | 16 | 4 | 9 | 19 | 20 | 0 | 8 | 12 | 20 |
| ARAN | 6 | 8 | 14 | 1 | 6 | 11 | 16 | 22 | 0 | 8 | 8 | 16 |

st(s) evenly to end.

| | | | | | | | | | | | | |
|---|---|---|---|---|---|---|---|---|---|---|---|---|
| SPORT | 132 | 132 | 136 | 140 | 140 | 140 | 140 | 144 | 144 | 148 | 152 | 152 |
| WORSTED | 108 | 112 | 112 | 116 | 116 | 116 | 116 | 120 | 120 | 124 | 124 | 128 |
| ARAN | 96 | 100 | 100 | 104 | 104 | 104 | 104 | 108 | 108 | 112 | 112 | 116 |

sts remain.

Begin 2x2 Rib in the Rnd; work

| | |
|---|---|
| SPORT | 8 |
| WORSTED | 7 |
| ARAN | 6 |

rnds even. BO all sts in pattern.

## FINISHING

Block piece as desired. Sew underarm seams.

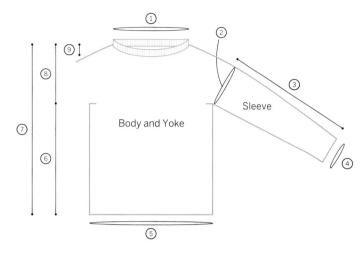

1   21½ (22½, 22½, 23¼, 23¼, 23¼, 23¼, 24, 24, 24¾, 24¾, 25½)"
    54.5 (57, 57, 59, 59, 59, 59, 61, 61, 63, 63, 65) cm

2   11½ (12, 12¾, 13¼, 14, 15¼, 16, 17¼, 18, 19¼, 20, 22)"
    29 (30.5, 32.5, 33.5, 35.5, 38.5, 40.5, 44, 45.5, 49, 51, 56) cm

3   18 (18, 18, 18½, 18½, 18½, 18½, 18½, 18, 18, 17½, 17)"
    45.5 (45.5, 45.5, 47, 47, 47, 47, 47, 45.5, 45.5, 44.5, 43) cm

4   8¾ (8¾, 8¾, 8¾, 8¾, 8¾, 9½, 9½, 9½, 10½, 10½, 10½)"
    22 (22, 22, 22, 22, 22, 24, 24, 24, 26.5, 26.5, 26.5) cm

5   33½ (36¾, 38½, 40, 41½, 44¾, 46½, 48, 52¾, 56, 60¾, 64)"
    85 (93.5, 98, 101.5, 105.5, 113.5, 118, 122, 134, 142, 154.5, 162.5) cm

6   16 (16, 16, 16½, 16½, 17, 17, 17, 17, 17, 17, 17)"
    40.5 (40.5, 40.5, 42, 42, 43, 43, 43, 43, 43, 43, 43) cm

7   23¾ (24¼, 24¾, 25¼, 26, 26¾, 26¾, 27½, 27¾, 28¼, 28¾, 29¼)"
    60.5 (61.5, 63, 64, 66, 68, 68, 70, 70.5, 72, 73, 74.5) cm

8   7¾ (8¼, 8¾, 8¾, 9½, 9¾, 9¾, 10½, 10¾, 11¼, 11¾, 12¼)"
    19.5 (21, 22, 22, 24, 25, 25, 26.5, 27.5, 28.5, 30, 31) cm

9   1¾"
    4.5 cm

1   22 (22, 22¾, 23¼, 23¼, 23¼, 23¼, 24, 24, 24¾, 25¼, 25¼)"
    56 (56, 58, 59, 59, 59, 59, 61, 61, 63, 64, 64) cm

2   11¾ (12, 12¾, 13, 14, 15, 16, 17, 18, 19, 20, 22)"
    30 (30.5, 32.5, 33, 35.5, 38, 40.5, 43, 45.5, 48.5, 51, 56) cm

3   18 (18, 18, 18½, 18½, 18½, 18½, 18½, 18, 18, 17½, 17)"
    45.5 (45.5, 45.5, 47, 47, 47, 47, 47, 45.5, 45.5, 44.5, 43) cm

4   8¾ (8¾, 8¾, 9¼, 9¼, 9¼, 9¼, 9¼, 9¼, 10, 10, 10¾)"
    22 (22, 22, 23.5, 23.5, 23.5, 23.5, 23.5, 23.5, 25.5, 25.5, 27.5) cm

5   33¼ (36, 38, 40, 42, 44, 46, 48, 52, 56, 60, 64)"
    84.5 (91.5, 96.5, 101.5, 106.5, 112, 117, 122, 132, 142, 152.5, 162.5) cm

6   16 (16, 16, 16½, 16½, 17, 17, 17, 17, 17, 17, 17)"
    40.5 (40.5, 40.5, 42, 42, 43, 43, 43, 43, 43, 43, 43) cm

7   23¾ (24¼, 24¾, 25½, 26, 26¾, 27, 27½, 27¾, 28¼, 28¾, 29¼)"
    60.5 (61.5, 63, 65, 66, 68, 68.5, 70, 70.5, 72, 73, 74.5) cm

8   7¾ (8¼, 8¾, 9, 9½, 9¾, 10, 10½, 10¾, 11¼, 11¾, 12¼)"
    19.5 (21, 22, 23, 24, 25, 25.5, 26.5, 27.5, 28.5, 30, 31) cm

9   1¾"
    4.5 cm

1   21¼ (22¼, 22¼, 23, 23, 23, 23, 24, 24, 25, 25, 25¾)"
    54 (56.5, 56.5, 58.5, 58.5, 58.5, 58.5, 61, 61, 63.5, 63.5, 65.5) cm

2   11½ (12, 13, 13¼, 14¼, 15, 16, 17¼, 18¼, 19, 20, 22¼)"
    29 (30.5, 33, 33.5, 36, 38, 40.5, 44, 46.5, 48.5, 51, 56.5) cm

3   18 (18, 18, 18½, 18½, 18½, 18½, 18½, 18, 18, 17½, 17)"
    45.5 (45.5, 45.5, 47, 47, 47, 47, 47, 45.5, 45.5, 44.5, 43) cm

4   9 (9, 9, 9, 9, 9, 9¾, 9¾, 9¾, 9¾, 9¾, 10¾)"
    23 (23, 23, 23, 23, 23, 25, 25, 25, 25, 25, 27.5) cm

5   33¾ (35½, 37¼, 41, 42¾, 44½, 46¼, 48, 51½, 57, 60½, 64)"
    85.5 (90, 94.5, 104, 108.5, 113, 117.5, 122, 131, 145, 153.5, 162.5) cm

6   16 (16, 16, 16½, 16½, 17, 17, 17, 17, 17, 17, 17)"
    40.5 (40.5, 40.5, 42, 42, 43, 43, 43, 43, 43, 43, 43) cm

7   23¾ (24¼, 24¾, 25½, 26, 26¾, 27, 27½, 28, 28½, 29, 29½)"
    60.5 (61.5, 63, 65, 66, 68, 68.5, 70, 71, 72.5, 73.5, 75) cm

8   7¾ (8¼, 8¾, 9, 9½, 9¾, 10, 10½, 11, 11½, 12, 12½)"
    19.5 (21, 22, 23, 24, 25, 25.5, 26.5, 28, 29, 30.5, 32) cm

9   1¾"
    4.5 cm

# Basic Cardigan: Yoke Construction

You'd typically steek to work a V-neck yoke sweater, so unlike the other basic cardigans, this one features the same crew neckline as the pullover. I've worked up the sample in a sturdy, soft, hard-wearing acrylic-wool blend. But I've also chosen some pure-wool options: a 100 percent worsted wool and an ultrafine alpaca blend.

This unisex garment is worked in pieces to the armholes, then joined and worked in one piece to the neckline. The sleeves are worked in the round, and the body is worked flat. The button band is then picked up and worked in two pieces. No waist shaping is included in any of the basic patterns, but should you choose to add some, please see pages 113–115 for details.

## FINISHED MEASUREMENTS

**FINGERING:** 34¾ (36¾, 38¾, 40¾, 42¾, 44¾, 46¾, 48¾, 53¾, 56¾, 60¾, 64¾)" [88.5 (93.5, 98.5, 103.5, 108.5, 113.5, 118.5, 124, 134, 144, 154.5, 164.5) cm] chest, buttoned

**DK:** 34½ (36¾, 38¾, 40¾, 42¼, 44¼, 46½, 48½, 52¾, 56¾, 60¼, 64½)" [87.5 (93.5, 98.5, 103.5, 107.5, 112.5, 118, 123, 134, 144, 153, 164) cm] chest, buttoned

**WORSTED:** 34¾ (36¼, 38¾, 40¼, 42¾, 44¼, 46¾, 48¼, 52¼, 56¼, 61, 64¼)" [88.5 (92, 98.5, 102, 108.5, 112.5, 118.5, 122.5, 132.5, 143, 155, 163) cm] chest, buttoned

*Note: Sweater is intended to be worn with 2–4" (5–10 cm) ease in the bust; shown in DK weight yarn and size 38¾" (98.5 cm).*

## YARN

**FINGERING:** Berroco Ultra Alpaca Fine [50% superwash wool, 30% nylon, 20% super fine alpaca; 433 yards (400 meters) / 100 grams]: 4 (4, 5, 5, 5, 6, 6, 6, 7, 7, 7, 8) hanks #1207 Salt and Pepper

**DK:** Berroco Vintage DK [52% acrylic, 40% wool, 8% nylon; 290 yards (265 meters) / 100 grams]: 5 (5, 5, 6, 6, 6, 7, 7, 7, 8, 8, 9) hanks #2107 Cracked Pepper

**WORSTED:** Rowan Pure Wool Superwash [100% superwash wool; 219 yards (200 meters) / 100 grams]: 6 (7, 7, 8, 8, 9, 9, 10, 11, 11, 12, 13) skeins #00111 Granite

## NEEDLES

**FINGERING:** One 40" (100 cm) long circular needle and one set of double-pointed needles size US 2 (2.75 mm)

**DK:** One 40" (100 cm) long circular needle and one set of double-pointed needles size US 6 (4 mm)

**WORSTED:** One 40" (100 cm) long circular needle and one set of double-pointed size US 7 (4.5 mm)

Change needle size if necessary to obtain correct gauge.

## NOTIONS

Stitch markers (including 1 in unique color or style), stitch holders or waste yarn, twelve ¾-inch (19-mm) buttons

## GAUGE

**FINGERING:** 32 sts and 40 rows = 4" (10 cm) in St st
**DK:** 23 sts and 32 rows = 4" (10 cm) in St st
**WORSTED:** 20 sts and 28 rows = 4" (10 cm) in St st

## NOTES

If your size gives the number 0 for a particular instruction, skip that instruction and proceed to the next instruction.

## BODY

Using circular needle, CO

| | | | | | | | | | | | | |
|---|---|---|---|---|---|---|---|---|---|---|---|---|
| FINGERING | 266 | 282 | 298 | 314 | 330 | 346 | 362 | 378 | 410 | 442 | 474 | 506 |
| DK | 190 | 202 | 214 | 226 | 234 | 246 | 258 | 270 | 294 | 318 | 338 | 362 |
| WORSTED | 166 | 174 | 186 | 194 | 206 | 214 | 226 | 234 | 254 | 274 | 298 | 314 |

sts.

Begin 2x2 Rib Flat; work even until piece measures 2¼" (5.5 cm), ending with a WS row.

Change to St st; work even until piece measures 16 (16½, 17, 17, 17, 17, 17, 17, 17, 17, 17, 17)" [40.5 (42, 43, 43, 43, 43, 43, 43, 43, 43, 43, 43) cm] from the beginning, ending with a WS row.

**DIVIDING ROW (RS):** Knit

| | | | | | | | | | | | | |
|---|---|---|---|---|---|---|---|---|---|---|---|---|
| FINGERING | 55 | 59 | 61 | 65 | 69 | 71 | 75 | 79 | 85 | 93 | 99 | 107 |
| DK | 38 | 41 | 43 | 46 | 48 | 49 | 52 | 55 | 60 | 66 | 70 | 76 |
| WORSTED | 33 | 35 | 37 | 39 | 42 | 43 | 46 | 48 | 52 | 57 | 61 | 65 |

sts, BO

| | | | | | | | | | | | | |
|---|---|---|---|---|---|---|---|---|---|---|---|---|
| FINGERING | 20 | 20 | 24 | 24 | 24 | 28 | 28 | 28 | 32 | 32 | 36 | 36 |
| DK | 16 | 16 | 18 | 18 | 18 | 22 | 22 | 22 | 24 | 24 | 26 | 26 |
| WORSTED | 14 | 14 | 16 | 16 | 16 | 18 | 18 | 18 | 20 | 20 | 24 | 24 |

sts, knit

| | | | | | | | | | | | | |
|---|---|---|---|---|---|---|---|---|---|---|---|---|
| FINGERING | 115 | 123 | 127 | 135 | 143 | 147 | 155 | 163 | 175 | 191 | 203 | 219 |
| DK | 81 | 87 | 91 | 97 | 101 | 103 | 109 | 115 | 125 | 137 | 145 | 157 |
| WORSTED | 71 | 75 | 79 | 83 | 89 | 91 | 97 | 101 | 109 | 119 | 127 | 135 |

sts (not including st on right-hand needle after binding off), BO

| | | | | | | | | | | | | |
|---|---|---|---|---|---|---|---|---|---|---|---|---|
| FINGERING | 20 | 20 | 24 | 24 | 24 | 28 | 28 | 28 | 32 | 32 | 36 | 36 |
| DK | 16 | 16 | 18 | 18 | 18 | 22 | 22 | 22 | 24 | 24 | 26 | 26 |
| WORSTED | 14 | 14 | 16 | 16 | 16 | 18 | 18 | 18 | 20 | 20 | 24 | 24 |

sts, knit to end.

| | | | | | | | | | | | | |
|---|---|---|---|---|---|---|---|---|---|---|---|---|
| FINGERING | 55 | 59 | 61 | 65 | 69 | 71 | 75 | 79 | 85 | 93 | 99 | 107 |
| DK | 38 | 41 | 43 | 46 | 48 | 49 | 52 | 55 | 60 | 66 | 70 | 76 |
| WORSTED | 33 | 35 | 37 | 39 | 42 | 43 | 46 | 48 | 52 | 57 | 61 | 65 |

sts remain for each Front;

| | | | | | | | | | | | | |
|---|---|---|---|---|---|---|---|---|---|---|---|---|
| FINGERING | 116 | 124 | 128 | 136 | 144 | 148 | 156 | 164 | 176 | 192 | 204 | 220 |
| DK | 82 | 88 | 92 | 98 | 102 | 104 | 110 | 116 | 126 | 138 | 146 | 158 |
| WORSTED | 72 | 76 | 80 | 84 | 90 | 92 | 98 | 102 | 110 | 120 | 128 | 136 |

sts remain for Back. Break yarn; transfer all sts to holders or waste yarn.

## SLEEVES

Using dpns, CO

| | | | | | | | | | | | | |
|---|---|---|---|---|---|---|---|---|---|---|---|---|
| FINGERING | 68 | 68 | 68 | 72 | 72 | 72 | 76 | 76 | 76 | 80 | 80 | 84 |
| DK | 48 | 48 | 48 | 52 | 52 | 52 | 56 | 56 | 56 | 56 | 56 | 60 |
| WORSTED | 44 | 44 | 44 | 44 | 44 | 44 | 48 | 48 | 48 | 52 | 52 | 52 |

sts.

Join for working in the rnd, being careful not to twist sts; pm for beginning of rnd.

Begin 2x2 Rib in the Rnd; work even until piece measures 3" (7.5 cm).

Change to St st; work 2 rnds even.

## SHAPE SLEEVE

Increase 2 sts every

| | | | | | | | | | | | | |
|---|---|---|---|---|---|---|---|---|---|---|---|---|
| FINGERING | 12 | 10 | 9 | 9 | 7 | 6 | 5 | 5 | 4 | 4 | 3 | 3 |
| DK | 11 | 10 | 9 | 10 | 8 | 6 | 6 | 5 | 5 | 4 | 3 | 3 |
| WORSTED | 14 | 12 | 10 | 9 | 8 | 6 | 6 | 5 | 5 | 4 | 4 | 3 |

rnds a total of

| FINGERING | 12 | 14 | 16 | 16 | 20 | 24 | 26 | 30 | 34 | 36 | 40 | 46 |
|---|---|---|---|---|---|---|---|---|---|---|---|---|
| DK | 10 | 11 | 12 | 12 | 15 | 18 | 18 | 21 | 24 | 27 | 30 | 34 |
| WORSTED | 7 | 8 | 10 | 11 | 13 | 16 | 16 | 19 | 21 | 22 | 24 | 29 |

times, as follows: K1, M1R, knit to last st, M1L, k1.

| FINGERING | 92 | 96 | 100 | 104 | 112 | 120 | 128 | 136 | 144 | 152 | 160 | 176 |
|---|---|---|---|---|---|---|---|---|---|---|---|---|
| DK | 68 | 70 | 72 | 76 | 82 | 88 | 92 | 98 | 104 | 110 | 116 | 128 |
| WORSTED | 58 | 60 | 64 | 66 | 70 | 76 | 80 | 86 | 90 | 96 | 100 | 110 |

sts.

Work even until piece measures 18 (18, 18, 18½, 18½, 18½, 18½, 18½, 18, 18, 17½, 17)" [45.5 (45.5, 45.5, 47, 47, 47, 47, 47, 45.5, 45.5, 44.5, 43) cm] from the beginning.

**NEXT RND:** BO

| FINGERING | 10 | 10 | 12 | 12 | 12 | 14 | 14 | 14 | 16 | 16 | 18 | 18 |
|---|---|---|---|---|---|---|---|---|---|---|---|---|
| DK | 8 | 8 | 9 | 9 | 9 | 11 | 11 | 11 | 12 | 12 | 13 | 13 |
| WORSTED | 7 | 7 | 8 | 8 | 8 | 9 | 9 | 9 | 10 | 10 | 12 | 12 |

sts, knit to last

| FINGERING | 10 | 10 | 12 | 12 | 12 | 14 | 14 | 14 | 16 | 16 | 18 | 18 |
|---|---|---|---|---|---|---|---|---|---|---|---|---|
| DK | 8 | 8 | 9 | 9 | 9 | 11 | 11 | 11 | 12 | 12 | 13 | 13 |
| WORSTED | 7 | 7 | 8 | 8 | 8 | 9 | 9 | 9 | 10 | 10 | 12 | 12 |

sts, BO to end.

| FINGERING | 72 | 76 | 76 | 80 | 88 | 92 | 100 | 108 | 112 | 120 | 124 | 140 |
|---|---|---|---|---|---|---|---|---|---|---|---|---|
| DK | 52 | 54 | 54 | 58 | 64 | 66 | 70 | 76 | 80 | 86 | 90 | 102 |
| WORSTED | 44 | 46 | 48 | 50 | 54 | 58 | 62 | 68 | 70 | 76 | 76 | 86 |

sts remain. Break yarn; transfer sts to holder or waste yarn.

## YOKE

**JOINING ROW (RS):** Using circular needle, knit across

| FINGERING | 55 | 59 | 61 | 65 | 69 | 71 | 75 | 79 | 85 | 93 | 99 | 107 |
|---|---|---|---|---|---|---|---|---|---|---|---|---|
| DK | 38 | 41 | 43 | 46 | 48 | 49 | 52 | 55 | 60 | 66 | 70 | 76 |
| WORSTED | 33 | 35 | 37 | 39 | 42 | 43 | 46 | 48 | 52 | 57 | 61 | 65 |

Right Front sts, pm, knit across

| FINGERING | 72 | 76 | 76 | 80 | 88 | 92 | 100 | 108 | 112 | 120 | 124 | 140 |
|---|---|---|---|---|---|---|---|---|---|---|---|---|
| DK | 52 | 54 | 54 | 58 | 64 | 66 | 70 | 76 | 80 | 86 | 90 | 102 |
| WORSTED | 44 | 46 | 48 | 50 | 54 | 58 | 62 | 68 | 70 | 76 | 76 | 86 |

Right Sleeve sts, pm, knit across

| FINGERING | 58 | 62 | 64 | 68 | 72 | 74 | 78 | 82 | 88 | 96 | 102 | 110 |
|---|---|---|---|---|---|---|---|---|---|---|---|---|
| DK | 41 | 44 | 46 | 49 | 51 | 52 | 55 | 58 | 63 | 69 | 73 | 79 |
| WORSTED | 36 | 38 | 40 | 42 | 45 | 46 | 49 | 51 | 55 | 60 | 64 | 68 |

sts (first half of Back), pm in unique color or style for center Back, knit across

| FINGERING | 58 | 62 | 64 | 68 | 72 | 74 | 78 | 82 | 88 | 96 | 102 | 110 |
|---|---|---|---|---|---|---|---|---|---|---|---|---|
| DK | 41 | 44 | 46 | 49 | 51 | 52 | 55 | 58 | 63 | 69 | 73 | 79 |
| WORSTED | 36 | 38 | 40 | 42 | 45 | 46 | 49 | 51 | 55 | 60 | 64 | 68 |

sts (second half of Back), pm, knit across

| FINGERING | 72 | 76 | 76 | 80 | 88 | 92 | 100 | 108 | 112 | 120 | 124 | 140 |
|---|---|---|---|---|---|---|---|---|---|---|---|---|
| DK | 52 | 54 | 54 | 58 | 64 | 66 | 70 | 76 | 80 | 86 | 90 | 102 |
| WORSTED | 44 | 46 | 48 | 50 | 54 | 58 | 62 | 68 | 70 | 76 | 76 | 86 |

Left Sleeve sts, pm, knit across

| FINGERING | 55 | 59 | 61 | 65 | 69 | 71 | 75 | 79 | 85 | 93 | 99 | 107 |
|---|---|---|---|---|---|---|---|---|---|---|---|---|
| DK | 38 | 41 | 43 | 46 | 48 | 49 | 52 | 55 | 60 | 66 | 70 | 76 |
| WORSTED | 33 | 35 | 37 | 39 | 42 | 43 | 46 | 48 | 52 | 57 | 61 | 65 |

Left Front sts.

| FINGERING | 370 | 394 | 402 | 426 | 458 | 474 | 506 | 538 | 570 | 618 | 650 | 714 |
|---|---|---|---|---|---|---|---|---|---|---|---|---|
| DK | 262 | 278 | 286 | 306 | 326 | 334 | 354 | 378 | 406 | 442 | 466 | 514 |
| WORSTED | 226 | 238 | 250 | 262 | 282 | 294 | 314 | 334 | 354 | 386 | 402 | 438 |

sts.

**NEXT ROW (WS):** Purl 1 row, increasing or decreasing sts as indicated below. If the number is positive, work that many increases; if the number is negative, work that many decreases. Work the increases or decreases on the Back and/or Fronts, working at the markers between Body and Sleeves.

| | | | | | | | | | | | | |
|---|---|---|---|---|---|---|---|---|---|---|---|---|
| FINGERING | 2 | 2 | 6 | 6 | -2 | 6 | -2 | 2 | 6 | 6 | -2 | 6 |
| DK | 2 | -2 | 2 | 6 | -2 | 2 | 6 | 6 | 2 | 2 | 2 | 2 |
| WORSTED | 2 | 2 | 2 | 2 | -6 | 6 | -2 | 2 | 6 | -2 | 6 | 6 |
| | | | | | | | | | | | | |
| FINGERING | 372 | 396 | 408 | 432 | 456 | 480 | 504 | 540 | 576 | 624 | 648 | 720 |
| DK | 264 | 276 | 288 | 312 | 324 | 336 | 360 | 384 | 408 | 444 | 468 | 516 |
| WORSTED | 228 | 240 | 252 | 264 | 276 | 300 | 312 | 336 | 360 | 384 | 408 | 444 |

sts.

## SHAPE BACK NECK (OPTIONAL)

*Note: Back neck is shaped using short rows (see Special Techniques, page 188).*

**SHORT ROW 1:** Knit to 1 st before Left Sleeve marker, w&t.

**SHORT ROW 2:** Purl to 1 st before Right Sleeve marker, w&t.

**SHORT ROW 3:** Knit to

| | |
|---|---|
| FINGERING | 8 |
| DK | 6 |
| WORSTED | 5 |

sts before wrapped st from previous RS row, w&t.

**SHORT ROW 4:** Purl to

| | |
|---|---|
| FINGERING | 8 |
| DK | 6 |
| WORSTED | 5 |

sts before wrapped st from previous WS row, w&t.

Repeat Short Rows 3 and 4

| | |
|---|---|
| FINGERING | 7 |
| DK | 5 |
| WORSTED | 4 |

times.

Knit to end, working wraps together with wrapped sts as you come to them, and removing all markers except center Back marker.

Work

| | | | | | | | | | | | | |
|---|---|---|---|---|---|---|---|---|---|---|---|---|
| FINGERING | 24 | 28 | 30 | 30 | 34 | 34 | 36 | 38 | 40 | 42 | 44 | 48 |
| DK | 18 | 20 | 22 | 24 | 26 | 26 | 28 | 30 | 30 | 32 | 34 | 36 |
| WORSTED | 16 | 18 | 20 | 20 | 22 | 22 | 24 | 26 | 26 | 28 | 30 | 32 |

rows even, working remaining wraps together with wrapped sts as you come to them on first row.

**NEXT ROW (WS):** *K12, pm for shaping; repeat from * to last 12 sts, knit to end. *Note: Some sizes will place a marker at the same place as the center Back marker. If that is the case, keep both markers in place. The number of markers you have at the center Back will determine how you work Yoke Decrease Rows.*

**YOKE DECREASE ROW (RS):** *K2tog, knit to shaping marker, sm; repeat from * to center Back marker if you have a double marker at center Back (or to shaping marker just past center Back marker if you have a single marker at center Back), sm, **knit to 2 sts before shaping marker, ssk, sm; repeat from ** to last marker, knit to last 2 sts, ssk.

| | | | | | | | | | | | | |
|---|---|---|---|---|---|---|---|---|---|---|---|---|
| FINGERING | 31 | 33 | 34 | 36 | 38 | 40 | 42 | 45 | 48 | 52 | 54 | 60 |
| DK | 22 | 23 | 24 | 26 | 27 | 28 | 30 | 32 | 34 | 37 | 39 | 43 |
| WORSTED | 19 | 20 | 21 | 22 | 23 | 25 | 26 | 28 | 30 | 32 | 34 | 37 |

sts decreased.

Work

| FINGERING | 7 | 7 | 9 | 9 | 9 | 9 | 9 | 11 | 11 | 11 | 13 | 13 |
|---|---|---|---|---|---|---|---|---|---|---|---|---|
| DK | 5 | 7 | 7 | 7 | 7 | 7 | 7 | 9 | 9 | 9 | 9 | 11 |
| WORSTED | 5 | 5 | 5 | 5 | 7 | 7 | 7 | 7 | 7 | 7 | 9 | 9 |

rows even.

Repeat Yoke Decrease Row.

Work

| FINGERING | 7 | 7 | 7 | 7 | 5 | 5 | 5 | 5 | 5 | 5 | 5 | 5 |
|---|---|---|---|---|---|---|---|---|---|---|---|---|
| DK | 5 | 5 | 5 | 5 | 3 | 3 | 3 | 3 | 3 | 5 | 5 | 5 |
| WORSTED | 3 | 5 | 5 | 5 | 5 | 3 | 3 | 3 | 3 | 3 | 3 | 3 |

rows even.

Repeat Yoke Decrease Row.

**SELECTED SIZES ONLY (PROCEED TO *ALL SIZES* IF YOUR SIZE IS 0):**
Work

| FINGERING | 0 | 0 | 0 | 0 | 3 | 3 | 3 | 3 | 3 | 5 | 5 | 5 |
|---|---|---|---|---|---|---|---|---|---|---|---|---|
| DK | 0 | 0 | 0 | 0 | 3 | 3 | 3 | 3 | 3 | 3 | 3 | 3 |
| WORSTED | 0 | 0 | 0 | 0 | 0 | 1 | 1 | 3 | 3 | 3 | 3 | 3 |

row(s) even.

Repeat Yoke Decrease Row.

**ALL SIZES:**
Work

| FINGERING | 5 | 5 | 5 | 5 | 5 | 7 | 7 | 7 | 5 | 5 | 5 | 7 |
|---|---|---|---|---|---|---|---|---|---|---|---|---|
| DK | 3 | 3 | 5 | 5 | 5 | 5 | 5 | 5 | 5 | 5 | 5 | 5 |
| WORSTED | 3 | 3 | 3 | 3 | 3 | 5 | 5 | 5 | 3 | 3 | 3 | 5 |

rows even.

Repeat Yoke Decrease Row. *Note: For sizes with a single marker at center Back, when you have just 1 st remaining between the shaping marker and center Back marker, on next Yoke Decrease Row, work k2tog on 1 st before and after center Back marker, repositioning center Back marker to before k2tog.*

Work

| FINGERING | 3 | 5 | 5 | 5 | 5 | 5 | 5 | 7 | 5 | 5 | 5 | 5 |
|---|---|---|---|---|---|---|---|---|---|---|---|---|
| DK | 3 | 3 | 3 | 3 | 3 | 5 | 5 | 5 | 5 | 3 | 5 | 5 |
| WORSTED | 3 | 3 | 3 | 3 | 3 | 3 | 3 | 3 | 3 | 3 | 3 | 3 |

rows even.

Repeat Yoke Decrease Row.

Work

| FINGERING | 3 | 3 | 3 | 5 | 5 | 5 | 5 | 5 | 5 | 5 | 5 | 5 |
|---|---|---|---|---|---|---|---|---|---|---|---|---|
| DK | 3 | 3 | 3 | 3 | 3 | 3 | 3 | 3 | 5 | 3 | 3 | 3 |
| WORSTED | 1 | 1 | 3 | 3 | 3 | 3 | 3 | 3 | 3 | 3 | 3 | 3 |

row(s) even.

Repeat Yoke Decrease Row.

**SELECTED SIZES ONLY (PROCEED TO *ALL SIZES* IF YOUR SIZE IS 0):**
Work

| FINGERING | 0 | 0 | 0 | 0 | 0 | 0 | 0 | 0 | 3 | 5 | 5 | 5 |
|---|---|---|---|---|---|---|---|---|---|---|---|---|
| DK | 0 | 0 | 0 | 0 | 0 | 0 | 0 | 0 | 0 | 3 | 3 | 3 |
| WORSTED | 0 | 0 | 0 | 0 | 0 | 0 | 0 | 0 | 3 | 3 | 3 | 3 |

rows even.

Repeat Yoke Decrease Row.

**ALL SIZES:**

| | | | | | | | | | | | | |
|---|---|---|---|---|---|---|---|---|---|---|---|---|
| FINGERING | 186 | 198 | 204 | 216 | 190 | 200 | 210 | 225 | 192 | 208 | 216 | 240 |
| DK | 132 | 138 | 144 | 156 | 135 | 140 | 150 | 160 | 170 | 148 | 156 | 172 |
| WORSTED | 114 | 120 | 126 | 132 | 138 | 125 | 130 | 140 | 120 | 128 | 136 | 148 |

sts remain.

Knit 1 row, decreasing

| | | | | | | | | | | | | |
|---|---|---|---|---|---|---|---|---|---|---|---|---|
| FINGERING | 10 | 22 | 24 | 32 | 6 | 12 | 22 | 33 | 0 | 12 | 16 | 36 |
| DK | 8 | 10 | 16 | 24 | 3 | 4 | 14 | 20 | 30 | 8 | 12 | 24 |
| WORSTED | 6 | 8 | 14 | 16 | 22 | 9 | 14 | 20 | 0 | 4 | 12 | 20 |

sts evenly across.

| | | | | | | | | | | | | |
|---|---|---|---|---|---|---|---|---|---|---|---|---|
| FINGERING | 176 | 176 | 180 | 184 | 184 | 188 | 188 | 192 | 192 | 196 | 200 | 204 |
| DK | 124 | 128 | 128 | 132 | 132 | 136 | 136 | 140 | 140 | 140 | 144 | 148 |
| WORSTED | 108 | 112 | 112 | 116 | 116 | 116 | 116 | 120 | 120 | 124 | 124 | 128 |

sts remain.

Begin 2x2 Rib Flat; work

| | |
|---|---|
| FINGERING | 8 |
| DK | 6 |
| WORSTED | 5 |

rows even. BO all sts in pattern.

## FINISHING

Block piece as desired. Sew underarm seams.

**BUTTONHOLE BAND**

With RS facing, and beginning at Right Front Hem, pick up and knit

| | | | | | | | | | | | | |
|---|---|---|---|---|---|---|---|---|---|---|---|---|
| FINGERING | 186 | 194 | 202 | 206 | 210 | 210 | 214 | 218 | 218 | 222 | 226 | 230 |
| DK | 134 | 142 | 146 | 146 | 150 | 150 | 154 | 154 | 158 | 162 | 162 | 166 |
| WORSTED | 118 | 122 | 126 | 130 | 130 | 134 | 134 | 134 | 138 | 138 | 142 | 146 |

sts along Right Front.
*Note: Exact st count is not essential, but be sure to end with a multiple of 4 sts + 2 for ribbing to work out evenly.* Begin 2x2 Rib Flat; work

| | |
|---|---|
| FINGERING | 7 |
| DK | 5 |
| WORSTED | 4 |

rows even.

**BUTTONHOLE ROW (RS):** Work

| | | | | | | | | | | | | |
|---|---|---|---|---|---|---|---|---|---|---|---|---|
| FINGERING | 10 | 9 | 13 | 9 | 11 | 11 | 13 | 10 | 10 | 12 | 14 | 10 |
| DK | 6 | 10 | 7 | 7 | 9 | 9 | 11 | 11 | 7 | 9 | 9 | 11 |
| WORSTED | 9 | 6 | 8 | 10 | 10 | 6 | 6 | 6 | 8 | 8 | 10 | 7 |

sts, [BO 2 sts, work

| | | | | | | | | | | | | |
|---|---|---|---|---|---|---|---|---|---|---|---|---|
| FINGERING | 13 | 14 | 14 | 15 | 15 | 15 | 15 | 16 | 16 | 16 | 16 | 17 |
| DK | 9 | 9 | 10 | 10 | 10 | 10 | 10 | 10 | 11 | 11 | 11 | 11 |
| WORSTED | 7 | 8 | 8 | 8 | 8 | 9 | 9 | 9 | 9 | 9 | 9 | 10 |

sts] 11 times, BO 2 sts, work to end.

Work

| | |
|---|---|
| FINGERING | 7 |
| DK | 5 |
| WORSTED | 4 |

rows even, CO 2 sts over BO sts on first row using Backward Loop CO (see Special Techniques, page 188). BO all sts in pattern.

**BUTTON BAND**
Work as for Buttonhole Band, beginning at Left Front neck edge and eliminating buttonholes.
Sew buttons opposite buttonholes.

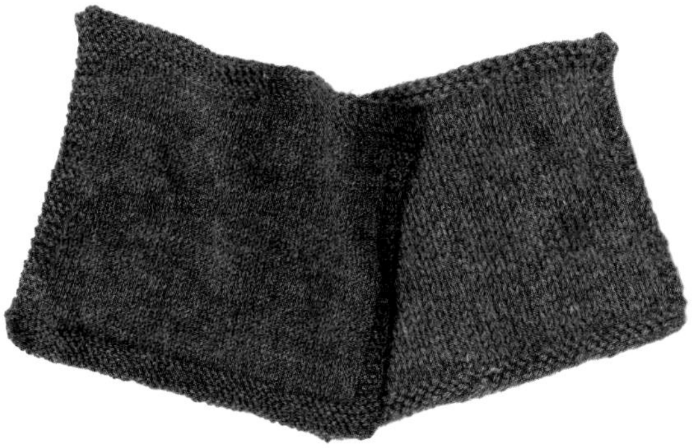

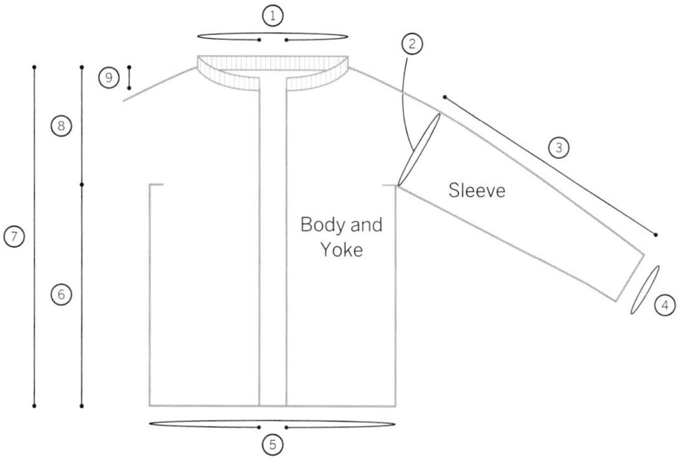


### FINGERING WEIGHT

1 22 (22, 22½, 23, 23, 23½, 23½, 24, 24, 24½, 25, 25½)"
56 (56, 57, 58.5, 58.5, 59.5, 59.5, 61, 61, 62, 63.5, 65) cm

2 11½ (12, 12½, 13, 14, 15, 16, 17, 18, 19, 20, 22)"
29 (30.5, 32, 33, 35.5, 38, 40.5, 43, 45.5, 48.5, 51, 56) cm

3 18 (18, 18, 18½, 18½, 18½, 18½, 18½, 18, 18, 17½, 17)"
45.5 (45.5, 45.5, 47, 47, 47, 47, 47, 45.5, 45.5, 44.5, 43) cm

4 8½ (8½, 8½, 9, 9, 9, 9½, 9½, 9½, 10, 10, 10½)"
21.5 (21.5, 21.5, 23, 23, 23, 24, 24, 24, 25.5, 25.5, 26.5) cm

5 33¼ (35¼, 37¼, 39¼, 41¼, 43¼, 45¼, 47¼, 51¼, 55¼, 59¼, 63¼)"
84.5 (89.5, 94.5, 99.5, 105, 110, 115, 120, 130, 140.5, 150.5, 160.5) cm

6 16 (16½, 17, 17, 17, 17, 17, 17, 17, 17, 17, 17)"
40.5 (42, 43, 43, 43, 43, 43, 43, 43, 43, 43, 43) cm

7 23¾ (25, 25¾, 26, 26½, 26¾, 27, 27½, 27¾, 28½, 28¾, 29½)"
60.5 (63.5, 65.5, 66, 67.5, 68, 68.5, 70, 70.5, 72.5, 73, 75) cm

8 7¾ (8½, 8¾, 9, 9½, 9¾, 10, 10½, 10¾, 11½, 11¾, 12½)"
19.5 (21.5, 22, 23, 24, 25, 25.5, 26.5, 27.5, 29, 30, 32) cm

9 1¾"
4.5 cm

### DK WEIGHT

1 21½ (22¼, 22¼, 23, 23, 23¾, 23¾, 24¼, 24¼, 24¼, 25, 25¾)"
54.5 (56.5, 56.5, 58.5, 58.5, 60.5, 60.5, 61.5, 61.5, 61.5, 63.5, 65.5) cm

2 11¾ (12¼, 12½, 13¼, 14¼, 15¼, 16, 17, 18, 19¼, 20¼, 22¼)"
30 (31, 32, 33.5, 36, 38.5, 40.5, 43, 45.5, 49, 51.5, 56.5) cm

3 18 (18, 18, 18½, 18½, 18½, 18½, 18½, 18, 18, 17½, 17)"
45.5 (45.5, 45.5, 47, 47, 47, 47, 47, 45.5, 45.5, 44.5, 43) cm

4 8¼ (8¼, 8¼, 9, 9, 9, 9¾, 9¾, 9¾, 9¾, 9¾, 10½)"
21 (21, 21, 23, 23, 23, 25, 25, 25, 25, 25, 26.5) cm

5 33 (35¼, 37¼, 39¼, 40¾, 42¾, 44¾, 47, 51¼, 55¼, 58¾, 63)"
84 (89.5, 94.5, 99.5, 103.5, 108.5, 113.5, 119.5, 130, 140.5, 149, 160) cm

6 16 (16½, 17, 17, 17, 17, 17, 17, 17, 17, 17, 17)"
40.5 (42, 43, 43, 43, 43, 43, 43, 43, 43, 43, 43) cm

7 23¾ (24¾, 25¾, 26, 26½, 26¾, 27, 27½, 27¾, 28¼, 28¾, 29¼)"
60.5 (63, 65.5, 66, 67.5, 68, 68.5, 70, 70.5, 72, 73, 74.5) cm

8 7¾ (8¼, 8¾, 9, 9½, 9¾, 10, 10½, 10¾, 11¼, 11¾, 12¼)"
19.5 (21, 22, 23, 24, 25, 25.5, 26.5, 27.5, 28.5, 30, 31) cm

9 1¾"
4.5 cm

### WORSTED WEIGHT

1 21½ (22½, 22½, 23¼, 23¼, 23¼, 23¼, 24, 24, 24¾, 24¾, 25½)"
54.5 (57, 57, 59, 59, 59, 59, 61, 61, 63, 63, 65) cm

2 11½ (12, 12¾, 13¼, 14, 15¼, 16, 17¼, 18, 19¼, 20, 22)"
29 (30.5, 32.5, 33.5, 35.5, 38.5, 40.5, 44, 45.5, 49, 51, 56) cm

3 18 (18, 18, 18½, 18½, 18½, 18½, 18½, 18, 18, 17½, 17)"
45.5 (45.5, 45.5, 47, 47, 47, 47, 47, 45.5, 45.5, 44.5, 43) cm

4 8¾ (8¾, 8¾, 8¾, 8¾, 8¾, 9½, 9½, 9½, 10½, 10½, 10½)"
22 (22, 22, 22, 22, 22, 24, 24, 24, 26.5, 26.5, 26.5) cm

5 33¼ (34¾, 37¼, 38¾, 41¼, 42¾, 45¼, 46¾, 50¾, 54¾, 59½, 62¾)"
84.5 (88.5, 94.5, 98.5, 105, 108.5, 115, 118.5, 129, 139, 151, 159.5) cm

6 16 (16½, 17, 17, 17, 17, 17, 17, 17, 17, 17, 17)"
40.5 (42, 43, 43, 43, 43, 43, 43, 43, 43, 43, 43) cm

7 23¾ (24¾, 25¾, 25¾, 26½, 26¾, 27, 27½, 27¾, 28¼, 28¾, 29¼)"
60.5 (63, 65.5, 65.5, 67.5, 68, 68.5, 70, 70.5, 72, 73, 74.5) cm

8 7¾ (8¼, 8¾, 8¾, 9½, 9¾, 10, 10½, 10¾, 11¼, 11¾, 12¼)"
19.5 (21, 22, 22, 24, 25, 25.5, 26.5, 27.5, 28.5, 30, 31) cm

9 1¾"
4.5 cm

# 5

....................................................................................................

# Set-In-Sleeve Sweaters

Of all hand-knit constructions, the set-in sleeve produces a garment that most closely matches our body's topography. The curves of a set-in sleeve are shaped like our shoulders' curves; and when the set-in-sleeve garment fits well, the seams sit in the places we pivot and move. They also have a clean, tailored look—if you're thinking of a more formal or "dressier" sweater, there's a good chance you're thinking of a set-in sleeve.

Unlike the other constructions, set-in-sleeve sweaters need to fit fairly close to the body in order to feel great (and look right). Too large through the armhole, and your sweater looks like a bathrobe!

When drafting a set-in-sleeve sweater, ensure the armhole edges sit just inside your shoulder muscles, on your torso. As you move your arms in a wide circle, those seams should stay in place, and either the fabric stretch, or the sleeves pull up on your arms. The torso of the sweater should stay stable on your body.

## WHAT MAKES A SET-IN SLEEVE A SET-IN SLEEVE?

The armholes/sleeve caps of hand-knit set-in-sleeve sweaters have a few important characteristics:

- The curve of the armhole is dictated entirely by the body's difference between bust and shoulders.

- The curve of the top of the sleeve is bell shaped, and its height is dictated by the length around the edge of the armhole curve.

- In hand-knit sweaters, for ease of knitting instructions, the cap and armholes are *symmetrical*—the back and front are the same.

Set-in-sleeve sweaters are most flexible when worked in pieces and then seamed—this allows for the shapes of the armhole and sleeve cap curves to differ, as long as their lengths are the same. This makes it possible to draft a set-in-sleeve cap to fit not only a "Mr./Ms. Average" body, but a body with longer armholes and smaller arms, or a shorter armhole and larger arms.

Longer body,
narrower arms

"Average"

Shorter body,
wider arms

There are some guidelines to drafting a set-in-sleeve pattern, but for the most part, the shaping is dictated by the needs of the body wearing the sweater: The cross-chest distance and bust width are determined by the body. The biceps width and armhole depth are determined by the body. The curves are constructed based on those waypoints.

$$a + b + c = a + z + y$$

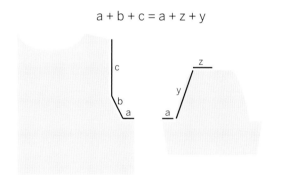

Generally, I'd *strongly* recommend working your set-in-sleeve sweater from the bottom up, in pieces, and then seaming. (And when I wrote my CustomFit custom sweater pattern software, that's how I wrote it!) There's just no better way to guarantee that your sweater will fit, *and* look great, in the armhole area than taking each part of the body as is.

That said, if you fall into the realm of "typical" in terms of your armhole depth and biceps width,

you've got a few more options. In the simplest variation, instead of knitting the sleeve separately and then seaming it on, you pick up your biceps stitches around the armhole opening and work a top-down sleeve cap using short rows. Once the short rows are complete, you join the stitches for working in the round and then work the sleeve in the round down toward the wrist.

You can take this "mostly seamless" approach one step further and work the body in the round to the armholes, then back and forth in two pieces to the shoulder. Seam the shoulders and work the sleeves top-down, and you've got a set-in-sleeve sweater that has only a few inches of mattress stitch. The pick-up approach around the armhole, and those seamed shoulders, provide a strong base, and this is almost as sturdy as a classic seamed sweater.

Beyond this method, there are a number of other top-down approaches, the most popular of which might be the "contiguous" method. Generally speaking, I think these work best:

- On bodies that hew closely to the "Mr./Ms. Average" standards (for fit reasons).
- When they rely more on picking up stitches than increases or decreases (for stability reasons).

This chapter will focus on drafting set-in-sleeve patterns in pieces; I'll discuss going from there to a more seamless version at the end.

## DESIGN AND FABRIC CONSIDERATIONS FOR SET-IN SLEEVES

Set-in sleeves are one of the most structured sweater constructions, with seams everywhere—so you can use pretty much any fabric you like and get a great sweater. Much like with any other construction:

- Seamed sweaters are more structured than all-in-one versions.

- Pullovers are more structured than cardigans.

- Shallow necklines are more structured than deep necklines.

That said, you really don't need to worry about it too much—the stability in the armhole area will support just about whatever you'd like to do. I worked the deep-V-neck basic cardigan on page 100 in a drapey wool-silk with no worries; the set-in construction is also strong enough to support the weight of heavy cables and full pockets of the Campfire Cardigan on page 181.

The structure of the set-in-sleeve sweater also supports the full range of shapes for your sweater's body, from the straight-sided silhouettes of the basics to the A-line of the Mill Pond Cardigan on page 133 to the delicate waist shaping of the Spring Rain Tee on 177. I haven't included a tapered-body set-in-sleeve sweater in this book, but they work wonderfully, too. (The basic designs in this chapter, and the Campfire Cardigan on page 181, lack any torso shaping at all.)

### *Drafting a set-in-sleeve pattern.*

Much like the other constructions, I recommend starting to draft your set-in-sleeve pattern by filling in a personal schematic for the front, back, and sleeves of your sweater—filling in the arrows labeled here:

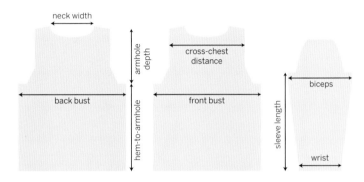

Most of the measurements listed here can be taken straight from your very first personal schematic.

- The **wrist**, **biceps**, front and back **bust** (and waist, and hip, if you're not making a straight sweater).

- The armhole depth, sleeve length, and hem-to-armhole length.

But we haven't yet talked about two more measurements:

- The cross-chest distance.

- The neck width.

And you'll need to determine those. The **cross-chest distance** is the distance between the armhole edges on your *front*—unlike when sewing clothing, you'll want to use a front rather than a back measurement for this. (Since the armholes are symmetrical, it's far better to ask the back to stretch a few inches—no problem for a hand-knit!—than have bunches of extra fabric in your armpits on the front.) You can either measure this on your body or on a sweater that fits you well in the shoulders:

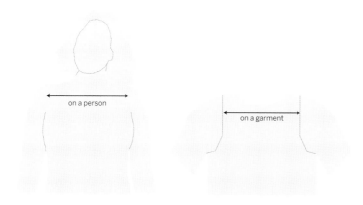

Once you have the cross-chest distance, the neck width will follow. For set-in-sleeve sweaters, the neck width is typically a percentage of the cross-chest distance:

- A *narrow neckline* is typically 40–45 percent of the cross-chest distance.

- An *average neckline* is typically 45–55 percent of the cross-chest distance.

- A *wide neckline* is typically 65–80 percent of the cross-chest distance.

It's a good idea to sanity-check your neck widths against some favorite store-bought pieces until you get a feel for what numbers are right for you. Just remember that these widths are before trim gets added!

***Once you've filled in your schematic, you're ready to draft your pattern.***

Let's follow this process with an example—a fairly wide crew-neck pullover, without waist shaping, for my measurements. (I'll work it in pieces, from the bottom up.) Here's my personal schematic for this sweater:

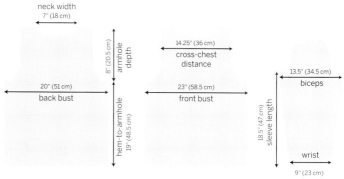

Note that compared to raglan, and even yoke, constructions, I'm going with a slightly slimmer sleeve—a 13½" (34.5 cm) biceps, just about 1" (2.5 cm) of ease through my arm. This is appropriate for a relatively close-fitting, tailored sweater with minimal ease through the bust—a larger arm might look out of place with the fit elsewhere in the garment.

Next, turn the measurements into stitch and row counts based on your gauge. Let's assume I'm working at a fairly typical gauge of 5 stitches and 7 rows to 1" (2.5 cm):

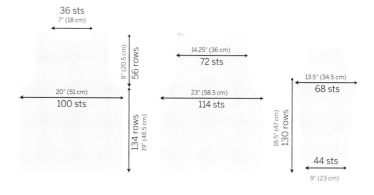

The body of my sweater is pretty simple—I cast on the appropriate number of stitches and work to the armhole shaping. The sleeves and neckline are similarly simple—you can see page 117 for more information on the sleeve.

For this section of the book, let's focus on **drafting the instructions for the armhole** on the back and front and the **sleeve cap**.

### Drafting an armhole.

Drafting the armhole is a fairly simple process—first, identify the number of stitches you need to remove on each side, total:

> (bust count − cross-chest count) ÷ 2
>
> *My example: 100 sts − 72 sts = 28 sts total*
>
> Then divide by 2 to determine how many stitches to remove on each side (28 ÷ 2 = 14 stitches to remove on each side).

You'll split this number up into a combination of bind-offs and every-RS-row armhole decreases. Ideally, you'll have at least 1" (2.5 cm) of bind-off, and the entire shaped part should take up no more than 25–33 percent of the armhole's total height. How you approach this depends on how many decreases you have to work:

- Start by placing about 1" (2.5 cm) of stitches in initial bind-offs and ½" (1.5 cm) of stitches in a secondary bind-off.
- Calculate the height, in inches (cm), of the decrease section if you remove the rest of the stitches in every-RS-row decreases. If this height is under a third of the armhole depth, you're done!

- If not, add stitches to the initial and secondary bind-offs, one at a time, until the height of the decreases *is* less than a third of the armhole depth.
- Once you've settled the numbers, call the initial bind-offs "A," the secondary bind-offs "B," and the decreases "C."

**For my example**, I'll start with binding off 5 stitches initially and then 3 additional stitches, leaving 6 to remove with every-RS-row decreases. This takes 16 rows total (4 for bind-offs and 12 for decreases), which is less than a third of my armhole depth—so I'm done! **My "A" is 5, my "B" is 3, and my "C" is 6.**

After decreases, work straight at the armhole edge (shaping neck as desired) until the armhole reaches the desired depth. Here's a pattern text example:

> When piece reaches *(length to armhole—mine is 19" [48.5 cm])*, shape armholes:
>
> BO A *(mine is 5)* sts at the beginning of the next 2 rows.
>
> BO B *(mine is 3)* sts at the beginning of the following 2 rows.
>
> Decrease 1 st at each end of every RS row C *(mine is 6)* times total as follows:
>
> Armhole Decrease Row (RS): Knit 2, ssk, work to last 4 sts, k2tog, k2. *(Or see other edge shaping options in chapter 11.)*
>
> Work even until armhole measures *(armhole depth—mine is 8" [20 cm])* from start of bind-offs, then shape shoulders.

In the most basic form, shoulders are shaped with stepped bind-offs halfway through: On your first shoulder-shaping row, bind off half of the stitches, then work to the end. Work one row even. Bind off remaining stitches.

**Drafting a sleeve cap.**

Drafting a sleeve cap gets a little hairier—although not massively hairy, since as hand-knitters we get to make a *lot* of approximations! *(The math-inclined reader might notice some possible refinements to the methods described in this section, but I promise these calculations will make you the greatest hand-knit sweater you've ever worn.)*

The intuition behind making a sleeve cap is fairly simple, but there are several steps involved in the calculations. As you read through the rest of this section and work through your own cap, remember the goal: The length of the edge of the sleeve cap should match the length of the edge of the armhole.

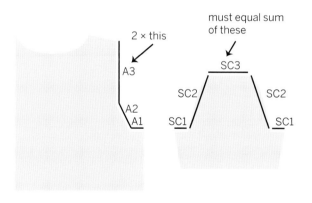

Here's a bird's-eye view of the overall process of making the calculations:

■ First, calculate the length around the armhole. We'll call this L, and the sleeve cap length must match it.

The *height of the cap* is the bit you'll be able to adjust. So after finding your target length for the cap's curve, you need to work backward from that target length to the cap height:

■ Calculate the length of the straight (bound-off) sections of the cap (labeled SC3 and SC1 in the diagram at left).

■ Subtract them from the overall target length.

■ Divide by 2—this is the length of the edge of the curved part of the cap (SC2 in diagram).

■ Approximate the curved part of the cap with a right triangle, and calculate the width of the base of that triangle.

■ You can now work backward to the cap height.

Once you have the cap height, you can turn it into rows—and you're almost done. There's just one more step:

■ Distribute the decreases you'll need to work over the height you've just calculated.

If you're reading these words and hyperventilating, please breathe! It's not as crazy as it seems, once you're dealing with real numbers, and on my website I've given you a blank worksheet to keep track of your calculations.

(Alternatively, the basic patterns for this chapter span gauges from fingering to bulky, and I've also written a bunch of software to help you with the caps: CustomFit will generate an entirely custom set-in-sleeve pattern based on your gauge and body, and monthly subscribers get access to a sleeve-cap generator that will do the same, but just for the sleeve-cap numbers instead of the whole pattern. So don't fret!)

Are you ready? OK, here we go!

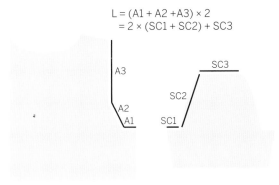

$$L = (A1 + A2 + A3) \times 2$$
$$= 2 \times (SC1 + SC2) + SC3$$

In this diagram, I've replaced the "make the edges the same length" words with some arithmetic. Those two edges being the same length means that:

$$2 \times (A1 + A2 + A3) = 2 \times (SC1 + SC2) + SC3$$

We've calculated A1, and the numbers that give us A2 and A3, in the previous step. Since the armhole depth, bust, and cross-chest distance are based on your body and can't change, the left-hand side of this equation is fixed. The number of stitches you bind off on the sleeve cap (at the beginning of the cap shaping, and the top) is also (mostly) fixed—as are the number of stitches you need to remove in the "curved" portion of the cap.

In fact, the only thing that *isn't* fixed in the sleeve cap is the number of rows you work! That's what we'll be trying to figure out. In this diagram, I've labeled all the dimensions that come from your body in green—these are fixed. The orange height is the only bit we get to change to ensure the equal sign remains true.

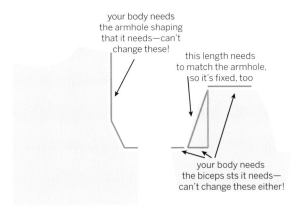

Feel like you have a handle on how this should work? Great! Let's get messy with the numbers, bit by bit.

## Armhole length.

The total length around the armhole is the individual lengths labeled here, multiplied by 2 (for the front and back of your sweater):

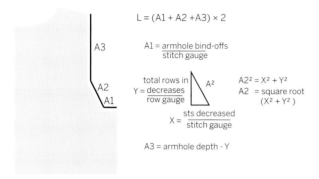

Breaking down the armhole

$L = (A1 + A2 + A3) \times 2$

$A1 = \dfrac{\text{armhole bind-offs}}{\text{stitch gauge}}$

$Y = \dfrac{\text{total rows in decreases}}{\text{row gauge}}$

$A2^2 = X^2 + Y^2$

$A2 = \text{square root} (X^2 + Y^2)$

$X = \dfrac{\text{sts decreased}}{\text{stitch gauge}}$

$A3 = \text{armhole depth} - Y$

Here's how that math breaks out. I'll include my own calculations as an example, done in Imperial measurements only for brevity.

- A1 = the number of stitches bound off at the armhole, divided by your stitch gauge:

    *My example: A1 = 8 sts bound off ÷ 5 sts per inch = 1.6"*

- A3 = the total armhole depth, minus the length of the rows in your shaping:

    Your pattern lists the number of shaping rows: There will be twice as many rows as shaping rows (since you shape every RS row).

    My example: 6 every-RS-row decreases makes 12 shaping rows

    Divide by your (actual) row gauge. This is the height of the "shaped" portion of the armhole. (Remember this for later, because you'll need it again! I've called it "Y" in the diagram above.)

    My example: Y = 12 shaping rows ÷ 7 rows per inch = 1.7"

Subtract this height from your full armhole depth. This is A3.

My example: A3 = armhole depth − Y = 8" − 1.7" = 6.3"

- A2: You'll need your calculator for this one. A2 is the hypotenuse of a right triangle, seen in the "Breaking down the armhole" diagram at left. Before we can figure out its length, we need to know the lengths of the two sides.

    Side 1, called "Y": Figured out in previous step

    My example: 1.7"

    Side 2, called "X": Number of stitches decreased in this part of the armhole (from pattern) divided by the stitch gauge.

    My example: X = 6 sts removed ÷ 5 sts per inch = 1.2"

The length of the hypotenuse is related to the sides in this way:

$$X^2 + Y^2 = A2^2$$

(I know. You'll only have to do this once more before you're done, though!)

*My example: $1.2^2 + 1.7^2 = A2^2$*

*$1.44 + 2.89 = A2^2$*

*$4.33 = A2^2$*

*$\sqrt{4.33} = A2$*

*$2.08 = A2$*

To get the total length of the armhole, add A1, A2, and A3 together. Multiply by 2. Remember this number—I'll call it "L"—for your target length.

*My example: L = (A1 + A2 + A3) × 2 = (1.6 + 2.08 + 6.3) × 2 = 19.96"*

### Sleeve cap.

Still with me? Excellent!

You know the total length, L, from the armhole we just finished. Let's work backward to figure out the height of the sleeve cap—then we can turn that height into some knitting instructions. Here's another diagram, getting you through the first few steps below:

Breaking down the sleeve cap

$$L = SC3 + 2 \times (SC1 + SC2)$$

$SC1 = \dfrac{\text{cap bind-offs}}{\text{stitch gauge}}$

$SC2 = \dfrac{L - (SC3 + SC1 + SC1)}{2}$ (the total length, minus straight bits, divided by 2 since there are two sides)

$SC3 = \dfrac{\text{final top-of-cap bind-offs}}{\text{stitch gauge}}$

The first part we need to calculate is SC2—the length of the diagonal portion of the cap. To do so, we need to subtract the other components from the total length. Here's the continuation of my example:

- The number of bind-offs at the beginning of the sleeve cap should usually match the armholes. So SC1 is (likely) equal to A1.

   *My example: The bind-offs do match, so SC1 = 1.6"*

- The number of bind-offs at the top of the sleeve cap is either written in the pattern, or should be around 25-40 percent of the total biceps stitches. Divide by your stitch gauge to get SC3.

   *My example: I'll want to bind off roughly 24 stitches at the top of my cap. 24 sts ÷ 5 sts to the inch = 4.8"*

- Now we can subtract SC1 and SC3 from L to find SC2: SC2 = (L – ([2 × SC1] + SC3) ÷ 2)

*My example: 19.96" is my target length, so:*

*19.96 = 4.8 + (2 × [1.6 + SC2])*

*19.96 = 4.8 + 3.2 + (2 × SC2)*

*19.96 = 8 + (2 × SC2)*

*19.96 – 8 = 2 × SC2*

*11.96 = 2 × SC2*

*11.96 ÷ 2 = SC2*

*5.98 = SC2*

Hang on, we're not done yet! We've now labeled the entire curve of the sleeve cap with the lengths it needs to measure to fit into the armhole . . .

. . . but we still don't have knitting instructions! To get *knitting* instructions, we'll need to know **how to work the decreases on the curved part of the cap so that the edge will be SC2 inches (cm) long**. To make those calculations, we're back in triangle land:

Calculating your cap's height

$W = $ cap height (this is what we're looking for!)

$Z = \dfrac{\text{sts to decrease}}{\text{stitch gauge}}$

WHERE

stitches to decrease = (biceps stitches – bound-off sts) ÷ 2
= (biceps sts – (SC1 + SC1 + SC3)) ÷ 2

AND

$SC2^2 = Z^2 + W^2$
$SC2^2 – Z^2 = W^2$
$W = \sqrt{(SC2^2 – Z^2)}$

This time we *know* the hypotenuse of the triangle (SC2) and can figure out one of the sides (Z), and must calculate the other—the cap height (W). Here's the final formula for W (though I break it down in the image above):

$$W = \sqrt{(SC2^2 – Z^2)}$$

(Time for that calculator again!) You know SC2 already; now calculate how many stitches you have to decrease in the curved section of the cap on each side: Take the biceps stitches, remove all the stitches that get bound-off, then divide by 2 since you'll remove half of the stitches on each side.

*My example:*

*I have 68 biceps stitches to start; 8 get bound off at the start of the cap on each side, and 24 stitches get bound off at the end. So,*

*sts to decrease, total = 68 − (8 + 8 + 24) = 68 − 40 = 28*

*sts to decrease, each side = 28 ÷ 2 = 14*

*And Z = 14 stitches ÷ 5 sts per inch = 2.8"*

Now you know SC2 and you know Z, so you can find the cap height with the formula above:

*My example:*
$$W = \sqrt{(SC2^2 - Z^2)} = \sqrt{(5.98^2 - 2.8^2)} = \sqrt{(35.76 - 7.84)} = \sqrt{27.92} = 5.28"$$

So the curved part of my cap should be 5.28" tall, which is appropriate for an 8" armhole. (Generally speaking, and there are *definitely* exceptions to this; you'll want to see a cap that's somewhere between half and two-thirds of your armhole's vertical height.)

Multiply the height by your row gauge to get the number of rows in the cap.

*My example: 5.28" tall × 7 rows per inch = 36.9 rows; round to 36 rows for shaping*

Congratulations, you're almost there!

### Putting it together: sleeve cap instructions.

Forgotten where you are? Don't worry—that's a lot of calculations! Here's a recap:

- We drafted armhole instructions to match the body's needs, then
- Figured out how many stitches to remove in the curved part of the cap on each side (Z), and
- How tall the cap must be, in rows.

Now, we'll distribute the decreases you need to work in the "curved" part of the cap along the rows in the curved part of the cap.

*My example: I have to distribute 14 decrease rows over 36 total rows.*

Here's how I recommend going about it—though you can always get old school and draw things out on a piece of graph paper:

- Make sure you have at least twice as many rows as decreases. If not, you'll need to work some every-row shaping.

  *My example: I'm good here. Working decrease rows every RS row will use up 28 of my needed 36 rows.*

- Figure out the number of extra rows you will have left *if you shape every RS row*. Round down to an even number.

  *My example: I have 36 total rows to fill, minus 28 rows if I shape every RS row = 8 extra rows*

- Make as many of the shaping rows every third RS row as possible—this will use up 4 of your "extra" rows apiece.

  *My example: I can work my decreases every third RS row twice, and use up all 8 of my extras. So I'll work 2 every-third-RS-row shaping rows, and 12 every-RS-row shaping rows, to remove all 14 stitches per side.*

- If you have extra rows left, make as many of the shaping rows every-other-RS row as possible—each will use up 2 from your "extra" rows.

*My example: I don't need this step.*

You're now ready to put all of this hard work into knitting-instruction form! You've got your initial bind-offs from the body, the curved part of the cap you've just figured out, and the final bind-offs.

Your eventual sleeve cap instructions will look something like this (my numbers are in parentheses):

Shape sleeve cap:

Bind off X (5) sts at the beginning of the next two rows.

Bind off Y (3) sts at the beginning of the following two rows.

Decrease 1 stitch at each end of every 3rd RS row X (2) times, then every other RS row X times (*skip this section*), then every RS row X (12) times, then every row X times (*skip this section*).

BO X (24) sts.

Voilà! A cap that fits into its armhole perfectly—and fits your body perfectly, too.

## FURTHER THINKING
### A "MOSTLY SEAMLESS" SET-IN-SLEEVE CONSTRUCTION

Truly, I think seams are the greatest and that it's more than worth your energy and resources to learn how to mattress stitch well. (In my observation, the knitters I know who mattress stitch well don't put it off or dread it—even though some of us like doing it more than others!)

However, if you'd like to try to work your set-in-sleeve garment without seams, you can—if you're lucky in your combination of biceps and armhole depth. Here's how to tell:

- Work the body in the round to the armholes, then split the front and back and work them flat to the shoulders.

- Seam the shoulders.

- Pick up your biceps stitches around the armhole, starting at the armhole seam—**here's where you find out if you're lucky** in terms of your combination of biceps and armhole depth.

  - If the picked-up stitches look good, you're all clear!

  - If there are too many or too few stitches for the armhole opening, there's not a simple way to salvage this process. You're better off working the cap flat and seaming it in.

- Place four markers—at the top of the shoulder, one on either side of the final sleeve cap bind-offs; and at the armhole, one on either side of the initial armhole bind-offs.
  Work short rows to shape your cap, like this:

- *Set-Up Row 1:* Knit to third marker (just past the shoulder seam), sm, wrap and turn.

- *Set-Up Row 2:* Purl back to the second marker placed (just past the shoulder seam), sm, wrap and turn.

- *Short Row 1:* Knit to 1 st past the last wrapped st, working the wrapped st with its wrap, wrap and turn.

- *Short Row 2:* Purl to 1 st past the last wrapped st, working the wrapped st with its wrap, wrap and turn.

- Continue Short Rows 1 and 2 until you reach the armhole markers.

  - Knit 1 round, working the final wrapped stitches with their wraps. You're now at the bottom of the armhole and ready to work the sleeve down to the cuff.

Provided the number of stitches you need to pick up for the biceps looks good around the armhole, this is a perfectly structural and stable way to knit a sleeve cap.

### "SNEAKING IN" SOME DIFFERENCES IN THE FRONT AND BACK ARMHOLES

Larger-busted women will have a different number of stitches on the front bust than the back bust. If the differences are not large, and/or you're working a deep neckline, you can calculate the front neck decreases based on this larger bust count, and leave the armholes truly symmetrical, with no downside. (That's how I've personally been removing the roughly 3" (7.5 cm) of extra width I have in the front of my own sweaters, for years.)

However, for the particularly narrow-shouldered large-busted figure, or someone who wants a high neckline, it's tempting to try to remove a few more stitches in the front armholes than the back armholes. Can you do this without giving yourself fits when you're seaming in the sleeve cap?

It depends. In most cases, you can probably get away with:

- Working every *other* armhole decrease row as a double decrease—k3tog, or sssk.

- Working the last stitch of each bind-off "step" as a k2tog before binding off.

- Adding one extra decrease row (or two, if your yarn is on the thin side) after completing the armhole decreases as for the back.

- This "sneak some decreases in" approach will allow you to remove 4-8 additional stitches in the front armhole shaping vs. the back, without hurting your cap seaming.

In drastic cases, you might also be able to work an internal dart line around 1" (2.5 cm) in from the existing armhole decreases, matching the armhole decreases one for one—though this does tend to bias the fabric, so you'll want to avoid this approach if you're using anything especially drapey.

And if all this sleeve cap math makes you reach for your knitting, no worries! I've written some great basic patterns for you to use.

These simple straight-sided sweaters are in three gauges and twelve sizes, so you've got a great starting point. I've shown them with recommended yarns, but I encourage you to experiment, too! The set-in-sleeve construction works well with just about any fabric. If you'd like a worksheet to help you tame the numbers as you knit, you can download one from my website.

# Basic Pullover: Set-In-Sleeve Construction

Classic, tailored, and utterly wearable, a crew-neck set-in-sleeve pullover is the ultimate blank canvas. I've shown it in an equally classic sport weight wool (so soft), but I offer some variations that are a bit further afield: a heathered wool with a more rustic look and an exquisitely soft Aran-weight tweed.

This unisex garment is worked in pieces from the bottom up, and then seamed for stability. No waist shaping is included in any of the basic patterns, but should you choose to add some, please see pages 113–115 for details.

## FINISHED MEASUREMENTS

**SPORT:** 31½ (32½, 35½, 36½, 39½, 40½, 43½, 44½, 48½, 52½, 56½, 60½)" [80 (82.5, 90, 92.5, 100.5, 103, 110.5, 113, 123, 133.5, 143.5, 153.5) cm] chest

**WORSTED:** 31½ (32½, 35½, 37, 40, 41½, 43, 46, 48½, 53, 57½, 62)" [80 (82.5, 90, 94, 101.5, 105.5, 109, 117, 123, 134.5, 146, 157.5) cm] chest

**ARAN:** 31 (33, 35, 37, 39, 41, 43, 45, 49, 53, 57, 61)" [78.5 (84, 89, 94, 99, 104, 109, 114.5, 124.5, 134.5, 145, 155) cm] chest

*Note: Sweater is intended to be worn with 1–2" (2.5–5 cm) ease in the bust; shown in sport weight yarn and size 36½" (92.5 cm).*

## YARN

**SPORT:** Quince & Co. Chickadee [100% American wool; 181 yards (166 meters) / 50 grams]: 6 (6, 7, 7, 8, 8, 9, 9, 10, 11, 12, 14) hanks Camel

**WORSTED:** Blue Sky Fibers Woolstok [100% fine highland wool; 123 yards (112 meters) / 50 grams]: 9 (9, 10, 10, 11, 12, 13, 14, 15, 16, 18, 20) hanks #1302 Gravel Road

**ARAN:** The Fibre Company Arranmore [80% wool / 10% silk / 10% cashmere; 175 yards (160 meters) / 100 grams]: 5 (5, 6, 6, 7, 7, 7, 8, 8, 9, 10, 11) hanks Cronan

## NEEDLES

**SPORT:** One pair straight needles and one 24" (60 cm) long circular needle (for Neckband) size US 5 (3.75 mm)

**WORSTED:** One pair straight needles and one 24" (60 cm) long circular needle (for Neckband) size US 6 (4 mm)

**ARAN:** One pair straight needles and one 24" (60 cm) long circular needle (for Neckband) size US 8 (5 mm)

Change needle size if necessary to obtain correct gauge.

## NOTIONS

Stitch markers

## GAUGE

**SPORT:** 24 sts and 32 rows = 4" (10 cm) in St st
**WORSTED:** 22 sts and 32 rows = 4" (10 cm) in St st
**ARAN:** 16 sts and 24 rows = 4" (10 cm) in St st

## NOTES

If your size gives the number 0 for a particular instruction, skip that instruction and proceed to the next instruction.

Unless otherwise specified, decreases should be worked to match the slant of the edge being shaped, as follows: For left-slanting edges: On RS rows, k2, ssk, knit to end; on WS rows, p2, p2tog, purl to end. For right-slanting edges: On RS rows, knit to last 4 sts, k2tog, k2; on WS rows, purl to last 4 sts, ssp, p2. Increases should also be worked to match the slant of the edge being shaped, as follows: For right-slanting edges: On RS rows, k1, M1R, knit to end; on WS rows, p1, M1PR, purl to end. For left-slanting edges: On RS rows, knit to last st, M1L, k1; on WS rows, p1, M1PL, purl to end.

# BACK

CO

| | | | | | | | | | | | | |
|---|---|---|---|---|---|---|---|---|---|---|---|---|
| SPORT | 94 | 98 | 106 | 110 | 118 | 122 | 130 | 134 | 146 | 158 | 170 | 182 |
| WORSTED | 86 | 90 | 98 | 102 | 110 | 114 | 118 | 126 | 134 | 146 | 158 | 170 |
| ARAN | 62 | 66 | 70 | 74 | 78 | 82 | 86 | 90 | 98 | 106 | 114 | 122 |

sts.

Begin 2x2 Rib Flat; work even until piece measures 2¼" (5.5 cm), ending with a WS row.

Change to St st; work even until piece measures 16 (16, 16½, 16½, 17, 17, 17, 17½, 17½, 17½, 17½, 18)" [40.5 (40.5, 42, 42, 43, 43, 43, 44.5, 44.5, 44.5, 44.5, 45.5) cm] from the beginning, ending with a WS row.

## SHAPE ARMHOLES

BO

| | | | | | | | | | | | | |
|---|---|---|---|---|---|---|---|---|---|---|---|---|
| SPORT | 8 | 8 | 8 | 9 | 9 | 9 | 9 | 9 | 11 | 11 | 12 | 15 |
| WORSTED | 7 | 7 | 7 | 9 | 9 | 9 | 9 | 9 | 10 | 10 | 11 | 14 |
| ARAN | 5 | 5 | 5 | 6 | 6 | 6 | 6 | 6 | 7 | 7 | 8 | 10 |

sts at the beginning of the next 2 rows, then

| | | | | | | | | | | | | |
|---|---|---|---|---|---|---|---|---|---|---|---|---|
| SPORT | 0 | 0 | 3 | 3 | 5 | 5 | 6 | 6 | 6 | 8 | 9 | 9 |
| WORSTED | 0 | 0 | 3 | 3 | 5 | 5 | 6 | 6 | 6 | 7 | 9 | 9 |
| ARAN | 0 | 0 | 2 | 2 | 3 | 3 | 4 | 4 | 4 | 5 | 6 | 6 |

sts at the beginning of the following 2 rows.

| | | | | | | | | | | | | |
|---|---|---|---|---|---|---|---|---|---|---|---|---|
| SPORT | 78 | 82 | 84 | 86 | 90 | 94 | 100 | 104 | 112 | 120 | 128 | 134 |
| WORSTED | 72 | 76 | 78 | 78 | 82 | 86 | 88 | 96 | 102 | 112 | 118 | 124 |
| ARAN | 52 | 56 | 56 | 58 | 60 | 64 | 66 | 70 | 76 | 82 | 86 | 90 |

sts remain.

Decrease 1 st each side every RS row

| | | | | | | | | | | | | |
|---|---|---|---|---|---|---|---|---|---|---|---|---|
| SPORT | 4 | 5 | 5 | 4 | 5 | 4 | 5 | 5 | 8 | 9 | 12 | 13 |
| WORSTED | 4 | 5 | 5 | 3 | 4 | 3 | 2 | 5 | 7 | 9 | 11 | 12 |
| ARAN | 3 | 4 | 3 | 3 | 3 | 3 | 3 | 4 | 6 | 7 | 8 | 9 |

times.

| | | | | | | | | | | | | |
|---|---|---|---|---|---|---|---|---|---|---|---|---|
| SPORT | 70 | 72 | 74 | 78 | 80 | 86 | 90 | 94 | 96 | 102 | 104 | 108 |
| WORSTED | 64 | 66 | 68 | 72 | 74 | 80 | 84 | 86 | 88 | 94 | 96 | 100 |
| ARAN | 46 | 48 | 50 | 52 | 54 | 58 | 60 | 62 | 64 | 68 | 70 | 72 |

sts remain.

Work even until armholes measure 5½ (6, 6¼, 6½, 7, 7¼, 7½, 8, 8½, 9½, 10, 11)" [14 (15, 16, 16.5, 18, 18.5, 19, 20.5, 21.5, 24, 25.5, 28) cm], ending with a WS row.

## SHAPE NECK

**NEXT ROW (RS):** Knit

| | | | | | | | | | | | | |
|---|---|---|---|---|---|---|---|---|---|---|---|---|
| SPORT | 21 | 22 | 22 | 23 | 24 | 25 | 26 | 28 | 28 | 30 | 30 | 31 |
| WORSTED | 19 | 20 | 20 | 22 | 22 | 24 | 25 | 25 | 26 | 28 | 28 | 29 |
| ARAN | 14 | 15 | 15 | 16 | 17 | 18 | 18 | 19 | 19 | 20 | 21 | 21 |

sts, join a second ball of yarn, BO center

| | | | | | | | | | | | | |
|---|---|---|---|---|---|---|---|---|---|---|---|---|
| SPORT | 28 | 28 | 30 | 32 | 32 | 36 | 38 | 38 | 40 | 42 | 44 | 46 |
| WORSTED | 26 | 26 | 28 | 28 | 30 | 32 | 34 | 36 | 36 | 38 | 40 | 42 |
| ARAN | 18 | 18 | 20 | 20 | 20 | 22 | 24 | 24 | 26 | 28 | 28 | 30 |

sts, knit to end.

Working both sides at the same time, decrease 1 st at each neck edge every RS row twice.

| | | | | | | | | | | | | |
|---|---|---|---|---|---|---|---|---|---|---|---|---|
| SPORT | 19 | 20 | 20 | 21 | 22 | 23 | 24 | 26 | 26 | 28 | 28 | 29 |
| WORSTED | 17 | 18 | 18 | 20 | 20 | 22 | 23 | 23 | 24 | 26 | 26 | 27 |
| ARAN | 12 | 13 | 13 | 14 | 15 | 16 | 16 | 17 | 17 | 18 | 19 | 19 |

sts remain each shoulder.

Work even until armholes measure 6½ (7, 7¼, 7½, 8, 8¼, 8½, 9, 9½, 10½, 11, 12)" [16.5 (18, 18.5, 19, 20.5, 21, 21.5, 23, 24, 26.5, 28, 30.5) cm], ending with a WS row.

## SHAPE SHOULDERS

BO

| | | | | | | | | | | | | |
|---|---|---|---|---|---|---|---|---|---|---|---|---|
| SPORT | 10 | 10 | 10 | 11 | 11 | 12 | 12 | 13 | 13 | 14 | 14 | 15 |
| WORSTED | 9 | 9 | 9 | 10 | 10 | 11 | 12 | 12 | 12 | 13 | 13 | 14 |
| ARAN | 6 | 7 | 7 | 7 | 8 | 8 | 8 | 9 | 9 | 9 | 10 | 10 |

sts at each armhole edge once, then BO

| | | | | | | | | | | | | |
|---|---|---|---|---|---|---|---|---|---|---|---|---|
| SPORT | 9 | 10 | 10 | 10 | 11 | 11 | 12 | 13 | 13 | 14 | 14 | 14 |
| WORSTED | 8 | 9 | 9 | 10 | 10 | 11 | 11 | 11 | 12 | 13 | 13 | 13 |
| ARAN | 6 | 6 | 6 | 7 | 7 | 8 | 8 | 8 | 8 | 9 | 9 | 9 |

sts once.

# FRONT

Work as for Back until armholes measure 3¾ (4¼, 4½, 4¾, 5¼, 5½, 5¾, 6¼, 6¾, 7¾, 8¼, 9¼)" [9.5 (11, 11.5, 12, 13.5, 14, 14.5, 16, 17, 19.5, 21, 23.5) cm], ending with a WS row.

| | | | | | | | | | | | | |
|---|---|---|---|---|---|---|---|---|---|---|---|---|
| SPORT | 70 | 72 | 74 | 78 | 80 | 86 | 90 | 94 | 96 | 102 | 104 | 108 |
| WORSTED | 64 | 66 | 68 | 72 | 74 | 80 | 84 | 86 | 88 | 94 | 96 | 100 |
| ARAN | 46 | 48 | 50 | 52 | 54 | 58 | 60 | 62 | 64 | 68 | 70 | 72 |

sts remain after armhole shaping is complete.

## SHAPE NECK

**NEXT ROW (RS):** Knit

| | | | | | | | | | | | | |
|---|---|---|---|---|---|---|---|---|---|---|---|---|
| SPORT | 27 | 28 | 29 | 30 | 31 | 34 | 35 | 37 | 38 | 40 | 41 | 42 |
| WORSTED | 25 | 26 | 26 | 28 | 29 | 31 | 33 | 34 | 35 | 37 | 38 | 39 |
| ARAN | 18 | 19 | 19 | 20 | 21 | 23 | 23 | 24 | 25 | 26 | 27 | 28 |

sts, join a second ball of yarn, BO center

| | | | | | | | | | | | | |
|---|---|---|---|---|---|---|---|---|---|---|---|---|
| SPORT | 16 | 16 | 16 | 18 | 18 | 18 | 20 | 20 | 20 | 22 | 22 | 24 |
| WORSTED | 14 | 14 | 16 | 16 | 16 | 18 | 18 | 18 | 18 | 20 | 20 | 22 |
| ARAN | 10 | 10 | 12 | 12 | 12 | 12 | 14 | 14 | 14 | 16 | 16 | 16 |

sts, knit to end.

Working both sides at the same time, decrease 1 st at each neck edge every row

| | | | | | | | | | | | | |
|---|---|---|---|---|---|---|---|---|---|---|---|---|
| SPORT | 4 | 4 | 5 | 5 | 5 | 6 | 6 | 6 | 6 | 6 | 7 | 7 |
| WORSTED | 4 | 4 | 4 | 4 | 5 | 5 | 5 | 6 | 6 | 6 | 6 | 6 |
| ARAN | 3 | 3 | 3 | 3 | 3 | 4 | 4 | 4 | 4 | 4 | 4 | 5 |

times, then every RS row

| | | | | | | | | | | | | |
|---|---|---|---|---|---|---|---|---|---|---|---|---|
| SPORT | 4 | 4 | 4 | 4 | 4 | 5 | 5 | 5 | 6 | 6 | 6 | 6 |
| WORSTED | 4 | 4 | 4 | 4 | 4 | 4 | 5 | 5 | 5 | 5 | 6 | 6 |
| ARAN | 3 | 3 | 3 | 3 | 3 | 3 | 3 | 3 | 4 | 4 | 4 | 4 |

times.

| | | | | | | | | | | | | |
|---|---|---|---|---|---|---|---|---|---|---|---|---|
| SPORT | 19 | 20 | 20 | 21 | 22 | 23 | 24 | 26 | 26 | 28 | 28 | 29 |
| WORSTED | 17 | 18 | 18 | 20 | 20 | 22 | 23 | 23 | 24 | 26 | 26 | 27 |
| ARAN | 12 | 13 | 13 | 14 | 15 | 16 | 16 | 17 | 17 | 18 | 19 | 19 |

sts remain each shoulder.

Work even until armholes measure 6½ (7, 7¼, 7½, 8, 8¼, 8½, 9, 9½, 10½, 11, 12)" [16.5 (18, 18.5, 19, 20.5, 21, 21.5, 23, 24, 26.5, 28, 30.5) cm], ending with a WS row.

## SHAPE SHOULDERS
BO

|  | | | | | | | | | | | | |
|---|---|---|---|---|---|---|---|---|---|---|---|
| SPORT | 10 | 10 | 10 | 11 | 11 | 12 | 12 | 13 | 13 | 14 | 14 | 15 |
| WORSTED | 9 | 9 | 9 | 10 | 10 | 11 | 12 | 12 | 12 | 13 | 13 | 14 |
| ARAN | 6 | 7 | 7 | 7 | 8 | 8 | 8 | 9 | 9 | 9 | 10 | 10 |

sts at each armhole edge once, then BO

|  | | | | | | | | | | | | |
|---|---|---|---|---|---|---|---|---|---|---|---|
| SPORT | 9 | 10 | 10 | 10 | 11 | 11 | 12 | 13 | 13 | 14 | 14 | 14 |
| WORSTED | 8 | 9 | 9 | 10 | 10 | 11 | 11 | 11 | 12 | 13 | 13 | 13 |
| ARAN | 6 | 6 | 6 | 7 | 7 | 8 | 8 | 8 | 8 | 9 | 9 | 9 |

sts once.

# SLEEVES

CO

|  | | | | | | | | | | | | |
|---|---|---|---|---|---|---|---|---|---|---|---|
| SPORT | 50 | 50 | 50 | 54 | 54 | 54 | 58 | 58 | 58 | 62 | 62 | 62 |
| WORSTED | 46 | 46 | 46 | 50 | 50 | 50 | 54 | 54 | 54 | 58 | 58 | 58 |
| ARAN | 34 | 34 | 34 | 38 | 38 | 38 | 38 | 38 | 38 | 42 | 42 | 42 |

sts.

Begin 2x2 Rib Flat; work even until piece measures 3" (7.5 cm), ending with a WS row.

Change to St st; work 2 rows even.

## SHAPE SLEEVE
Beginning on the next RS row, increase 1 st each side every

|  | | | | | | | | | | | | |
|---|---|---|---|---|---|---|---|---|---|---|---|
| SPORT | 13 | 12 | 9 | 11 | 9 | 8 | 7 | 6 | 5 | 4 | 3 | 3 |
| WORSTED | 15 | 13 | 10 | 12 | 10 | 8 | 8 | 7 | 5 | 4 | 4 | 3 |
| ARAN | 16 | 13 | 11 | 14 | 12 | 10 | 8 | 7 | 5 | 5 | 4 | 3 |

rows a total of

|  | | | | | | | | | | | | |
|---|---|---|---|---|---|---|---|---|---|---|---|
| SPORT | 8 | 9 | 11 | 10 | 12 | 14 | 15 | 18 | 22 | 26 | 32 | 38 |
| WORSTED | 7 | 8 | 10 | 9 | 11 | 13 | 13 | 16 | 20 | 24 | 29 | 35 |
| ARAN | 5 | 6 | 7 | 6 | 7 | 8 | 10 | 12 | 15 | 17 | 21 | 25 |

times.

|  | | | | | | | | | | | | |
|---|---|---|---|---|---|---|---|---|---|---|---|
| SPORT | 66 | 68 | 72 | 74 | 78 | 82 | 88 | 94 | 102 | 114 | 126 | 138 |
| WORSTED | 60 | 62 | 66 | 68 | 72 | 76 | 80 | 86 | 94 | 106 | 116 | 128 |
| ARAN | 44 | 46 | 48 | 50 | 52 | 54 | 58 | 62 | 68 | 76 | 84 | 92 |

sts.

Work even until piece measures 18 (18, 18, 18½, 18½, 18½, 19, 19, 19, 19, 19½, 19½)" [45.5 (45.5, 45.5, 47, 47, 47, 48.5, 48.5, 48.5, 48.5, 49.5, 49.5) cm] from the beginning, ending with a WS row.

## SHAPE CAP
BO

|  | | | | | | | | | | | | |
|---|---|---|---|---|---|---|---|---|---|---|---|
| SPORT | 8 | 8 | 8 | 9 | 9 | 9 | 9 | 9 | 11 | 11 | 12 | 15 |
| WORSTED | 7 | 7 | 7 | 9 | 9 | 9 | 9 | 9 | 10 | 10 | 11 | 14 |
| ARAN | 5 | 5 | 5 | 6 | 6 | 6 | 6 | 6 | 7 | 7 | 8 | 10 |

sts at the beginning of the next 2 rows, then

|  | | | | | | | | | | | | |
|---|---|---|---|---|---|---|---|---|---|---|---|
| SPORT | 0 | 0 | 3 | 3 | 5 | 5 | 6 | 6 | 6 | 8 | 6 | 6 |
| WORSTED | 0 | 0 | 3 | 3 | 5 | 5 | 6 | 6 | 6 | 7 | 6 | 6 |
| ARAN | 0 | 0 | 2 | 2 | 3 | 3 | 4 | 4 | 4 | 5 | 4 | 4 |

sts at the beginning of the following 2 rows.

Decrease 1 st each side of every third RS row

| | | | | | | | | | | | | |
|---|---|---|---|---|---|---|---|---|---|---|---|---|
| SPORT | 1 | 1 | 2 | 3 | 4 | 4 | 3 | 3 | 3 | 3 | 2 | 3 |
| WORSTED | 1 | 2 | 3 | 4 | 5 | 5 | 5 | 4 | 4 | 4 | 4 | 4 |
| ARAN | 1 | 1 | 2 | 2 | 3 | 3 | 3 | 3 | 3 | 3 | 2 | 3 |

time(s), then every other RS row

| | | | | | | | | | | | | |
|---|---|---|---|---|---|---|---|---|---|---|---|---|
| SPORT | 0 | 1 | 1 | 0 | 1 | 0 | 1 | 0 | 1 | 1 | 0 | 0 |
| WORSTED | 1 | 1 | 0 | 0 | 1 | 0 | 0 | 1 | 1 | 0 | 0 | 1 |
| ARAN | 0 | 1 | 0 | 1 | 1 | 0 | 0 | 0 | 0 | 0 | 1 | 1 |

time(s), then every RS row

| | | | | | | | | | | | | |
|---|---|---|---|---|---|---|---|---|---|---|---|---|
| SPORT | 13 | 12 | 10 | 9 | 7 | 9 | 10 | 13 | 13 | 15 | 22 | 22 |
| WORSTED | 11 | 10 | 9 | 6 | 4 | 6 | 6 | 8 | 10 | 14 | 17 | 17 |
| ARAN | 8 | 8 | 7 | 5 | 4 | 6 | 6 | 7 | 8 | 10 | 13 | 12 |

times.

BO

| | | | | | | | | | | | | |
|---|---|---|---|---|---|---|---|---|---|---|---|---|
| SPORT | 2 | 2 | 2 | 3 | 3 | 3 | 3 | 3 | 4 | 5 | 6 | 6 |
| WORSTED | 2 | 2 | 2 | 2 | 2 | 3 | 3 | 3 | 4 | 5 | 6 | 6 |
| ARAN | 2 | 2 | 2 | 2 | 2 | 2 | 2 | 2 | 3 | 3 | 3 | 4 |

sts at the beginning of the next 4 rows.

BO remaining

| | | | | | | | | | | | | |
|---|---|---|---|---|---|---|---|---|---|---|---|---|
| SPORT | 14 | 16 | 16 | 14 | 14 | 16 | 18 | 20 | 18 | 18 | 18 | 22 |
| WORSTED | 12 | 14 | 14 | 16 | 16 | 14 | 16 | 18 | 16 | 16 | 16 | 20 |
| ARAN | 8 | 8 | 8 | 10 | 10 | 10 | 12 | 14 | 12 | 14 | 16 | 16 |

sts.

## FINISHING

Block pieces as desired. Sew shoulder seams. Set in Sleeves; sew side and Sleeve seams.

### NECKBAND

With RS facing, using circular needle and beginning at right shoulder, pick up and knit approximately 1 st in each BO st, 2 sts for every 3 rows along vertical edges, and 3 sts for every 4 rows along diagonal edges. You will pick up approximately

| | | | | | | | | | | | | |
|---|---|---|---|---|---|---|---|---|---|---|---|---|
| SPORT | 100 | 100 | 100 | 104 | 104 | 112 | 116 | 116 | 120 | 124 | 128 | 132 |
| WORSTED | 92 | 92 | 96 | 96 | 96 | 100 | 104 | 108 | 108 | 112 | 116 | 120 |
| ARAN | 64 | 64 | 68 | 68 | 68 | 72 | 76 | 76 | 80 | 84 | 84 | 88 |

sts. *Note: Exact st count is not essential, but be sure to end with a multiple of 4 sts for ribbing to work out evenly.* Join for working in the rnd; pm for beginning of rnd. Begin 2x2 Rib in the Rnd; work even for ¾" (2 cm). BO all sts in pattern.

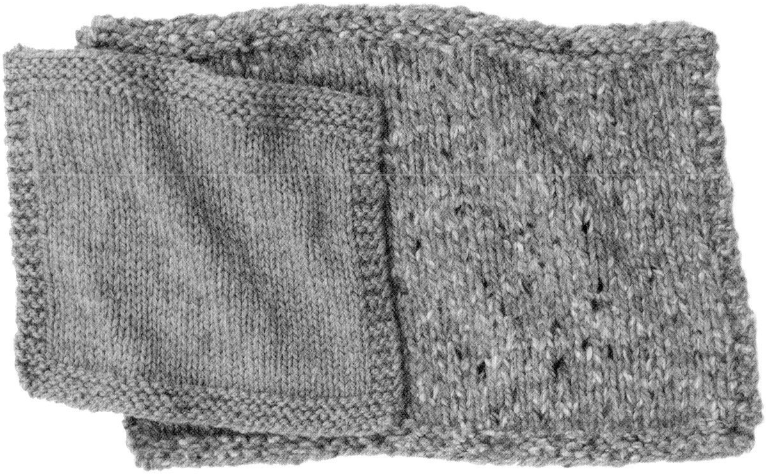

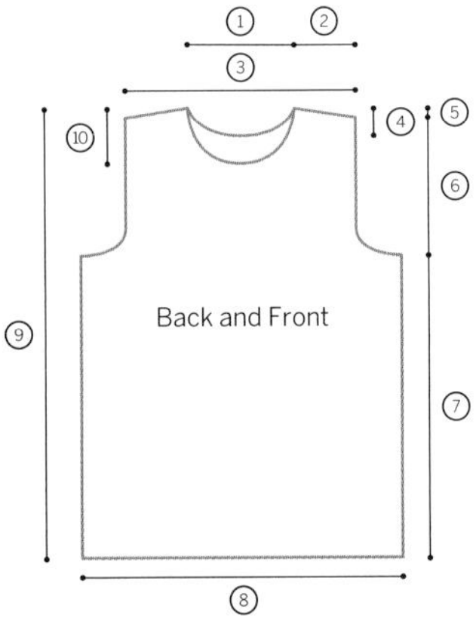


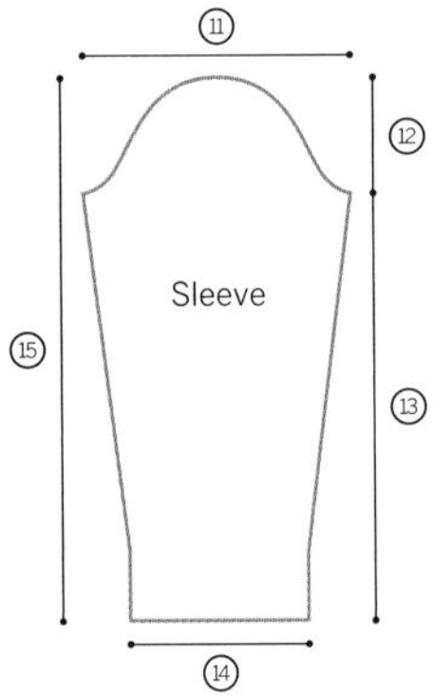


### SPORT WEIGHT

1 5¼ (5¼, 5¾, 6, 6, 6¾, 7, 7, 7¼, 7¾, 8, 8¼)"
13.5 (13.5, 14.5, 15, 15, 17, 18, 18, 18.5, 19.5, 20.5, 21) cm

2 3¼ (3¼, 3¼, 3½, 3¾, 3¾, 4, 4¼, 4¼, 4¾, 4¾, 4¾)"
8.5 (8.5, 8.5, 9, 9.5, 9.5, 10, 11, 11, 12, 12, 12) cm

3 11½ (12, 12½, 13, 13½, 14½, 15, 15½, 16, 17, 17½, 18)"
29 (30.5, 32, 33, 34.5, 37, 38, 39.5, 40.5, 43, 44.5, 45.5) cm

4 1½"
4 cm

5 ½"
1.5 cm

6 6½ (7, 7¼, 7½, 8, 8¼, 8½, 9, 9½, 10½, 11, 12)"
16.5 (18, 18.5, 19, 20.5, 21, 21.5, 23, 24, 26.5, 28, 30.5) cm

7 16 (16, 16½, 16½, 17, 17, 17, 17½, 17½, 17½, 17½, 18)"
40.5 (40.5, 42, 42, 43, 43, 43, 44.5, 44.5, 44.5, 44.5, 45.5) cm

8 15¾ (16¼, 17¾, 18¼, 19¾, 20¼, 21¾, 22¼, 24¼, 26¼, 28¼, 30¼)"
40 (41.5, 45, 46.5, 50, 51.5, 55, 56.5, 61.5, 66.5, 72, 77) cm

9 23 (23½, 24¼, 24½, 25½, 25¾, 26, 27, 27½, 28½, 29, 30½)"
58.5 (59.5, 61.5, 62, 65, 65.5, 66, 68.5, 70, 72.5, 73.5, 77.5) cm

10 3¼"
8.5 cm

11 11 (11¼, 12, 12¼, 13, 13¾, 14¾, 15¾, 17, 19, 21, 23)"
28 (28.5, 30.5, 31, 33, 35, 37.5, 40, 43, 48.5, 53.5, 58.5) cm

12 4¾ (5, 5½, 5½, 6¼, 6¼, 6¼, 6½, 7, 7½, 8, 8¾)"
12 (12.5, 14, 14, 16, 16, 16, 16.5, 18, 19, 20.5, 22) cm

13 18 (18, 18, 18½, 18½, 18½, 19, 19, 19, 19, 19½, 19½)"
45.5 (45.5, 45.5, 47, 47, 47, 48.5, 48.5, 48.5, 48.5, 49.5, 49.5) cm

14 8¼ (8¼, 8¼, 9, 9, 9, 9¾, 9¾, 9¾, 10¼, 10¼, 10¼)"
21 (21, 21, 23, 23, 23, 25, 25, 25, 26, 26, 26) cm

15 22¼ (22½, 23, 23½, 24¼, 24¼, 24¾, 25, 25½, 26, 27, 27¾)"
56.5 (57, 58.5, 59.5, 61.5, 61.5, 63, 63.5, 65, 66, 68.5, 70.5) cm

## WORSTED WEIGHT

1 5½ (5½, 5¾, 5¾, 6¼, 6½, 7, 7¼, 7¼, 7¾, 8, 8¼)"
14 (14, 14.5, 14.5, 16, 16.5, 18, 18.5, 18.5, 19.5, 20.5, 21) cm

2 3 (3¼, 3¼, 3¾, 3¾, 4, 4¼, 4¼, 4¼, 4¾, 4¾, 5)"
7.5 (8.5, 8.5, 9.5, 9.5, 10, 11, 11, 11, 12, 12, 12.5) cm

3 11¾ (12, 12¼, 13, 13½, 14½, 15¼, 15¾, 16, 17, 17½, 18¼)"
30 (30.5, 31, 33, 34.5, 37, 38.5, 40, 40.5, 43, 44.5, 46.5) cm

4 1½"
4 cm

5 ½"
1.5 cm

6 6½ (7, 7¼, 7½, 8, 8¼, 8½, 9, 9½, 10½, 11, 12)"
16.5 (18, 18.5, 19, 20.5, 21, 21.5, 23, 24, 26.5, 28, 30.5) cm

7 16 (16, 16½, 16½, 17, 17, 17, 17½, 17½, 17½, 17½, 18)"
40.5 (40.5, 42, 42, 43, 43, 43, 44.5, 44.5, 44.5, 44.5, 45.5) cm

8 15¾ (16¼, 17¾, 18½, 20, 20¾, 21½, 23, 24¼, 26½, 28¾, 31)"
40 (41.5, 45, 47, 51, 52.5, 54.5, 58.5, 61.5, 67.5, 73, 78.5) cm

9 23 (23½, 24¼, 24½, 25½, 25¾, 26, 27, 27½, 28½, 29, 30½)"
58.5 (59.5, 61.5, 62, 65, 65.5, 66, 68.5, 70, 72.5, 73.5, 77.5) cm

10 3¼"
8.5 cm

11 11 (11¼, 12, 12¼, 13, 13¾, 14½, 15¾, 17, 19¼, 21, 23¼)"
28 (28.5, 30.5, 31, 33, 35, 37, 40, 43, 49, 53.5, 59) cm

12 4¾ (5¼, 5½, 5½, 6¼, 6¼, 6¼, 6½, 7, 7½, 8¼, 8¾)"
12 (13.5, 14, 14, 16, 16, 16, 16.5, 18, 19, 21, 22) cm

13 18 (18, 18, 18½, 18½, 18½, 19, 19, 19, 19, 19½, 19½)"
45.5 (45.5, 45.5, 47, 47, 47, 48.5, 48.5, 48.5, 48.5, 49.5, 49.5) cm

14 8¼ (8¼, 8¼, 9, 9, 9, 9¾, 9¾, 9¾, 10½, 10½, 10½)"
21 (21, 21, 23, 23, 23, 25, 25, 25, 26.5, 26.5, 26.5) cm

15 22¼ (22¾, 23, 23½, 24¼, 24¼, 24¾, 25, 25½, 26, 27¼, 27¾)"
56.5 (58, 58.5, 59.5, 61.5, 61.5, 63, 63.5, 65, 66, 69, 70.5) cm

## ARAN WEIGHT

1 5½ (5½, 6, 6, 6, 6½, 7, 7, 7½, 8, 8, 8½)"
14 (14, 15, 15, 15, 16.5, 18, 18, 19, 20.5, 20.5, 21.5) cm

2 3 (3¼, 3¼, 3½, 3¾, 4, 4, 4¼, 4¼, 4½, 4¾, 4¾)"
7.5 (8.5, 8.5, 9, 9.5, 10, 10, 11, 11, 11.5, 12, 12) cm

3 11½ (12, 12½, 13, 13½, 14½, 15, 15½, 16, 17, 17½, 18)"
29 (30.5, 32, 33, 34.5, 37, 38, 39.5, 40.5, 43, 44.5, 45.5) cm

4 1½"
4 cm

5 ½"
1.5 cm

6 6½ (7, 7¼, 7½, 8, 8¼, 8½, 9, 9½, 10½, 11, 12)"
16.5 (18, 18.5, 19, 20.5, 21, 21.5, 23, 24, 26.5, 28, 30.5) cm

7 16 (16, 16½, 16½, 17, 17, 17, 17½, 17½, 17½, 17½, 18)"
40.5 (40.5, 42, 42, 43, 43, 43, 44.5, 44.5, 44.5, 44.5, 45.5) cm

8 15½ (16½, 17½, 18½, 19½, 20½, 21½, 22½, 24½, 26½, 28½, 30½)"
39.5 (42, 44.5, 47, 49.5, 52, 54.5, 57, 62, 67.5, 72.5, 77.5) cm

9 23 (23½, 24¼, 24½, 25½, 25¾, 26, 27, 27½, 28½, 29, 30½)"
58.5 (59.5, 61.5, 62, 65, 65.5, 66, 68.5, 70, 72.5, 73.5, 77.5) cm

10 3¼"
8.5 cm

11 11 (11½, 12, 12½, 13, 13½, 14½, 15½, 17, 19, 21, 23)"
28 (29, 30.5, 32, 33, 34.5, 37, 39.5, 43, 48.5, 53.5, 58.5) cm

12 4½ (5¼, 5½, 5½, 6¼, 6¼, 6¼, 6½, 6¾, 7½, 8¼, 8¾)"
11.5 (13.5, 14, 14, 16, 16, 16, 16.5, 17, 19, 21, 22) cm

13 18 (18, 18, 18½, 18½, 18½, 19, 19, 19, 19, 19½, 19½)"
45.5 (45.5, 45.5, 47, 47, 47, 48.5, 48.5, 48.5, 48.5, 49.5, 49.5) cm

14 8½ (8½, 8½, 9½, 9½, 9½, 9½, 9½, 9½, 10½, 10½, 10½)"
21.5 (21.5, 21.5, 24, 24, 24, 24, 24, 24, 26.5, 26.5, 26.5) cm

15 21¾ (22½, 22¾, 23¼, 24, 24, 24½, 24¾, 25¼, 25¾, 27, 27¾)"
55 (57, 58, 59, 61, 61, 62, 63, 64, 65.5, 68.5, 70.5) cm

# Basic Cardigan: Set-In-Sleeve Construction

The tailored, V-neck, set-in-sleeve cardigan is twin to the pullover in terms of wearability. I've chosen a fine wool-silk yarn for the sample, but offer a couple of variations: a drapey, soft, wool-alpaca blend and a rough-and-tumble, hard-wearing wool-acrylic blend.

This unisex garment is worked in pieces from the bottom up, and then seamed for stability. The button band is then picked up and worked in one piece. No waist shaping is included in any of the basic patterns, but should you choose to add some, please see pages 113–115 for details.

## FINISHED MEASUREMENTS

**FINGERING:** 31¼ (32¾, 35¼, 36½, 38¾, 40¼, 42¾, 45, 48¾, 52½, 56¼, 61)" [79.5 (83, 89.5, 92.5, 98.5, 102, 108.5, 114.5, 124, 133.5, 143, 155) cm] chest, buttoned

**SPORT:** 32¾ (33¼, 36¼, 38¼, 40¾, 41¼, 44¼, 46¼, 49¼, 54¼, 57¼, 62¼)" [83 (84.5, 92, 97, 103.5, 105, 112.5, 117.5, 125, 138, 145.5, 158) cm] chest, buttoned

**WORSTED:** 32½ (35, 36½, 39¼, 40, 42½, 45½, 46¼, 51, 55¼, 58½, 62¼)" [82.5 (89, 92.5, 99.5, 101.5, 108, 115.5, 117.5, 129.5, 140.5, 148.5, 158) cm] chest, buttoned

*Note: Sweater is intended to be worn with 1–2" (2.5–5 cm) ease in the bust; shown in fingering weight yarn and size 36½" (92.5 cm).*

## YARN

**FINGERING:** Valley Yarns Charlemont [60% superwash merino wool / 20% silk / 20% polyamide; 439 yards (401 meters) / 100 grams]: 3 (3, 4, 4, 4, 4, 4, 5, 5, 6, 6, 7) hanks Cocoa

**SPORT:** The Fibre Company Knightsbridge [65% baby llama / 25% merino wool / 10% silk; 120 yards (110 meters) / 50 grams]: 11 (11, 12, 13, 14, 14, 15, 16, 18, 20, 21, 24) hanks High Tea

**WORSTED:** Berroco Vintage [52% acrylic / 40% wool / 8% nylon; 218 yards (199 meters) / 100 grams]: 5 (5, 5, 6, 6, 6, 7, 7, 8, 9, 10, 11) hanks #5103 Mocha

## NEEDLES

**FINGERING:** One pair straight needles and one 40" (100 cm) long circular needle (for Front Bands/Collar) size US 2 (2.75 mm)

**SPORT:** One pair straight needles and one 40" (100 cm) long circular needle (for Front Bands/Collar) size US 5 (3.75 mm)

**WORSTED:** One pair straight needles and one 40" (100 cm) long circular needle (for Front Bands/Collar) size US 7 (4.5 mm)

Change needle size if necessary to obtain correct gauge.

## NOTIONS

Stitch markers, seven ¾-inch (19-mm) buttons

## GAUGE

**FINGERING:** 28 sts and 38 rows = 4" (10 cm) in St st
**SPORT:** 24 sts and 32 rows = 4" (10 cm) in St st
**WORSTED:** 20 sts and 28 rows = 4" (10 cm) in St st

## NOTES

If your size gives the number 0 for a particular instruction, skip that instruction and proceed to the next instruction.

Unless otherwise specified, decreases should be worked to match the slant of the edge being shaped, as follows: For left-slanting edges: On RS rows, k2, ssk, knit to end; on WS rows, p2, p2tog, purl to end. For right-slanting edges: On RS rows, knit to last 4 sts, k2tog, k2; on WS rows, purl to last 4 sts, ssp, p2. Increases should also be worked to match the slant of the edge being shaped, as follows: For right-slanting edges: On RS rows, k1, M1R, knit to end; on WS rows, p1, M1PR, purl to end. For left-slanting edges: On RS rows, knit to last st, M1L, k1; on WS rows, p1, M1PL, purl to end.

# BACK

## CO

| | | | | | | | | | | | | |
|---|---|---|---|---|---|---|---|---|---|---|---|---|
| FINGERING | 106 | 110 | 118 | 126 | 134 | 138 | 146 | 154 | 166 | 182 | 194 | 210 |
| SPORT | 94 | 98 | 106 | 110 | 118 | 122 | 130 | 134 | 146 | 158 | 170 | 182 |
| WORSTED | 78 | 82 | 90 | 94 | 98 | 102 | 110 | 114 | 122 | 134 | 142 | 154 |

sts.

Begin 2x2 Rib Flat; work even until piece measures 2¼" (5.5 cm), ending with a WS row.

Change to St st; work even until piece measures 16 (16, 16½, 16½, 17, 17, 17, 17½, 17½, 17½, 17½, 18)" [40.5 (40.5, 42, 42, 43, 43, 43, 44.5, 44.5, 44.5, 44.5, 45.5) cm] from the beginning, ending with a WS row.

## SHAPE ARMHOLES

### BO

| | | | | | | | | | | | | |
|---|---|---|---|---|---|---|---|---|---|---|---|---|
| FINGERING | 8 | 8 | 8 | 8 | 8 | 8 | 8 | 8 | 10 | 12 | 14 | 18 |
| SPORT | 8 | 8 | 8 | 9 | 9 | 9 | 9 | 9 | 11 | 11 | 12 | 15 |
| WORSTED | 7 | 7 | 7 | 8 | 8 | 8 | 8 | 8 | 9 | 9 | 10 | 13 |

sts at the beginning of the next 2 rows, then

| | | | | | | | | | | | | |
|---|---|---|---|---|---|---|---|---|---|---|---|---|
| FINGERING | 2 | 2 | 2 | 2 | 2 | 2 | 4 | 6 | 6 | 10 | 12 | 16 |
| SPORT | 0 | 0 | 3 | 3 | 3 | 3 | 3 | 3 | 5 | 6 | 8 | 9 |
| WORSTED | 0 | 0 | 3 | 3 | 3 | 3 | 3 | 3 | 4 | 5 | 7 | 8 |

sts at the beginning of following 2 rows.

| | | | | | | | | | | | | |
|---|---|---|---|---|---|---|---|---|---|---|---|---|
| FINGERING | 86 | 90 | 98 | 106 | 114 | 118 | 122 | 126 | 134 | 138 | 142 | 142 |
| SPORT | 78 | 82 | 84 | 86 | 94 | 98 | 106 | 110 | 114 | 124 | 130 | 134 |
| WORSTED | 64 | 68 | 70 | 72 | 76 | 80 | 88 | 92 | 96 | 106 | 108 | 112 |

sts remain.

Decrease 1 st each side every RS row

| | | | | | | | | | | | | |
|---|---|---|---|---|---|---|---|---|---|---|---|---|
| FINGERING | 2 | 2 | 5 | 7 | 8 | 8 | 8 | 8 | 9 | 8 | 8 | 8 |
| SPORT | 4 | 5 | 5 | 4 | 7 | 6 | 8 | 8 | 9 | 11 | 13 | 13 |
| WORSTED | 3 | 4 | 4 | 4 | 4 | 4 | 6 | 7 | 8 | 11 | 10 | 11 |

times.

| | | | | | | | | | | | | |
|---|---|---|---|---|---|---|---|---|---|---|---|---|
| FINGERING | 82 | 86 | 88 | 92 | 98 | 102 | 106 | 110 | 116 | 122 | 126 | 126 |
| SPORT | 70 | 72 | 74 | 78 | 80 | 86 | 90 | 94 | 96 | 102 | 104 | 108 |
| WORSTED | 58 | 60 | 62 | 64 | 68 | 72 | 76 | 78 | 80 | 84 | 88 | 90 |

sts remain.

Work even until armholes measure 5½ (6, 6¼, 6½, 7, 7¼, 7½, 8, 8½, 9½, 10, 11)" [14 (15, 16, 16.5, 18, 18.5, 19, 20.5, 21.5, 24, 25.5, 28) cm], ending with a WS row.

## SHAPE NECK

**NEXT ROW (RS):** Knit

| | | | | | | | | | | | | |
|---|---|---|---|---|---|---|---|---|---|---|---|---|
| FINGERING | 25 | 26 | 27 | 28 | 29 | 31 | 32 | 33 | 34 | 36 | 37 | 37 |
| SPORT | 21 | 22 | 22 | 23 | 24 | 25 | 26 | 28 | 28 | 30 | 30 | 31 |
| WORSTED | 18 | 18 | 19 | 19 | 21 | 21 | 23 | 23 | 24 | 25 | 26 | 26 |

sts, join a second ball of yarn, BO center

| | | | | | | | | | | | | |
|---|---|---|---|---|---|---|---|---|---|---|---|---|
| FINGERING | 32 | 34 | 34 | 36 | 40 | 40 | 42 | 44 | 48 | 50 | 52 | 52 |
| SPORT | 28 | 28 | 30 | 32 | 32 | 36 | 38 | 38 | 40 | 42 | 44 | 46 |
| WORSTED | 22 | 24 | 24 | 26 | 26 | 30 | 30 | 32 | 32 | 34 | 36 | 38 |

sts, knit to end.

Working both sides at the same time, decrease 1 st at each neck edge every RS row twice.

| | | | | | | | | | | | | |
|---|---|---|---|---|---|---|---|---|---|---|---|---|
| FINGERING | 23 | 24 | 25 | 26 | 27 | 29 | 30 | 31 | 32 | 34 | 35 | 35 |
| SPORT | 19 | 20 | 20 | 21 | 22 | 23 | 24 | 26 | 26 | 28 | 28 | 29 |
| WORSTED | 16 | 16 | 17 | 17 | 19 | 19 | 21 | 21 | 22 | 23 | 24 | 24 |

sts remain each shoulder.

Work even until armholes measure 6½ (7, 7¼, 7½, 8, 8¼, 8½, 9, 9½, 10½, 11, 12)" [16.5 (18, 18.5, 19, 20.5, 21, 21.5, 23, 24, 26.5, 28, 30.5) cm], ending with a WS row.

**SHAPE SHOULDERS**

BO

| | | | | | | | | | | | | |
|---|---|---|---|---|---|---|---|---|---|---|---|---|
| FINGERING | 12 | 12 | 13 | 13 | 14 | 15 | 15 | 16 | 16 | 17 | 18 | 18 |
| SPORT | 10 | 10 | 10 | 11 | 11 | 12 | 12 | 13 | 13 | 14 | 14 | 15 |
| WORSTED | 8 | 8 | 9 | 9 | 10 | 10 | 11 | 11 | 11 | 12 | 12 | 12 |

sts at each armhole edge once, then BO

| | | | | | | | | | | | | |
|---|---|---|---|---|---|---|---|---|---|---|---|---|
| FINGERING | 11 | 12 | 12 | 13 | 13 | 14 | 15 | 15 | 16 | 17 | 17 | 17 |
| SPORT | 9 | 10 | 10 | 10 | 11 | 11 | 12 | 13 | 13 | 14 | 14 | 14 |
| WORSTED | 8 | 8 | 8 | 8 | 9 | 9 | 10 | 10 | 11 | 11 | 12 | 12 |

sts once.

# LEFT AND RIGHT FRONTS

CO

| | | | | | | | | | | | | |
|---|---|---|---|---|---|---|---|---|---|---|---|---|
| FINGERING | 51 | 55 | 59 | 59 | 63 | 67 | 71 | 75 | 83 | 87 | 95 | 103 |
| SPORT | 47 | 47 | 51 | 55 | 59 | 59 | 63 | 67 | 71 | 79 | 83 | 91 |
| WORSTED | 39 | 43 | 43 | 47 | 47 | 51 | 55 | 55 | 63 | 67 | 71 | 75 |

sts.

*LEFT FRONT:*

**ROW 1 (RS):** *K2, p2; repeat from * to last 3 sts, k3.

**ROW 2:** P3, *k2, p2; repeat from * to end.

*RIGHT FRONT:*

**ROW 1 (RS):** K3, *p2, k2; repeat from * to end.

**ROW 2:** *P2, k2; repeat from * to last 3 sts, p3.

*BOTH FRONTS:*

Work even until piece measures 2¼" (5.5 cm), ending with a WS row.

Change to St st; work even until piece measures 14½ (14½, 15, 15, 15½, 15½, 15½, 16, 16, 16, 16, 16½)" [37 (37, 38, 38, 39.5, 39.5, 39.5, 40.5, 40.5, 40.5, 40.5, 42) cm] from the beginning, ending with a WS row.

**SHAPE NECK AND ARMHOLE**

*Note: Neck and armhole shaping are worked at the same time; please read entire section through before beginning.*

Beginning on the next RS row, decrease 1 st at neck edge every

| | | | | | | | | | | | | |
|---|---|---|---|---|---|---|---|---|---|---|---|---|
| FINGERING | 5 | 4 | 4 | 5 | 5 | 4 | 4 | 4 | 4 | 5 | 4 | 5 |
| SPORT | 4 | 5 | 4 | 4 | 4 | 4 | 4 | 4 | 4 | 4 | 4 | 4 |
| WORSTED | 4 | 3 | 5 | 4 | 5 | 4 | 4 | 4 | 4 | 4 | 4 | 5 |

rows a total of

| | | | | | | | | | | | | |
|---|---|---|---|---|---|---|---|---|---|---|---|---|
| FINGERING | 16 | 19 | 19 | 16 | 18 | 20 | 21 | 22 | 26 | 23 | 26 | 26 |
| SPORT | 16 | 14 | 15 | 18 | 18 | 18 | 19 | 21 | 20 | 23 | 22 | 25 |
| WORSTED | 13 | 16 | 12 | 15 | 13 | 17 | 17 | 16 | 20 | 19 | 20 | 19 |

times.

AT THE SAME TIME, when piece measures 16 (16, 16½, 16½, 17, 17, 17, 17½, 17½, 17½, 17½, 18)" [40.5 (40.5, 42, 42, 43, 43, 43, 44.5, 44.5, 44.5, 44.5, 45.5) cm] from the beginning, ending at the armhole edge, shape armhole as follows:

Continuing to work neck shaping, BO

| | | | | | | | | | | | | |
|---|---|---|---|---|---|---|---|---|---|---|---|---|
| FINGERING | 8 | 8 | 8 | 8 | 8 | 8 | 8 | 8 | 10 | 12 | 14 | 18 |
| SPORT | 8 | 8 | 8 | 9 | 9 | 9 | 9 | 9 | 11 | 11 | 12 | 15 |
| WORSTED | 7 | 7 | 7 | 8 | 8 | 8 | 8 | 8 | 9 | 9 | 10 | 13 |

sts at armhole edge once, then

| | | | | | | | | | | | | |
|---|---|---|---|---|---|---|---|---|---|---|---|---|
| FINGERING | 2 | 2 | 2 | 2 | 2 | 2 | 4 | 6 | 6 | 10 | 12 | 16 |
| SPORT | 0 | 0 | 3 | 3 | 3 | 3 | 3 | 3 | 5 | 6 | 8 | 9 |
| WORSTED | 0 | 0 | 3 | 3 | 3 | 3 | 3 | 3 | 4 | 5 | 7 | 8 |

sts once.

Decrease 1 st at armhole edge every RS row

| | | | | | | | | | | | | |
|---|---|---|---|---|---|---|---|---|---|---|---|---|
| FINGERING | 2 | 2 | 5 | 7 | 8 | 8 | 8 | 8 | 9 | 8 | 8 | 8 |
| SPORT | 4 | 5 | 5 | 4 | 7 | 6 | 8 | 8 | 9 | 11 | 13 | 13 |
| WORSTED | 3 | 4 | 4 | 4 | 4 | 4 | 6 | 7 | 8 | 11 | 10 | 11 |

times.

| | | | | | | | | | | | | |
|---|---|---|---|---|---|---|---|---|---|---|---|---|
| FINGERING | 23 | 24 | 25 | 26 | 27 | 29 | 30 | 31 | 32 | 34 | 35 | 35 |
| SPORT | 19 | 20 | 20 | 21 | 22 | 23 | 24 | 26 | 26 | 28 | 28 | 29 |
| WORSTED | 16 | 16 | 17 | 17 | 19 | 19 | 21 | 21 | 22 | 23 | 24 | 24 |

sts remain.

Work even until armhole measures 6½ (7, 7¼, 7½, 8, 8¼, 8½, 9, 9½, 10½, 11, 12)" [16.5 (18, 18.5, 19, 20.5, 21, 21.5, 23, 24, 26.5, 28, 30.5) cm], ending at the armhole edge.

### SHAPE SHOULDER

BO

| | | | | | | | | | | | | |
|---|---|---|---|---|---|---|---|---|---|---|---|---|
| FINGERING | 12 | 12 | 13 | 13 | 14 | 15 | 15 | 16 | 16 | 17 | 18 | 18 |
| SPORT | 10 | 10 | 10 | 11 | 11 | 12 | 12 | 13 | 13 | 14 | 14 | 15 |
| WORSTED | 8 | 8 | 9 | 9 | 10 | 10 | 11 | 11 | 11 | 12 | 12 | 12 |

sts at armhole edge once, then

| | | | | | | | | | | | | |
|---|---|---|---|---|---|---|---|---|---|---|---|---|
| FINGERING | 11 | 12 | 12 | 13 | 13 | 14 | 15 | 15 | 16 | 17 | 17 | 17 |
| SPORT | 9 | 10 | 10 | 10 | 11 | 11 | 12 | 13 | 13 | 14 | 14 | 14 |
| WORSTED | 8 | 8 | 8 | 8 | 9 | 9 | 10 | 10 | 11 | 11 | 12 | 12 |

sts once.

## SLEEVES

CO

| | | | | | | | | | | | | |
|---|---|---|---|---|---|---|---|---|---|---|---|---|
| FINGERING | 62 | 62 | 62 | 66 | 66 | 66 | 66 | 70 | 70 | 70 | 74 | 74 |
| SPORT | 50 | 50 | 50 | 54 | 54 | 54 | 58 | 58 | 58 | 62 | 62 | 62 |
| WORSTED | 42 | 42 | 42 | 46 | 46 | 46 | 50 | 50 | 50 | 50 | 50 | 50 |

sts.

Begin 2x2 Rib Flat; work even until piece measures 3" (7.5 cm), ending with a WS row.

Change to St st; work 2 rows even.

### SHAPE SLEEVE

Beginning on the next RS row, increase 1 st each side every

| | | | | | | | | | | | | |
|---|---|---|---|---|---|---|---|---|---|---|---|---|
| FINGERING | 16 | 12 | 10 | 10 | 10 | 8 | 6 | 6 | 6 | 4 | 4 | 4 |
| SPORT | 13 | 12 | 9 | 11 | 9 | 8 | 7 | 6 | 5 | 4 | 3 | 3 |
| WORSTED | 15 | 11 | 10 | 12 | 10 | 8 | 8 | 7 | 5 | 4 | 3 | 3 |

rows a total of

| | | | | | | | | | | | | |
|---|---|---|---|---|---|---|---|---|---|---|---|---|
| FINGERING | 7 | 9 | 11 | 11 | 13 | 16 | 18 | 21 | 25 | 28 | 29 | 33 |
| SPORT | 8 | 9 | 11 | 10 | 12 | 14 | 15 | 18 | 22 | 26 | 32 | 38 |
| WORSTED | 6 | 8 | 9 | 8 | 9 | 11 | 12 | 14 | 18 | 23 | 28 | 33 |

times.

| | | | | | | | | | | | | |
|---|---|---|---|---|---|---|---|---|---|---|---|---|
| FINGERING | 76 | 80 | 84 | 88 | 92 | 98 | 102 | 112 | 120 | 126 | 132 | 140 |
| SPORT | 66 | 68 | 72 | 74 | 78 | 82 | 88 | 94 | 102 | 114 | 126 | 138 |
| WORSTED | 54 | 58 | 60 | 62 | 64 | 68 | 74 | 78 | 86 | 96 | 106 | 116 |

sts.

Work even until piece measures 18 (18, 18, 18½, 18½, 18½, 19, 19, 19, 19, 19½, 19½)" [45.5 (45.5, 45.5, 47, 47, 47, 48.5, 48.5, 48.5, 48.5, 49.5, 49.5) cm] from the beginning, ending with a WS row.

### SHAPE CAP

BO

| | | | | | | | | | | | | |
|---|---|---|---|---|---|---|---|---|---|---|---|---|
| FINGERING | 8 | 8 | 8 | 8 | 8 | 8 | 8 | 8 | 10 | 12 | 14 | 18 |
| SPORT | 8 | 8 | 8 | 9 | 9 | 9 | 9 | 9 | 11 | 11 | 12 | 15 |
| WORSTED | 7 | 7 | 7 | 8 | 8 | 8 | 8 | 8 | 9 | 9 | 10 | 13 |

sts at the beginning of the next 2 rows, then

| | | | | | | | | | | | | |
|---|---|---|---|---|---|---|---|---|---|---|---|---|
| FINGERING | 2 | 2 | 2 | 2 | 2 | 2 | 0 | 6 | 6 | 10 | 10 | 8 |
| SPORT | 0 | 0 | 3 | 3 | 3 | 3 | 3 | 3 | 5 | 6 | 6 | 6 |
| WORSTED | 0 | 0 | 3 | 3 | 3 | 3 | 3 | 3 | 4 | 5 | 5 | 5 |

sts at the beginning of the following 2 rows.

Decrease 1 st each side of every third RS row

| | | | | | | | | | | | | |
|---|---|---|---|---|---|---|---|---|---|---|---|---|
| FINGERING | 2 | 2 | 1 | 1 | 1 | 0 | 0 | 0 | 2 | 7 | 10 | 13 |
| SPORT | 1 | 1 | 2 | 3 | 3 | 2 | 2 | 1 | 3 | 2 | 2 | 3 |
| WORSTED | 1 | 1 | 3 | 3 | 4 | 3 | 2 | 2 | 2 | 2 | 2 | 3 |

time(s), then every other RS row

| | | | | | | | | | | | | |
|---|---|---|---|---|---|---|---|---|---|---|---|---|
| FINGERING | 0 | 0 | 1 | 0 | 1 | 0 | 1 | 0 | 1 | 0 | 0 | 1 |
| SPORT | 0 | 1 | 1 | 0 | 1 | 1 | 0 | 0 | 0 | 1 | 0 | 0 |
| WORSTED | 1 | 1 | 0 | 1 | 0 | 1 | 1 | 0 | 1 | 1 | 0 | 1 |

time(s), then every RS row

| | | | | | | | | | | | | |
|---|---|---|---|---|---|---|---|---|---|---|---|---|
| FINGERING | 11 | 13 | 15 | 18 | 19 | 24 | 23 | 27 | 18 | 11 | 2 | 0 |
| SPORT | 13 | 12 | 10 | 9 | 10 | 12 | 15 | 18 | 15 | 18 | 22 | 22 |
| WORSTED | 9 | 10 | 7 | 5 | 6 | 7 | 10 | 13 | 12 | 15 | 18 | 16 |

times.

BO

| | | | | | | | | | | | | |
|---|---|---|---|---|---|---|---|---|---|---|---|---|
| FINGERING | 3 | 3 | 3 | 3 | 3 | 3 | 3 | 3 | 5 | 5 | 7 | 7 |
| SPORT | 2 | 2 | 2 | 2 | 2 | 2 | 3 | 3 | 3 | 4 | 4 | 5 |
| WORSTED | 2 | 2 | 2 | 2 | 2 | 2 | 3 | 3 | 3 | 4 | 4 | 5 |

sts at the beginning of the next 4 rows.

BO remaining

| | | | | | | | | | | | | |
|---|---|---|---|---|---|---|---|---|---|---|---|---|
| FINGERING | 18 | 18 | 18 | 18 | 18 | 18 | 18 | 18 | 26 | 26 | 32 | 32 |
| SPORT | 14 | 16 | 16 | 18 | 18 | 20 | 18 | 20 | 22 | 22 | 26 | 26 |
| WORSTED | 10 | 12 | 12 | 14 | 14 | 16 | 14 | 14 | 18 | 16 | 20 | 20 |

sts.

## FINISHING

Block pieces as desired. Sew shoulder seams. Set in Sleeves. Sew side and Sleeve seams.

### FRONT BANDS/COLLAR

With RS facing, using circular needle and beginning at lower Right Front edge, pick up and knit approximately 1 st in each BO st, 2 sts for every 3 rows along vertical edges, and 3 sts for every 4 rows along diagonal edges. You will pick up approximately

| | | | | | | | | | | | | |
|---|---|---|---|---|---|---|---|---|---|---|---|---|
| FINGERING | 102 | 102 | 105 | 105 | 109 | 109 | 109 | 112 | 112 | 112 | 112 | 116 |
| SPORT | 87 | 87 | 90 | 90 | 93 | 93 | 93 | 96 | 96 | 96 | 96 | 99 |
| WORSTED | 72 | 72 | 75 | 75 | 77 | 77 | 77 | 80 | 80 | 80 | 80 | 82 |

sts along the straight edges of the Fronts,

| | | | | | | | | | | | | |
|---|---|---|---|---|---|---|---|---|---|---|---|---|
| FINGERING | 59 | 64 | 65 | 66 | 70 | 72 | 74 | 78 | 82 | 88 | 93 | 99 |
| SPORT | 50 | 52 | 54 | 56 | 59 | 61 | 62 | 66 | 68 | 75 | 78 | 84 |
| WORSTED | 42 | 45 | 45 | 47 | 49 | 51 | 52 | 54 | 58 | 62 | 65 | 70 |

sts along each shaped neck edge, and

| | | | | | | | | | | | | |
|---|---|---|---|---|---|---|---|---|---|---|---|---|
| FINGERING | 52 | 54 | 54 | 56 | 60 | 60 | 60 | 62 | 66 | 70 | 72 | 72 |
| SPORT | 44 | 44 | 46 | 46 | 46 | 50 | 52 | 54 | 54 | 56 | 58 | 60 |
| WORSTED | 38 | 40 | 38 | 42 | 42 | 46 | 44 | 46 | 46 | 50 | 52 | 54 |

sts along Back neck. You will have approximately

| | | | | | | | | | | | | |
|---|---|---|---|---|---|---|---|---|---|---|---|---|
| FINGERING | 374 | 386 | 394 | 398 | 418 | 422 | 426 | 442 | 454 | 470 | 482 | 502 |
| SPORT | 318 | 322 | 334 | 338 | 350 | 358 | 362 | 378 | 382 | 398 | 406 | 426 |
| WORSTED | 266 | 274 | 278 | 286 | 294 | 302 | 302 | 314 | 322 | 334 | 342 | 358 |

sts. *Note: Exact st count is not essential, but be sure to end with a multiple of 4 sts + 2 for ribbing to work out evenly.* Begin 2x2 Rib Flat; work

| | |
|---|---|
| FINGERING | 6 |
| SPORT | 5 |
| WORSTED | 4 |

rows even.

**BUTTONHOLE ROW (RS):** Work

| | |
|---|---|
| FINGERING | 8 |
| SPORT | 7 |
| WORSTED | 6 |

sts, [BO 2 sts, work

| | | | | | | | | | | | | |
|---|---|---|---|---|---|---|---|---|---|---|---|---|
| FINGERING | 13 | 13 | 13 | 13 | 14 | 14 | 14 | 15 | 15 | 15 | 15 | 15 |
| SPORT | 10 | 10 | 10 | 10 | 11 | 11 | 11 | 11 | 11 | 11 | 11 | 12 |
| WORSTED | 8 | 8 | 8 | 8 | 9 | 9 | 9 | 9 | 9 | 9 | 9 | 9 |

sts] 7 times, work to end.

Work

| | |
|---|---|
| FINGERING | 7 |
| SPORT | 6 |
| WORSTED | 5 |

rows even, CO 2 sts over BO sts on first row using Backward Loop CO (see Special Techniques, page 188). BO all sts in pattern.

Sew buttons opposite buttonholes.

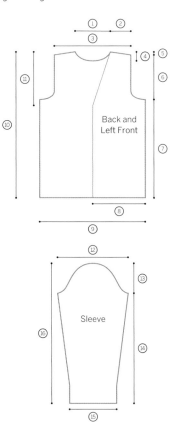

Back and Left Front

Sleeve

## FINGERING WEIGHT

1  5¼ (5½, 5½, 5¾, 6¼, 6¼, 6½, 6¾, 7½, 7¾, 8, 8)"
   13.5 (14, 14, 14.5, 16, 16, 16.5, 17, 19, 19.5, 20.5, 20.5) cm

2  3¼ (3½, 3½, 3¾, 3¾, 4¼, 4¼, 4½, 4½, 4¾, 5, 5)"
   8.5 (9, 9, 9.5, 9.5, 11, 11, 11.5, 11.5, 12, 12.5, 12.5) cm

3  11¾ (12¼, 12½, 13¼, 14, 14½, 15¼, 15¾, 16½, 17½, 18, 18)"
   30 (31, 32, 33.5, 35.5, 37, 38.5, 40, 42, 44.5, 45.5, 45.5) cm

4  1½"
   4 cm

5  ½"
   1.5 cm

6  6½ (7, 7¼, 7½, 8, 8¼, 8½, 9, 9½, 10½, 11, 12)"
   16.5 (18, 18.5, 19, 20.5, 21, 21.5, 23, 24, 26.5, 28, 30.5) cm

7  16 (16, 16½, 16½, 17, 17, 17, 17½, 17½, 17½, 17½, 18)"
   40.5 (40.5, 42, 42, 43, 43, 43, 44.5, 44.5, 44.5, 44.5, 45.5) cm

8  7¼ (7¾, 8½, 8½, 9, 9½, 10¼, 10¾, 11¾, 12½, 13½, 14¾)"
   18.5 (19.5, 21.5, 21.5, 23, 24, 26, 27.5, 30, 32, 34.5, 37.5) cm

9  15¼ (15¾, 16¾, 18, 19¼, 19¾, 20¾, 22, 23¾, 26, 27¾, 30)"
   38.5 (40, 42.5, 45.5, 49, 50, 52.5, 56, 60.5, 66, 70.5, 76) cm

10 23 (23½, 24¼, 24½, 25½, 25¾, 26, 27, 27½, 28½, 29, 30½)"
   58.5 (59.5, 61.5, 62, 65, 65.5, 66, 68.5, 70, 72.5, 73.5, 77.5) cm

11 8½ (9, 9¼, 9½, 10, 10¼, 10½, 11, 11½, 12½, 13, 14)"
   21.5 (23, 23.5, 24, 25.5, 26, 26.5, 28, 29, 32, 33, 35.5) cm

12 10¾ (11½, 12, 12½, 13¼, 14, 14½, 16, 17¼, 18, 18¾, 20)"
   27.5 (29, 30.5, 32, 33.5, 35.5, 37, 40.5, 44, 45.5, 47.5, 51) cm

13 4¼ (4¾, 5, 5¼, 5¾, 5¾, 5¾, 6½, 6¼, 7½, 7½, 9¼)"
   11 (12, 12.5, 13.5, 14.5, 14.5, 14.5, 16.5, 16, 19, 19, 23.5) cm

14 18 (18, 18, 18½, 18½, 18½, 19, 19, 19, 19, 19½, 19½)"
   45.5 (45.5, 45.5, 47, 47, 47, 48.5, 48.5, 48.5, 48.5, 49.5, 49.5) cm

15 8¾ (8¾, 8¾, 9½, 9½, 9½, 9½, 10, 10, 10, 10½, 10½)"
   22 (22, 22, 24, 24, 24, 24, 25.5, 25.5, 25.5, 26.5, 26.5) cm

16 22¼ (22¾, 23, 23¾, 24¼, 24¼, 24¾, 25½, 25¼, 26½, 27, 28¾)"
   56.5 (58, 58.5, 60.5, 61.5, 61.5, 63, 65, 64, 67.5, 68.5, 73) cm

## SPORT WEIGHT

1  5¼ (5¼, 5¾, 6, 6, 6¾, 7, 7, 7¼, 7¾, 8, 8¼)"
   13.5 (13.5, 14.5, 15, 15, 17, 18, 18, 18.5, 19.5, 20.5, 21) cm

2  3¼ (3¼, 3¼, 3½, 3¾, 3¾, 4, 4¼, 4¼, 4¾, 4¾, 4¾)"
   8.5 (8.5, 8.5, 9, 9.5, 9.5, 10, 11, 11, 12, 12, 12) cm

3  11¾ (12, 12¼, 13, 13¼, 14¼, 15, 15¾, 16, 17, 17¼, 18)"
   30 (30.5, 31, 33, 33.5, 36, 38, 40, 40.5, 43, 44, 45.5) cm

4  1½"
   4 cm

5  ½"
   1.5 cm

6  6½ (7, 7¼, 7½, 8, 8¼, 8½, 9, 9½, 10½, 11, 12)"
   16.5 (18, 18.5, 19, 20.5, 21, 21.5, 23, 24, 26.5, 28, 30.5) cm

7  16 (16, 16½, 16½, 17, 17, 17, 17½, 17½, 17½, 17½, 18)"
   40.5 (40.5, 42, 42, 43, 43, 43, 44.5, 44.5, 44.5, 44.5, 45.5) cm

8  7¾ (7¾, 8½, 9¼, 9¾, 9¾, 10½, 11¼, 11¾, 13¼, 13¾, 15¼)"
   19.5 (19.5, 21.5, 23.5, 25, 25, 26.5, 28.5, 30, 33.5, 35, 38.5) cm

9  15¾ (16¼, 17¾, 18¼, 19¾, 20¼, 21¾, 22¼, 24¼, 26¼, 28¼, 30¼)"
   40 (41.5, 45, 46.5, 50, 51.5, 55, 56.5, 61.5, 66.5, 72, 77) cm

10 23 (23½, 24¼, 24½, 25½, 25¾, 26, 27, 27½, 28½, 29, 30½)"
   58.5 (59.5, 61.5, 62, 65, 65.5, 66, 68.5, 70, 72.5, 73.5, 77.5) cm

11 8½ (9, 9¼, 9½, 10, 10¼, 10½, 11, 11½, 12½, 13, 14)"
   21.5 (23, 23.5, 24, 25.5, 26, 26.5, 28, 29, 32, 33, 35.5) cm

12 11 (11¼, 12, 12¼, 13, 13¾, 14¾, 15¾, 17, 19, 21, 23)"
   28 (28.5, 30.5, 31, 33, 35, 37.5, 40, 43, 48.5, 53.5, 58.5) cm

13 4¾ (5, 5½, 5½, 6¼, 6, 6¼, 6¼, 7, 7½, 8, 8¾)"
   12 (12.5, 14, 14, 16, 15, 16, 16, 18, 19, 20.5, 22) cm

14 18 (18, 18, 18½, 18½, 18½, 19, 19, 19, 19, 19½, 19½)"
   45.5 (45.5, 45.5, 47, 47, 47, 48.5, 48.5, 48.5, 48.5, 49.5, 49.5) cm

15 8¼ (8¼, 8¼, 9, 9, 9, 9¾, 9¾, 9¾, 10¼, 10¼, 10¼)"
   21 (21, 21, 23, 23, 23, 25, 25, 25, 26, 26, 26) cm

16 22¾ (23, 23½, 24, 24¾, 24½, 25¼, 25¼, 26, 26½, 27½, 28¼)"
   58 (58.5, 59.5, 61, 63, 62, 64, 64, 66, 67.5, 70, 72) cm

## WORSTED WEIGHT

1  5¼ (5½, 5½, 6, 6, 6¾, 6¾, 7¼, 7¼, 7½, 8, 8½)"
   13.5 (14, 14, 15, 15, 17, 17, 18.5, 18.5, 19, 20.5, 21.5) cm

2  3¼ (3¼, 3½, 3½, 3¾, 3¾, 4¼, 4¼, 4½, 4½, 4¾, 4¾)"
   8.5 (8.5, 9, 9, 9.5, 9.5, 11, 11, 11.5, 11.5, 12, 12) cm

3  11½ (12, 12½, 12¾, 13½, 14½, 15¼, 15½, 16, 16¾, 17½, 18)"
   29 (30.5, 32, 32.5, 34.5, 37, 38.5, 39.5, 40.5, 42.5, 44.5, 45.5) cm

4  1½"
   4 cm

5  ½"
   1.5 cm

6  6½ (7, 7¼, 7½, 8, 8¼, 8½, 9, 9½, 10½, 11, 12)"
   16.5 (18, 18.5, 19, 20.5, 21, 21.5, 23, 24, 26.5, 28, 30.5) cm

7  16 (16, 16½, 16½, 17, 17, 17, 17½, 17½, 17½, 17½, 18)"
   40.5 (40.5, 42, 42, 43, 43, 43, 44.5, 44.5, 44.5, 44.5, 45.5) cm

8  7¾ (8½, 8½, 9½, 9½, 10¼, 11, 11, 12½, 13½, 14¼, 15)"
   19.5 (21.5, 21.5, 24, 24, 26, 28, 28, 32, 34.5, 36, 38) cm

9  15½ (16½, 18, 18¾, 19½, 20½, 22, 22¾, 24½, 26¾, 28½, 30¾)"
   39.5 (42, 45.5, 47.5, 49.5, 52, 56, 58, 62, 68, 72.5, 78) cm

10 23 (23½, 24¼, 24½, 25½, 25¾, 26, 27, 27½, 28½, 29, 30½)"
   58.5 (59.5, 61.5, 62, 65, 65.5, 66, 68.5, 70, 72.5, 73.5, 77.5) cm

11 8½ (9, 9¼, 9½, 10, 10¼, 10½, 11, 11½, 12½, 13, 14)"
   21.5 (23, 23.5, 24, 25.5, 26, 26.5, 28, 29, 32, 33, 35.5) cm

12 10¾ (11½, 12, 12½, 12¾, 13½, 14¾, 15½, 17¼, 19¼, 21¼, 23¼)"
   27.5 (29, 30.5, 32, 32.5, 34.5, 37.5, 39.5, 44, 49, 54, 59) cm

13 4¾ (5, 5½, 5½, 6¼, 6¼, 6¼, 6½, 6¾, 7½, 7¾, 8¾)"
   12 (12.5, 14, 14, 16, 16, 16, 16.5, 17, 19, 19.5, 22) cm

14 18 (18, 18, 18½, 18½, 18½, 19, 19, 19, 19, 19½, 19½)"
   45.5 (45.5, 45.5, 47, 47, 47, 48.5, 48.5, 48.5, 48.5, 49.5, 49.5) cm

15 8½ (8½, 8½, 9¼, 9¼, 9¼, 10, 10, 10, 10, 10, 10)"
   21.5 (21.5, 21.5, 23.5, 23.5, 23.5, 25.5, 25.5, 25.5, 25.5, 25.5, 25.5) cm

16 22¾ (23, 23½, 24, 24¾, 24¾, 25¼, 25½, 25¾, 26½, 27¼, 28¼)"
   58 (58.5, 59.5, 61, 63, 63, 64, 65, 65.5, 67.5, 69, 72) cm

# PART TWO

# ADJUSTMENTS

Congratulations!

At this point you've got a beautiful basic sweater template as a starting point. (Either because you wrote it yourself, or because you've chosen one of the basics from part 1.) Now comes the truly fun part—adjusting your pattern to create the sweater of your dreams.

In this section of the book, I'll step you through all the changes you can make to the silhouette of your sweater—from the body to the sleeves to the neck. I'll show you how to calculate shaping and what your options are.

These kinds of adjustments offer another great chance to raid your closet for ideas. When you lay your favorite garments out on a table, what shape do they have? How might you use those shapes in your next sweater? It can be a lot less intimidating to make these kinds of modifications when they're based on a garment you adore.

# 6

·············································

# Working with Traditional Patterns

Although it's *completely fine* if you'd like to write your own pattern (also: let's go grab a coffee together sometime), it's *also* completely fine if you'd like to start with a traditionally written pattern instead. The best place to start with a traditional pattern is **choosing a size**.

For most men, all children, and some women, choosing a size in a traditional pattern is a simple process: Compare your chest/full bust circumference to the finished circumferences in the pattern, and choose the number with the ease you'd like. So if you're making a sweater for a man with a 42" (107 cm) chest, and you know he likes 4" (10 cm) of ease, choose a size 46" (117 cm). But the amount of ease needed is affected by the construction, too:

**Drop-shoulder** sweaters want a minimum of 4" (10 cm) of positive ease; **raglans** want 3-6" (7.5-15 cm) of positive ease; **yokes** want 2" (5 cm) or more of positive ease; **set-in-sleeve** sweaters can be worn with zero ease for a fitted garment, or up to 3" (7.5 cm) of ease for a woman and up to 4" (10 cm) of ease for men or kids.

The problem with this approach is that if a bustier woman chooses a size this way, she gets a garment

that's crazy oversize through the shoulders—because she's adding that ease to a circumference that's *already* a good bit larger than her frame.

A better approach for this knitter is to *start* by choosing a size that fits her shoulders appropriately and then use the adjustments described in this chapter to fiddle with the body and sleeve dimensions if necessary. Here's how that works:

**For the purposes of choosing a starting size only**, pretend your upper torso is your full bust—and choose a finished bust circumference equal to your upper torso *plus the appropriate amount of ease for the construction:*

- **DROP SHOULDER:** 4-8" (10-20.5 cm) for traditional drop-shoulder patterns with larger armholes (at least 8" [20.5 cm] for slim-armed patterns)

- **RAGLANS:** 3-6" (7.5-15 cm)

- **YOKES:** 2-4" (5-10 cm), unless the yoke depth is particularly short (your set-in-sleeve armhole depth or shorter)—then you can go smaller if you'd like

- **SET-IN SLEEVES:** 0-3" (0-7.5 cm)

Let's step through that with my own numbers: I have an upper torso of 38" (96.5 cm), and a full bust of 42¼" (107.5 cm). In traditional patterns, I'd choose the following sizes **to start with**:

- Drop shoulder: 42-46" (106.5-117 cm)
- Raglan: 41-44" (104-112 cm)
- Yoke: 40-42" (101.5-106.5 cm)
- Set-in sleeve: 38-41" (96.5-104 cm)

Choosing a **starting** size this way will ensure that the construction math—all the calculations we covered in part 1—will work out for your shoulders, the most important place for a sweater to fit. But you're likely not done yet!

**Now disregard your upper torso and go back to your actual full bust** to see what adjustments you'll need. After all, the bust doesn't go away just because we ignored it to start! You *won't* need adjustments to the back or sleeves to accommodate a large bust, though—they're only on the front, and that's where your adjustments should focus, too.

Here's how: Compare the finished bust size you chose to your actual full bust—the difference between the two is how much positive or negative ease you'll have **if you make no further changes**.

To make changes, first calculate the full finished bust circumference you'd like the sweater to have.

- Then take the difference between that number and your starting size—this is the additional width you need on your sweater front.
- Add that width to the front bust. This change is the adjustment you'll need to make while knitting—exactly how you do it depends on the shape of the body.

Let's make this concrete with my own numbers: Suppose I want at least 1" (2.5 cm) of positive ease in my sweater at the full bust, no matter what construction I'm knitting.

- For **drop-shoulder** sweaters, I pick a size that's between 43½-46" (110.5-117 cm), and I have no further modifications to make.
- For **raglan** sweaters, I pick a size between 43½-44" (110.5-112 cm) if I can, and have no further modifications to make.
- For **yoke** sweaters, I pick a 42" (106.5 cm) size if I can, and add ½" (1.5 cm) to the front.
- For **set-in-sleeve** sweaters, I'll definitely have to add between 1½-5½" (4-14 cm) to the front.

If you're busty, the more tailored and fitted a construction you choose, the more likely it is that you'll have to make some fit adjustments. As for how to do so . . . well, that's what we'll talk about next!

Set-in-sleeve sweaters offer a next-to-the-body fit.

Drop-shoulder sweaters need to be roomy in the shoulder area.

..........................................

# Working with the Sweater Body

In terms of the finished product, there are thousands of different sweater bodies out there. If we restrict our focus to just the *shapes* of the sweater body, things get a lot simpler: There are only a handful of lengths, and shapes, for any sweater out there.

I think of sweater bodies as having five basic **lengths** and three basic **shapes**:

## SWEATER LENGTHS

- **CROPPED**—Cropped sweaters end above the wearer's waist.

- **SHORT**—Short sweaters have a hem that lands below the waist, but high on the hip/low on the belly. For women, these might be sweaters you only wear with skirts.

- **'VERAGE**—Average sweaters have a hem that lands comfortably on the hip, so you don't have to tug it down and can wear it with pants. But an average sweater does not touch the front of your legs.

- **LONG**—The hem of a long sweater *does* touch the front of your legs, but it does not clear the curve of your bum on the back.

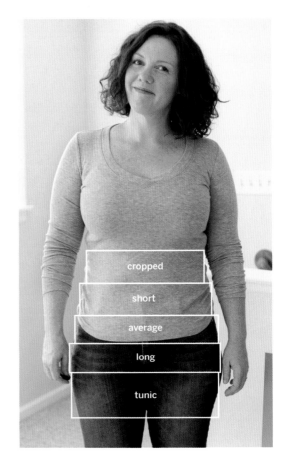

- **TUNIC**—Tunic sweaters have a hem that lands fully below the curve of your bum on the back, and as far down your body as mid-thigh on the front.

I've included a quick illustration of the different sweater lengths on the opposite page.

These are all ranges, of course, and should *absolutely* be based on your own preferences! (And when considering a sweater, I'd urge you to think about which of these lengths you enjoy wearing in store-bought clothes. A bit of self-reflection on the styles you like to wear can save tons of heartbreak when you realize you don't like the length of the project you just completed.)

For each range, the actual, number-of-inches length of your sweater should match your body (for more information on measuring, see page 14). I think it's a good idea to measure the five sweater lengths on your body once and then double-check them against your store-bought faves. (To measure the length of a store-bought garment, simply lay it flat on a table and measure straight up the body from the hem to the outside edge of the shoulder.)

Which length you choose for your sweater is up to you; once you've chosen a length, you can fill in this crucial bit of your personal schematic.

## SWEATER SHAPES

In addition to your sweater's length, you'll also want to choose your sweater's *shape*:

- **Straight** sweaters have no shaping at all from hem to bust/chest. (I'd recommend choosing a straight sweater circumference based on your largest body circumference.)

- **A-line** sweaters have a hem that is wider than the bust/chest. When worn, this style can either look A-line or straight, depending on the ease at the hip versus the ease at the bust. For a garment to *look* A-line, the hips should have substantially more ease than the bust.

- **Tapered** sweaters have a hem that is narrower than the bust/chest. This is typically the style of fitted men's sweaters, but can also work nicely in other contexts: It's a natural shape for a woman with larger shoulders/bust than hips, for example. It also looks great as a larger cocoon-style sweater (see the Sunburst Cardigan, page 139), and makes a great choice for boleros as well.

- **Hourglass-shaped** sweaters have waist shaping, where the waist is smaller than the hip and/or bust/chest. How much smaller depends on the wearer—I'd recommend trying for a looser fit through the waist than at either the bust/chest or hip, and keeping the fits of the bust/chest and hip similar to each other. For example, I make my own hourglass-shaped sweaters with zero ease at the bust and hip and 3–4" (7.5–10 cm) of positive ease through the waist. You can work hourglass shaping either along dart lines (the Quiet Moment Cardigan on page 169 uses this type of dart on the back of the sweater, for example) or along the side seams (see the Spring Rain Tee, on page 177, for this style of dart).

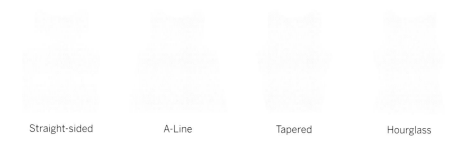

Straight-sided      A-Line      Tapered      Hourglass

## CALCULATING ADJUSTMENTS

Once you've chosen your sweater's length and shape, you're ready to actually make the numbers work!

The first thing to do is fill out your personal schematic, just like we did in part 1 for constructions. I'm going to show you pictures of set-in-sleeve sweater bodies through this section of the book to keep things consistent, but this approach works with any sweater construction—the armholes are irrelevant to calculating any shaping that happens on the body.

Remember the Master Shaping Formula from page 19? We'll use it again for body-shaping calculations:

$$\text{rate of shaping* } = \frac{\text{total number of rows}}{\text{number of shaping rows}}$$

\* rounded down to the nearest whole (even) number

***Body shaping for an A-line or tapered garment*** typically occurs along the sweater's side seams (see Edge Shaping, page 137), and is spread evenly between the sweater's hem ribbing (or other edge treatment) and a bit below the armhole shaping.

A-Line                    Tapered

Here's how to evenly distribute shaping on the body of a sweater:

- Your total rows available for shaping are the hem-to-armhole length, minus your bottom ribbing, minus a short "work straight" section just before the armholes.

*My example: I have a sweater body that's 19" (48.5 cm) long, but 4" (10 cm) of that length is taken up by ribbing and my "work straight" section before the armholes. So I have 15" (38 cm) of actual shaping length. At a gauge of 7 rows per inch, this is 106 rows (rounded to an even number).*

- Your total number of shaping rows is the difference between your hip and chest stitch counts divded by 2: You remove (or add) 1 stitch at each end of every shaping row.

*My example: I need to get from my cast-on count of 146 to my final bust count of 114—a difference of 32 stitches. Thus, I'll need to work 16 decrease rows over the course of the sweater body.*

- Use the Master Shaping Formula (see page 19) to determine your rate of shaping.

*My example: 106 total rows / 16 decrease rows = a rate of 6.62, which means I'll work my shaping every 6 rows, 16 times total.*

And here's a visual of my own shaping calculations:

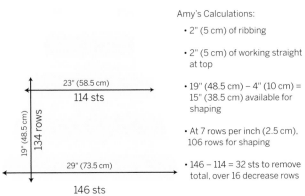

Amy's Calculations:
- 2" (5 cm) of ribbing
- 2" (5 cm) of working straight at top
- 19" (48.5 cm) – 4" (10 cm) = 15" (38.5 cm) available for shaping
- At 7 rows per inch (2.5 cm), 106 rows for shaping
- 146 – 114 = 32 sts to remove total, over 16 decrease rows

There's no real limit to how often (or infrequently) you can shape along an edge—so once you calculate this rate, you're done!

**Body shaping for an hourglass garment** isn't that much more complicated—you just need to calculate shaping rates more than once. Here's how an hourglass garment shaping might break down:

- Once you fill out your personal schematic, you'll have to calculate a rate of shaping from the hem to the waist on the back, waist to bust on the back, and the same places on the front.

- If your stitch counts at hip, waist, and bust are the same front to back (or the differences between them are the same), you have the option of working your shaping along the side seams at the edges, just like in the A-line or tapered sweater bodies. This kind of shaping is pictured in the diagram to the right.

- If your body's front needs are fundamentally different from your body's back needs, I recommend working your shaping along *internal dart lines* instead—this option is pictured on the right in the diagram to the right.

The phrase *internal dart* might seem intimidating, but working shaping away from the edges of your sweater body is no more difficult than working it at the edge. Instead of an instruction that reads:

*Decrease Row (RS):* Knit 1, ssk, knit to last 3 sts, k2tog, k1—2 sts decreased.

You'll place two markers, a bit away from the edge,* and work your shaping like this:

*Decrease Row (RS):* Knit to 2 sts before first marker, ssk, sm, knit to next marker, sm, k2tog, knit to end—2 sts decreased.

Working shaping along dart lines not only lets you adjust front and back, bust and hip, shaping to match

---

* How far away from the edge is "a bit away"? As long as you're at least an inch (2.5 cm) away from the side seams, it won't matter. But a good default is to split your stitches so that one-third of them fall between the markers on the back, and half fall between the markers on the front.

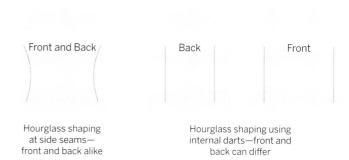

Front and Back | Back | Front

Hourglass shaping at side seams— front and back alike

Hourglass shaping using internal darts—front and back can differ

your body's measurements—it also lets you adjust shaping to match the look and feel of a sweater. Want a little bit of shaping to keep a more oversize garment from feeling too boxy, without making it look va-va-voom? Place a couple of inches' (5 cm or so) worth of shaping on the back only. Want to make a tailored-front, cascading-back tank? Place the shaping on the front only and leave the back straight.

## OTHER FIT ADJUSTMENTS

Most of the time, all you need to do is settle your lengths and bust, hip, and waist stitch counts. But there are a few adjustments that some knitters might want to make outside of those numbers:

- **ESPECIALLY SLOPING SHOULDERS.** If you find the two-step bind-off doesn't produce shoulders that are sloped enough for you, you might want to shape your shoulders with three or even four bind-off sections. Take your total shoulder stitch count and divide it into the number of sections you'd like to have—this is your new bind-off number. If you have remainders, make the initial bind-off sections longer than the later ones.

- **DOWAGER'S HUMP.** If you're knitting a sweater for someone with a very rounded upper back, you can improve the fit of the sweater in this area with a short-row dart at the upper back, just below the neck shaping: Place two markers, each about ½" (1.5 cm) in from the armhole edges. Set up your short rows by working to the second marker, wrapping and turning, then working back to the first marker, and wrapping and turning. Work short rows by working to ¾" (2 cm) before the next wrapped stitch, wrapping and turning. Repeat until you've added between 1-2" (2.5-5 cm) of rows total. Close the dart by working the end of the next 2 rows, working the wraps together with their wrapped stitches.

- **HORIZONTAL BUST DARTS/BELLY DARTS.** I have to admit, I'm not a huge fan of using short-row darts to adjust the front length for a bust or a belly—once the *width* of the belly or bust is accommodated, hand-knits will typically give you the length stretch you need. More curvature of the dart fabric can highlight the area, rather than allowing the fabric to skim unobtrusively over it. It's *possible*, though, that your knit fabric may not be able to give you the length stretch you need. In that case, to prevent a sweater from riding up in the front, you'll need a horizontal, or short-row, dart. This is only likely to be the case if:

  - You have a large bust **and** a very flat back **and**
  - You're knitting a fitted short sweater (giving the hem of the sweater no real opportunity to attach itself to your hips).

If any of those things aren't true—if your bust isn't especially large, or you have a bum to match your bust, or you're knitting a sweater that has a nice number of inches to attach to your hips, or you're knitting a looser construction—you can skip the next bit.

Otherwise, here's how to carry out a short-row dart:

- Measure your front length from shoulder to sweater hem, and subtract that from your back length from shoulder to sweater hem—the difference is the amount of short-row dart you should add. Multiply it by your row gauge and round it down to an even number, if necessary. Divide this number by 2; that's the number of wraps you'll work on each side.

- Vertically, you'll want the dart to be located just on the **underside** of the bust (or belly)—that way, the wrapped stitches will be underneath the apex, where they're less visible. Start your dart at the base of the bust (or belly), vertically.

- Place four markers in your knitting—two innermost markers sitting to the *outside* of your nipple line (or belly); and two outermost markers, each about 1" (2.5 cm) away from the side seams. Count the number of stitches between an innermost and outermost markers—these are where you'll work your dart.

- Divide those stitches by the number of wraps you need to work on each side—this gives you the number of stitches in each wrapped "group." Place removable stitch markers where you'll work your wraps.

- Now work a short-row dart as for a dowager's hump, but instead of wrapping and turning every few stitches, wrap and turn every time you get to an openable stitch maker.

# 8

# Working with the Sweater Sleeve

Much like sweater bodies, most of the variation in sleeve design comes in the form of embellishments. Sleeves have just four basic lengths and three basic shapes, though you can vary the look by adjusting how much of the sleeve is shaped!

## SLEEVE LENGTHS

There are four main regions on the arm where a sleeve's cuff might fall:

- A **short** sleeve has a cuff that lands below the sleeve-body join but well above the elbow.

- An **elbow-length** sleeve either ends just above, just below, or exactly at the elbow.

- A **three-quarter** sleeve ends somewhere in the middle of the forearm.

- A **long** sleeve ends down toward the wrist—either just above the wrist bone for a bracelet-length sleeve, at the top of the hand, at the break of the thumb, or all the way down at the knuckles. (The Penobscot Pullover on page 147 has extra-extra-long sleeves that even include thumbholes!)

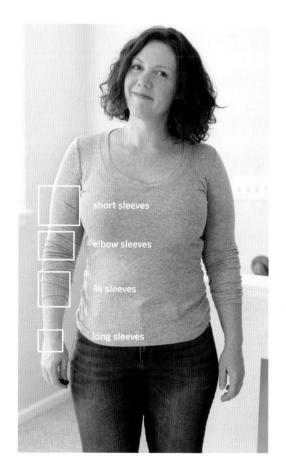

There is no right or wrong way to knit a sleeve, and no right or wrong preferences about what you like to wear. As with sweater lengths, it's a good idea to take an honest look at your most-worn store-bought pieces and use that to inform your sweater knitting.

Whatever length category you choose, the off-the-needles length of your sleeve should match your body. (For more information on measuring a sleeve length, see page 14.) I think it's a good idea to take four sleeve lengths for a set-in-sleeve sweater once, and double-check them against your store-bought faves, if you have them.

### SLEEVE SHAPES

Once you've chosen your sleeve length, you'll also want to choose the sleeve's *shape*:

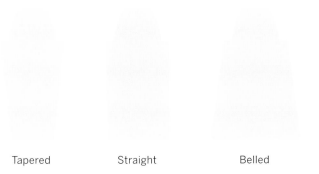

Tapered          Straight          Belled

- **Tapered** sleeves are the "default" sleeve shape, with a cuff that's smaller than the biceps.
- **Straight** sleeves are a good bet for very short sleeves, and look slightly belled when they're long.
- **Belled** sleeves exaggerate the difference between a snugger upper arm and an especially wide cuff.

All these shapes can work with any sleeve length, though the shorter the sleeve, the more aggressive the shaping lines will tend to be. I've stuck with a fairly traditional long belled sleeve for the Quiet Moment Cardigan on page 169, but in the past I've designed three-quarter and even elbow-length belled sleeves, and they make a really interesting design statement.

### CALCULATING ADJUSTMENTS

The math for sleeve adjustments is pretty simple—for straight sleeves, you choose a circumference based on your biceps, and you're done.

For belled sleeves and tapered sleeves, you'll use the Master Shaping Formula (see page 19) to calculate the rate of shaping just as you did on the body: Wait until the ribbing is complete before starting shaping (in most cases, anyway!) and ensure at least 1" (2.5 cm) of straight knitting before shaping the top of the sleeve.

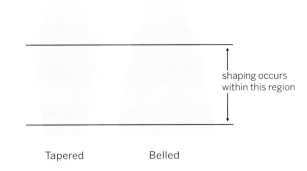

shaping occurs within this region

Tapered          Belled

Choosing the width of the cuff is your only decision to make: For tapered sleeves, I generally recommend a few inches of positive ease in the wrist, to give room for shirt cuffs and to avoid making the shaping too aggressive. For belled sleeves, how much ease to include in the cuff depends on how exaggerated you'd like the bell to look—but typically, a long belled sleeve will have at least 6" (15 cm) of positive ease in the wrist, and might have as much as 10" (25 cm) in an extreme case.

Here's an example of a sleeve-shaping calculation for a standard long, tapered sleeve:

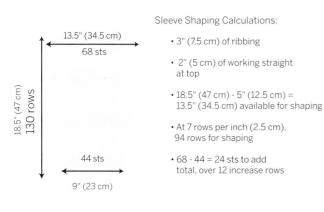

Sleeve Shaping Calculations:

• 3" (7.5 cm) of ribbing

• 2" (5 cm) of working straight at top

• 18.5" (47 cm) - 5" (12.5 cm) = 13.5" (34.5 cm) available for shaping

• At 7 rows per inch (2.5 cm), 94 rows for shaping

• 68 - 44 = 24 sts to add total, over 12 increase rows

Tapered sleeve

Suppose I know I want to cast on 44 stitches, and eventually wind up with 68 stitches at the top of the sleeve. This means I need to add 24 stitches total over the course of 12 increase rows.

With 130 rows total in my sleeve, if I work 3" (7.5 cm) of ribbing and want 2" (5 cm) of working straight at the top, I have at most 94 rows available for shaping.

Using the Master Shaping Formula:

$$\text{Rate of shaping} = \frac{\text{total rows}}{\text{shaping rows}} = \frac{94 \text{ rows}}{12 \text{ shaping rows}} = 7.8$$

**(increase every 7 rows 12 times total)**

For sleeve shaping, I like to leave the rate as is, even if it means I'll be shaping on WS rows as well as RS rows—I think the shaping looks better when it's smoothed out as evenly as possible.

Belled sleeve

# 9

····················································

# Working with Basic Neck Shaping

Once you've got the body and sleeves of your sweater settled, your last major decision, shape-wise, is the neckline. As you think about the neckline of your sweater, you're probably envisioning the finished garment as you'll wear it—but to get knitting instructions, we'll need to tease that final picture apart into two steps: how you **remove the stitches in the neckline, and (later) how you trim the neck opening.**

While there are lots of ways to trim a neck opening, there aren't actually that many ways to remove the stitches in the neckline of your sweater. There are four fundamental **neckline shapes**:

- **Square** necklines remove all the stitches at once in a single bind-off row.

- **Boat** necklines remove *almost* all the stitches in a single bind-off row, but smooth the corners out a bit with a handful of decrease rows on each side.

- **V** necklines remove all stitches evenly along the full depth of the neckline.

- **Round** necklines (crew, scoop, and everything in between) remove between 40 and 60 percent of the neckline stitches in an initial bind-off row, then decrease the remainder in two or more

rates of decreases—every row and every RS row for crew necklines; every RS row, every fourth row, and every sixth row for scoop necklines. Binding off 50 percent of the stitches is a good default; fewer stitches will result in a "pointier" round neckline, while more stitches will result in a "squared" round neckline.

There are, of course, a few variations on these shapes:

- A **shawl-collar pullover** requires a **squared-off V**, where there's a flat bind-off edge at the bottom, and then shaping distributed evenly to the shoulder.

- A **Henley pullover** starts with a round neck shape (somewhere between a crew and scoop in depth), with a thin notch bound off 2–5" (5–12.5 cm) below the neck's main bind-offs (see the Dockhouse Pullover on page 131).

- A **sweetheart** neckline is tough to truly accomplish in knitwear, but you can get close by working a V neckline with aggressive shaping at the bottom of the neckline, and then working straight to the shoulder.

## NECK DEPTHS

Theoretically, each neckline shape can be worked at any depth . . . but some shapes do play more nicely with some depths than others. When thinking about neck depth generally, I'd recommend thinking in terms of "shallow necklines" and "deep necklines," and imagining where you'd like the neck edge to fall on your body—it will help to have a picture in mind.

Shallow necklines still should have *some* depth to them, since you'll add trim; 2-4" (5-10 cm) below the shoulder shaping is a good range.

*Deep necklines* are often best thought of as being a certain amount above or below your armhole depth—envision the deepest part of the neckline on your own body. There's a big range determined by personal preference, but typically, a scoop neckline might be shaped an inch (2.5 cm) above armhole shaping, and a deep-V-neck cardigan might reach as low as 3" (7.5 cm) below armhole shaping.

## NECK WIDTHS

When thinking about neck width, it's also helpful to imagine where the neck edges will sit on your body—check with a tape measure in front of a mirror, if it helps! Wide necklines typically reach nearly to the sides of your torso, or even a tiny bit onto your shoulders; average necklines tend to leave a bit of space open on the sides of your neck, and narrow necklines tend to hug the sides of the neck. Different constructions have different considerations for neck widths; see part 1 for more information.

## SOME GENERALIZATIONS

Before diving into your own sweater design, it's helpful to know typical neck *widths* and *depths* for the four major shapes:

- **Square** necklines can be any width or depth, but their square edges are unstable, so they work best as narrow or average-width necklines that begin just a bit above the armhole shaping.

- **Boat** necklines tend to be wide and shallow—reaching the shoulders and starting just 2-3" (5-7.5 cm) below the shoulders. (For an example of a boat neck that's on the deeper end of that range, see the Spring Rain Tee on page 177.)

- **V** necklines can be any width, but read as deep necklines regardless of their actual depth in inches. My advice would be to ensure that they reach at least down as far as your armhole shaping, and probably an inch (2.5 cm) or more below the shaping (depending on what style of sweater you're making). For reference, the Campfire Cardigan on page 181 has a V neckline that starts 2" (5 cm) below the armhole shaping.

- **Round** necklines fall into three main categories:

  - **Crew necks** are typically narrow in width and not very deep: 3-3½" (7.5-9 cm) on average. They tend to be worked with half the stitches bound off in the center, and shaping every row and every RS row.

  - **Round necks** are just a bit deeper than crew necks: typically 4-5" (10-12.5 cm) below the shoulder shaping. They tend to be worked with wide or average widths, as they look somewhat square when worked with a narrow width. They also tend to use every-row and every-RS-row shaping, though this isn't hard and fast.

  - **Scoop necks** are deeper, typically 6" (15 cm) at the shallowest, with some reaching all the way to the armhole shaping. They can be worked narrow, average, or wide, and tend to use three shaping intervals to exaggerate the neckline's curve: every RS row, every other RS row, and every sixth row.

Once you've shaped your actual neck opening, the simplest way to finish it off is to pick up stitches around the neckline (after seaming, if appropriate) and work ¾-1¼" (2-3 cm) of ribbing before binding off. For other options, check out page 145.

PART THREE

......................................................

# EMBELLISHMENTS

I know I said this at the start of the last part, too, but . . . Now you're *really* at the fun bit! Playing around with fiber, stich patterns, funky collars, texture— nothing else gets at the heart of what we love about knitting like embellishing a basic silhouette.

This section assumes you've got that basic silhouette and dimensions settled, and are ready to amp up your design. Whether you're looking for a single key detail to elevate a basic into the sublime, or you're ready for a knitting challenge, this section probably has what you're looking for. I've separated everything into small chapters that you can look up later, and tried to make each a self-contained whole.

All these details and choices might start to feel overwhelming if you're reading this part of the book start to finish, though! So at the end of each chapter, I've included a few case studies from the designs in this book: Based on the basic patterns in part 1, these "recipes" quickly describe how I used an embellishment (or three) to amp up a simple silhouette. Some began with the yarn and grew around it; some started with a sketch. By talking through my design process for each, it's my hope that creating your own perfect sweater will seem more accessible.

CHAPTER

# 10

..............................................................

# Fabric: Yarns, Fibers, and Stitch Patterning

## YARN CHOICE

The yarn you use to make your sweater informs everything else about the garment: The yarn's texture, fiber(s), and color help determine whether the yarn itself, the silhouette, or the stitch patterning is the visual star. Let's take a brief spin through the different things you can play with in terms of yarn.

## YARN CONSTRUCTION

There are a few major ways the fiber we love turns into the yarn we use, and they all produce different fabric.

- **Worsted-spun** yarn is the most common variety—fibers are prepared so that they lay parallel, and in most cases, multiple strands, or plies, are twisted together into the final yarn. Worsted yarns produce a smooth fabric with great stitch definition and is heavy for its thickness.

- **Woolen-spun** yarn lets the fibers point in any and all directions before twisting it into plies; Relatively little fiber is used per inch of yarn, and the twist added provides the yarn's strength. These yarns are light as air and look nubby in the

hank. They produce a fabric that's slightly fuzzy looking, with hazy stitch definition and a rustic appearance. (They're also incredibly warm, as the loosely packed fibers trap a lot of air.)

- **Chainette** yarn is constructed by knitting the plies into a braid. This makes a yarn strand that's light, elastic, and strong—even when the *fibers* used are short and stiff. It's a great way to make fibers that can be rough on the hands pleasant to knit with. Fabric made from a chainette yarn isn't *quite* as crisp as worsted-spun, but it's close—and it's generally both light and soft.

- Finally, there are a bevy of **novelty constructions**, including bouclé, chenille, ribbon, and others (too many to list here!). My advice for creating a garment out of any novelty construction yarn is to *swatch*. Swatch with a few different needle sizes, and take your time evaluating the swatches before making any decisions. Think about the elasticity, memory, texture, and durability of the fabric you've produced before selecting a needle size to use and the silhouette for your sweater.

Even more than construction, the fiber (or fibers) in your yarn will dictate the kind of fabric you'll have to make your sweater. Want something with (or without) drape? That has a certain sheen? That takes color in this particular way? Your choice of fiber will give you what you're after. And what's more, as hand-knitters, we have access to an array of fibers that are *far* more luxe than you'll ever see in a store.

Here's a quick breakdown of the major materials used to make yarn and their primary characteristics:

- **Wool** is a lovely fiber from the knitter's perspective: It's relatively lightweight, elastic (the fiber can stretch and flex), and has good memory (it'll return to its original shape after being stretched out). All these qualities make it easy on the hands and pleasant to wear: Once it's knit into fabric, your stitches will remember where they're supposed to be and work to get back there. This is great news for any sweater that's putting an extra burden on its fabric—like ones with cables, or unstructured construction, or looser-than-ideal gauge. Varieties of wool differ from the coarse, hard-wearing, and (it's OK to say it) scratchy varieties we use for outerwear to the ultra-soft, ultra-thin, ultra-short hairs of an extra-fine merino that we might use for a next-to-the-skin turtleneck. But they all (more or less) share a relatively matte sheen, a somewhat soft texture, and a beautiful depth of color. Wool also tends to grip itself well, due to the structure of the hairs themselves—each is covered with an overlapping set of cuticle cells called scales.

- **Superwash wool** is wool from which the scales have either been removed completely or glued down. Compared to non-superwash wools, superwash has a smoother texture and won't felt when agitated in hot water. This makes them easy to care for, and I love a good superwash,

but be warned: Its super-smooth surface means a superwash wool will need to be knit more firmly than a non-superwash to produce a durable fabric that won't sag or "grow." (Passing the "poke" test from page 12 is a must for superwash wool.)

- **Alpaca** is one of my favorite fibers. It has a great luster, it's heavy and warm, and brings terrific drape to a fabric. It's on the slipperier side, and that plus its weight means alpaca is best either blended with something grippier and lighter in weight, like a strong sheep wool, or worked at a nice snug gauge for durability. It's not very elastic, which makes it doubly dangerous to knit loosely (unless sagging or stretching is part of the plan!). That said, a bit of alpaca blended with a nice wool is a great choice for just about any construction, and adds an upscale feel to otherwise simple designs.

- **Mohair** is a great fiber from a designer's perspective. It takes color beautifully, is incredibly light, and adds a distinctive fuzzy "halo" when introduced to a blend. Mohair yarns are grippy enough that you can knit them just about as loosely as you like without worrying about the structure of your fabric (if you can't rip it, you don't need to worry about structure!). It makes an ethereal, delicate fabric on its own and is naturally elastic, making it a lovely partner for silk. Most people find mohair to be very soft (though this depends on the quality of the fiber).

- **Cashmere** also deserves a special mention in a sweater context. A distinctive category of wool, cashmere comes from the downy undercoat of a goat, and each hair is both very short and exceedingly fine. It's warmer than typical sheep's wool (by a lot) and ultra, ultra soft. It has fuzzy, hazy stitch definition and a soft, short halo. Cashmere is undeniably luxurious, but, much as with silk, when I'm knitting a sweater I prefer it blended into my yarn in small amounts. Those teeny, tiny, supersoft fibers are absolutely *begging* to work their way out of your fabric (i.e., pill), and they felt pretty readily, too. For a cowl or a shawl, this doesn't matter—bring on the 100 percent cashmere! But we *move* a lot in our sweaters, and I want more durability than you're likely to find in most hand-knitting cashmere yarns. In my opinion, 5–15 percent cashmere in a merino (or merino-silk) blend is enough to get the lovely qualities cashmere brings to the table *without* endless pilling or felted armpits.

- **Silk** is another favorite of mine (I've never met a wool-silk blend without swooning). It's strong, has a drop-dead-gorgeous sheen, and imbues colors with an unmistakable luminance. It flows through your fingers smoothly and imparts luxury to all it creates. It's also drapey, inelastic, and heavy. In a sweater context, I think silk works best blended, and a little goes a long way—some of my favorite hand-knitting blends have 5–10 percent silk, and things get ultra-luxe ultra-quickly as the silk content rises. (I'd personally hesitate to go much above 15 percent silk in a sweater you'll wear regularly.)

- **Cotton** is soft. Its softness is often the primary reason we want to knit with it, followed closely by its ability to wick away moisture in warm weather. But cotton can be challenging to use in a hand-knitting context, as it is both heavy and entirely inelastic. (This means that a drop-shoulder cardigan in Aran-weight, worsted-spun cotton, like, oh, let's just call it *several* sweaters I knit in the late '80s, is unlikely to jump into heavy wardrobe rotation.) You can get past these challenges by choosing a cotton yarn that's been created to balance out these drawbacks: a chainette construction, or perhaps a blend with wool or other elastic fibers.

- **Linen** is another heavy, inelastic, moisture-wicking, durable fiber. I love working with it, though: For me, linen has both a beautiful, lustrous quality and exceptional drape without the warmth of something like alpaca. Fabrics made from linen have a gorgeous, fluid hand and get better and better the more you wear them. Like cotton, linen is often either worked up into a chainette yarn, or blended with another fiber to lighten the finished yarn and make it easier to work with.

- **Semi-synthetic fibers** like rayon, viscose, bamboo, Tencel, modal, and a number of others have been manufactured as alternatives to silk. They're typically smooth and slippery, and have a sheen like silk; they're also typically as drapey as silk. They are usually very lightweight, which makes them a nice addition to a cotton or linen blend. They tend to feel breathable in warmer weather and produce a fluid fabric. My only caution when working with a high-percentage rayon or bamboo yarn in a garment is that they need to be knit extra snug, much like superwash, to produce a garment that keeps its shape and has enough structure to get through the day.

- **Nylon** shines as a "helper" fiber in hand-knitting. It adds strength and durability to otherwise delicate yarns, and is often added to a novelty construction to form an (internal or external) skeleton. It's typically used sparingly—but a little goes a long way toward making your yarn resilient.

- **Acrylic** sometimes gets a bad rep, but it *does* offer advantages to the knitter. Acrylic (a petroleum product) is engineered to be soft, light, and durable. It's inexpensive and readily available. It can be washed with everything else in a regular machine-wash cycle, and will keep its shape even if your sweater has no structure. So for heavy fibers, unstructured constructions, or households where hand-knits get run through regular hot-water wash cycles, acrylic can be a helpful tool in your arsenal. For example, a superwash wool–acrylic blend can be knit a little more loosely than a straight-up superwash and remain durable. And a cotton-acrylic blend can be both soft *and* light. There's a flip side, though: Acrylic *does* melt, won't block, and can hold on to both water and odors—so I personally appreciate it most when used sparingly in a blend.

When considering a yarn for your sweater, read the label and untwist a bit of it to suss out the yarn's fiber content and construction. Swatch it in Stockinette to see how the yarn works up into fabric. Make a note of its sheen, stitch definition, and texture—and keep them in your mind as you read through the many ways you can embellish your sweater.

## STITCH PATTERNING

Incorporating a stitch pattern into your garment is one of my favorite ways to make a sweater your own. You can choose a stitch pattern from a stitch dictionary (I own several, including some chart-based Japanese stitch dictionaries that I adore) or make one up on your own, swatching. There are a few things to consider when using stitch patterns; I think they break down naturally into silhouette considerations and materials considerations.

### STITCH PATTERNS AND SILHOUETTES

I often think about the placement and scale of the stitch pattern within the sweater's silhouette first, in my own designs. There are a few ways to place stitch patterning in a silhouette:

- **Allover patterning** is a great choice for lots of silhouettes. If your stitch pattern is small in scale, using it all over will transform it, visually, into a texture (like a small-scale print in a store-bought piece). If it's large in scale, using it all over will

make a bold design statement. The only caution I'd give you when considering an allover pattern is that you'll need to work any *shaping* in pattern—so make sure you're comfortable doing so! To keep things as simple as possible, think about a straight-sided garment (the only shaping will be at the neck and sleeves). (That's what I did with the Dockhouse Pullover on page 131; you can make it even easier with a drop-shoulder construction.) If you're super-confident, go for a showstopper by making a dart-style sweater with waist shaping.

- **Patterning blocks**, either piece by piece or in more modular chunks, is a nice way to use a stitch pattern that looks best at scale, but within some limitations. This might either be because the stitch pattern can get overwhelming if used too much, or because you don't want to fuss with shaping in pattern. The slip-stitch colorwork on the top of the Mill Pond Cardigan (page 133) gives a nice touch of tweediness without becoming too visually overwhelming. (And as a bonus, you could make the sweater body hourglass-shaped, with internal darts, without fussing with slipped stitches.)

- **Vertical panels** or **horizontal stripes** of patterning present a nice opportunity to use a single motif sparingly, making a strong visual statement. (They also allow for the use of Stockinette around the stitch patterning, which can be great for shaping or sizing purposes.) Centered vertical panels of pattern, like the front of the Meadowbrook Cowl (page 159), create a slimming effect on the torso; asymmetrical panels draw the eye. Horizontal panels make a lovely alternative to color stripes.

Generally speaking, the size of the patterned portion of your sweater is inversely proportional to the amount of detailed attention the stitch pattern *itself* will get. Huge numbers of repeats turn a stitch pattern into a fabric texture; a single cable repeat really focuses the eye on every twist and turn in the cable. (Consider the difference between the allover Fiddler's Reach Cardigan on page 155 versus the eye-catching Campfire Cardigan motifs on page 181.)

*STITCH PATTERN STRUCTURE*

Another thing to consider when placing a stitch pattern within a garment is the interplay of the stitch pattern's structure and the silhouette's structure. A less-stable construction like an all-in-one raglan isn't the place for a stitch pattern that's inherently droopy, whereas a super-stable construction like a set-in sleeve can support just about anything you want. There are exceptions to every rule, but generally speaking:

- **Textured patterns of knits and purls** tend to be quite strong and structured, with the physics of the knits and purl stitches working to keep the fabric flat and stable.

- **Ribbings** grip and shrink widthwise.

- **Lace** tends to be fairly droopy and open—and the more yarn-overs in the lace, the more this is true.

- **Cables** can get very heavy since there's a double-thick fabric everywhere a cable crosses.

- **Slipped-stitch patterns** tend to be firm and very solid, with little stretch.

*MATERIALS*

Finally, it's a good idea to consider the combination of the yarn you'd like to use and the stitch pattern you've chosen. Will they play well together? When looking at your yarn and trying to imagine it within a stitch pattern, I recommend thinking about:

- **STITCH DEFINITION**. This refers to how crisply and quickly you can identify the outline of any particular stitch. Worsted-spun yarns tend to

have crisper definition than woolen-spuns, as I mentioned earlier; however, fiber and novelty textures can affect stitch definition, too. Generally, the more representational the stitch pattern is, the more important stitch definition is, and vice versa. A crisp lily-of-the-valley lace will be utterly obscured by highly fuzzy yarns, whereas a super-wide cable with no reverse Stockinette border might get translated into an interesting texture if worked in a fuzzy yarn.

- **OVERALL PATTERN VISIBILITY**. By overall visibility, I mean how well the pattern translates when viewed as a whole—if you're working the entire front of a sweater in an allover stitch pattern, or you're examining a set of cables from afar, how clear are they? This is related to stitch definition but isn't the same: A large-enough-scale cable will be visible even when worked in a fuzzy woolen spun, for example. When considering this, think about the bloom and halo of the yarn; how each repeat of the stitch pattern blends into the next, etc.

- **STRUCTURE**. This touches on the structural considerations I mentioned before; the less structured or heavier the stitch pattern is inherently, the more important it is to use a non-drapey yarn when making it. Cables demand something strong and durable to support their weight; lace wants something with good memory to keep each eyelet in shape; slipped stitches can tolerate a drapier yarn since they add so much structure on their own.

- **COLOR** is the final thing I'd consider when pairing a yarn with a stitch pattern. Is the color solid, semisolid, or variegated? If it's semisolid or variegated, you're likely to be happier pairing the yarn with simpler designs and simple or small-scale texture stitch patterns. Consider how the yarn looks knit up into fabric, rather than just in the hank, before making a firm decision on a yarn/design pairing. Finally, if the yarn is hand-painted, be sure to alternate hanks as you knit to keep the pooling and color differences between skeins to a minimum!

When considering a stitch pattern, I strongly suggest (you guessed it) swatching it in your intended yarn, to make sure you like the yarn/stitch pattern pairing (even if it obeys all the guidelines I've given you in this section).

In the picture below, I've swatched the same simple lace pattern in three different yarns. The flat color, smooth yarn, and small scale of Quince and Co.'s Tern gives a great view of the lace, with each stitch crisply defined. The gorgeously deep color of indigodragonfly's MerGoat Worsted is varied, and this variation obscures the lace pattern a bit, but the eyelets still show through. This gives the fabric a 3D, faggoted texture. The super-fuzzy Lana Grossa AM Alpaca completely obscures the lace aspect of the patterning, turning it into a basic (and lovely) texture. All three of these swatches will make a great sweater—but the sweaters will be very different!

# Recipe: Dockhouse Pullover

This Henley raglan pullover is the perfect sweater for days with a bit of bite in the air. I've spruced up the Basic Pullover (Raglan Construction) with a stitch pattern and a fun Henley neckline, but kept the body straight to keep the look casual. If that's not your thing, take this as inspiration and then run with it! I think the same idea would also look great with three-quarter sleeves and an A-line silhouette, in a super-long tunic length. Or the same stitch patterning, with a turtleneck, and a fitted body on a man's sweater.

I started with the Basic Raglan Pullover (worsted gauge) on page 45. From there, here's how I modified:

**MATERIALS:** Quince and Co. Lark in Root; 8 (9, 10, 11, 12, 12, 13, 14, 14, 15, 16, 18) hanks for sizes 32½ (34, 37, 38½, 40, 43, 44½, 47½, 50, 53, 56, 60½)" [82.5 (86.5, 94, 98, 101.5, 109, 113, 120.5, 127, 134.5, 142, 153.5) cm] chest
**SAMPLE SHOWN** is size 37" (94 cm)

## BASIC DIAMOND BROCADE
(multiple of 8 sts + 1; 8-row repeat)
**ROW 1 (RS):** *K4, p1, k3; repeat from * to last st, k1.
**ROW 2:** P1, *p2, k1, p1, k1, p3; repeat from * to end.
**ROW 3:** *K2, p1, k3, p1, k1; repeat from * to last st, k1.
**ROW 4:** P1, *k1, p5, k1, p1; repeat from * to end.
**ROW 5:** *P1, k7; repeat from * to last st, k1.
**ROW 6:** P1, *k1, p5, k1, p1; repeat from * to end.
**ROW 7:** *K2, p1, k3, p1, k1; repeat from * to last st, k1.
**ROW 8:** P1, *p2, k1, p1, k1, p3; repeat from * to end.
Repeat Rows 1–8 for Basic Diamond Brocade.

■ Ribbing changed to 1x1 Rib (see Basic Stitch Patterns, page 187) for all edges.

■ Instead of Stockinette, I worked the pieces in Basic Diamond Brocade, at the same gauge as Stockinette.

■ I changed the crew neck to a Henley.

 ■ 2" (5 cm) before starting the crew neck bind-offs, I bound off 5 stitches [or 1" (2.5 cm) of stitches] and then worked straight to the remainder of the neck shaping instructions.

 ■ I then bound off 5 fewer stitches in the pattern's initial neck shaping row, keeping all other neck shaping the same.

■ During finishing,

 ■ I first trimmed the notch with a button band;

 ■ Then, I picked up stitches around the entire neckline, including the tops of the plackets, and worked flat in 1x1 Rib until trim measured ¾" (2 cm) before binding off.

# Recipe: Mill Pond Cardigan

This sweet little cardigan keeps you cozy in style, dressing up a day at the shore. I've spruced up the Basic Cardigan (Set-In-Sleeve Construction) with a pop of color, an easy, body-skimming shape, and a flattering round neckline. I chose to keep the buttons all the way down the front of the cardigan, but this would also look great buttoned only at the top. Try out a few color combinations to see what you like!

I started with the Basic Set-In-Sleeve Cardigan (DK) from page 101. Here's how I modified:

**MATERIALS:** The Fibre Company Knightsbridge in Concordia (MC), Goldfirth (A), Stonehenge (B), and Poole (C); 11 (11, 12, 13, 14, 14, 15, 16, 18, 20, 21, 24) hanks MC and 1–2 hank(s) each in A, B, and C for sizes 32¾ (33¼, 36¼, 38¼, 40¾, 41¼ 44¼, 46¼, 49¼, 54¼, 57¼, 62¼)" [83 (84.5, 92, 97, 103.5, 105, 112.5, 117.5, 125, 138, 145.5, 158) cm] chest
**SAMPLE SHOWN** is size 41¼" (105 cm)

## FOUR-COLOR SLIP-STITCH TWEED
(multiple of 4 sts + 3; 4-row repeat)
**ROW 1 (RS):** K1, *slip 1 wyib, k3; repeat from * to last 2 sts, slip 1 wyib, k1.
**ROW 2:** P3, *slip 1 wyif, p3; repeat from * to end.
**ROW 3:** K1, *slip 1 wyib, k3; repeat from * to last 2 sts, slip 1 wyib, k1.
**ROW 4:** P3, *slip 1 wyif, p3; repeat from * to end.
Repeat Rows 1–4 for Four-Color Slip-Stitch Tweed.

■ I made the body pieces a slight A-line shape, rather than straight from hip to armhole.

　■ For the Back, I cast on 134 stitches instead of 120. I worked a decrease row every 12 rows 7 times after the ribbing, to get to the required 120 stitches for the bust.

　■ For the Fronts, I cast on 66 stitches instead of 59. I worked a decrease row every 12 rows 7 times after the ribbing, to get to the required 59 stitches for the bust.

■ I added the Four-Color Slip-Stitch Tweed to the body pieces, starting 4 rows before the armhole shaping.

■ I changed the front neckline to be a round shape, instead of a V:

　■ I began neck shaping when the armholes measured 2¼" (5.5 cm). There are 18 stitches to remove in the neck; I followed the scoop instructions on page 121.

　■ I started by binding off 9 stitches, then decreased 1 stitch at the neck edge every RS row 5 times, then every other RS row twice, then every 3rd RS row twice before working to the shoulder.

■ I changed the sleeves to be three-quarter sleeves instead of long:

　■ I cast on 62 stitches with MC, instead of the recommended 54.

　■ To get to the required biceps count of 82 stitches, I worked an increase row every 8 rows 10 times, and then knit until the sleeve measured 13" (33 cm) before shaping the cap as in the basic pattern on page 105.

■ During finishing, I trimmed the button-band plackets first, and then picked up around the entire neck edge (including button bands), and worked in 2x2 Rib for ¾" (2 cm) before binding off.

CHAPTER

# 11

Edges: Shaping, Trimming, and Adorning

## EDGE TRIMS

The edges of your knitting also represent great opportunities to embellish and personalize your sweater. Most of the garments in this book use traditional ribbing to edge necklines, sleeves, and sweater hems, but you have a bunch of other options:

- **OTHER SIMPLE STITCHES.** Consider swapping out ribbing with another simple stitch. My favorites include Garter stitch, Seed stitch, and Broken Rib; you can see some examples in the Spring Rain Tee (page 177), Meadowbrook Cowl (page 159), and Quiet Moment Cardigan (page 169). All of these stitches lie perfectly flat, so the only thing to consider before taking this plunge is whether you'll need to change your needle size for gauge. Your goal, gauge-wise, is a smooth transition between edge stitch and body stitch in your sweaters; you may need to go up or down a needle size when working one or more of these stitches. To figure out what *you* need, make this edge stitch swatch:

- CO 24 stitches.

- Work for 2" (5 cm) each in the following stitch sequence: 2x2 Rib, Stockinette, Seed stitch, Stockinette, Broken Rib, Stockinette, Garter stitch; BO all sts.

Edge stitch swatch

- Wash the swatch and lay flat to dry. If you notice any of the sections bowing outward or pulling inward excessively, that's a sign that you should go down (or up) a needle size when working that stitch.

■ **UNUSUAL EDGE TRIMS.** In addition to simply swapping out a stitch pattern, you can use a number of less-common trims on your edges.

■ A *folded hem* (see page 136) includes a facing worked on smaller needles than the main body; a turning ridge created by knitting one WS row (I switch to the main needle size at the ridge), and then knitting the body from there. I strongly prefer tacking down the faced hem with whip stitch rather than provisionally casting on the hem and knitting it to the sweater body; I think the latter approach tends to make the hem turn upward. For an extra bit of flair, work the hem and the turning ridge in a differently textured yarn and/or a contrasting color.

■ *Rolled Stockinette* (see page 136) can also be an attractive edge, but works best with yarns that have little to no elasticity. Plan on losing 5–8 rows to the roll.

■ *Applied I-cord* creates a smooth, Stockinette cord along any edge you trim. I used one vertically in the Jump Shot Hoodie (page 165), but it can also be used to trim sleeve or sweater hems. It makes a nice, neat look. To work an Applied I-cord, first pick up stitches along the row to be trimmed—one stitch for each row along the edge. Break your yarn. Cast on 3 sts onto a dpn (A, pictured at right). On your dpn, knit the first two stitches, slip the third stitch knitwise, then knit the first picked-up stitch. Pass the slipped stitch over the final stitch on the dpn. Slide the stitches back to the left end of the dpn. Repeat this process up the side of your knitting, using up one of the picked-up stitches for each row you knit on the dpn (B). At the end of your edge, break the yarn, pass it through the 3 sts on the dpn, and weave in ends (C).

A

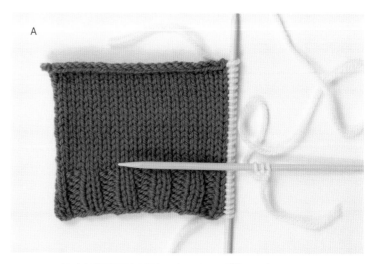

B

C

Rolled Stockinette edge and folded hem

Edge shaping

■ **ALTERING SYMMETRY AND SHAPE.** In addition to (or instead of) changing the stitch pattern at the edges of your garment, you can change the edge's *shape* as well:

■ *High-low asymmetry.* Making the back of your sweater longer than the front, or vice versa, from edge to edge is simple to work and dramatic in style. Typically, high-low garments are worked with a notch at the side seam, with the stitch pattern traveling up the notch, but this isn't necessary from a structural standpoint: You could absolutely simply seam the shorter piece to the longer piece with no separation.

■ *Adding curves with short rows.* You can also adjust the shape of any edge into a curve—symmetrically or asymmetrically—with short rows. I've included designs that do both in this book: The Spring Rain Tee (page 177) uses asymmetrical short rows to create tulip-shaped overlaps on the sweater body and sleeve cuffs, and the Sunburst Cardigan (page 139) uses short rows to scoop the back longer than the front in a shirt-tail fashion.

Short rows can be worked in the Stockinette sections of a sweater, as shown in these designs, or within the trim stitch itself, to create even more interest.

■ When adding short rows to a piece, start by deciding how deep you'd like the curve to extend. Multiply that depth by your per-inch (2.5 cm) row gauge, and round up to an even number if necessary. This is the number of short-row wraps you're going to work (half on each side). Then identify the stitches over which you'd like to work the curve: For something like the sleeve cuffs in the Spring Rain Tee, the wraps might be evenly spread over a large number of stitches; for a fully curved sweater bottom like the Sunburst Cardigan's back, the wraps happen over a small number of stitches on each side. Divide the wraps evenly over your stitches. (Or don't, and swatch to see what kind of curve you like best!)

■ Make things even more exciting, if you like, by working the short row wedges in a contrasting color.

## EDGE SHAPING

Any time you shape on an edge, you have a choice—hide the shaping inside the seam or picked-up stitches, or leave it visible. And if it *is* visible, you can also choose *how* visible it is. You essentially have two choices to make: *where* you work the shaping and *how* you shape. To see these options, check out the picture on the opposite page. From the bottom up, shaping is worked at the edge, then one stitch in from the edge, then 3 stitches in from the edge; on the right side of the swatch, the shaping slants with the edge; on the left side of the swatch, the shaping slants against the edge.

- *Where.* Shaping can be worked right on the edge, or one or more stitches in from the edge. When worked on the edge itself, the shaping is hidden within the seam of the finished garment, giving a very clean look. (The downside to this approach is that your seaming gets a bit trickier, but it's not awful.) Shaping worked one (or two, or three) stitches in makes for easier seaming, but the shaping then becomes part of the look of the finished piece. The farther your shaping is in from the edge, the more visually prominent the line of shaping will be.

- *How.* If you're shaping one or more stitches in from the edge, the direction your shaping *slants* makes for another choice. Shaping that slants *with* the edge being shaped (i.e., an ssk at the beginning of a RS row and a k2tog at the end) makes a streamlined, less-noticeable line. Shaping that slants *toward* the edge being shaped (i.e., a k2tog at the beginning of a RS row or an ssk at the end) is more noticeable. This technique was a sign of by-hand work in high-end clothing, and is called "fully fashioned" shaping.

Adding curves with short rows on the sleeve cuff.

The patterns in this book are written with shaping located 1 stitch away from the edge, slanting with the edge being shaped, but you should feel free to swap out edge shaping to please yourself! I tend to work shaping at the edge, hiding it, when the rest of the garment is busy (either in terms of yarn or stitch patterning). The plainer the rest of the garment, the more likely I am to use fully-fashioned shaping located two or three stitches away from the edge.

# Recipe: Sunburst Cardigan

I love big, cozy cardigans, and the deep-V, oversize silhouette of a drop shoulder is the coziest construction there is. Starting with the Basic Cardigan (Drop Shoulder), I upped the snuggle factor by making the body into a tapered cocoon shape, with short rows to help the back hem dip longer than the fronts. I used indigodragonfly's *amazingly* soft MerGoat Worsted yarn, and had some fun with the color variation by switching up the edge stitch a bit. I chose a single-button closure, but feel free to use this recipe as a starting point for your own imagination!

I started with the Basic Drop Shoulder Cardigan (worsted gauge) on page 33. From there, here's how I modified:

**MATERIALS:** indigodragonfly MerGoat Worsted in Aurumgami; 7 (8, 8, 9, 9, 10, 10, 10, 11, 12, 13, 13) hanks for size 37¼ (39½, 42, 42¾, 45¾, 46½, 49, 51¾, 53¼, 58, 61¾, 65)" [94.5 (100.5, 106.5, 108.5, 116, 118, 124.5, 131.5, 135.5, 147.5, 157, 165) cm] chest

**SAMPLE SHOWN** in size 45¾" (116 cm)

- I worked all edgings in Broken Rib (see Basic Stitch Patterns, page 187) instead of plain 2x2 Rib.
- I made the body pieces a slight tapered shape, rather than straight from hip to armhole.
  - I cast on 8 fewer stitches on the Back, and 4 fewer on each Front, and worked an increase row on the body every 20 rows 4 times, beginning approximately 1" (2.5 cm) after the ribbing.

- I added a short-row dart to the back of the sweater, 2 rows after completing the ribbing:
  - I placed markers 4 stitches in from the sides, then worked short rows as follows:

  **SHORT ROW 1 (RS):** Knit to marker, w&t.

  **SHORT ROW 2:** Purl to marker, w&t.

  **SHORT ROW 3:** Knit to 4 sts before wrapped st from previous RS row, w&t.

  **SHORT ROW 4:** Purl to 4 sts before wrapped st from previous WS row, w&t.

  Repeat Short Rows 3 and 4 three more times; 5 wrapped sts on each side of work.

  - Work two complete rows in Stockinette, working all wrapped stitches together with their wraps.
- When working the button band, I added only a single large buttonhole, just below the bust.

CHAPTER

# 12

......................................................

# Design Goodies: Cardigan Closures, Pockets, and Necklines

**BUTTON BANDS AND ZIPPERS**

Cardigans add their placket openings to the list of opportunities to embellish your sweater. When thinking about your cardigan's opening, you can independently adjust two things: how far apart the untrimmed edges of your cardigan rest, and how tall the cardigan opening trim is.

I call these two concepts the button band *allowance*, and the button band *trim height*. You can make changes to them independently of each other.

A *zero allowance* means that, when worn, the untrimmed edges of the cardigan front will touch each other (at least until you move!). This might be a good choice if you're planning on installing a zipper (as shown in the Jump Shot Hoodie on page 165), want an extra-snuggly collar on an open cardigan, or are going to trim the edge with I-cord and do something with frogs or hook-and-eye closures.

A *positive allowance* means that, when worn, the untrimmed edges of the cardigan will be separated from each other by the amount of the allowance.

Zero allowance          Positive allowance          Negative allowance

This is the default choice for cardigans with a button band, but might also be used when you want an open cardigan to always have a gap, or are planning on an especially luscious edge trim.

A *negative allowance* means that, when worn, the untrimmed edges of the cardigan will overlap each other by the amount of the allowance. The most obvious place you'd like to use a negative allowance is in a double-breasted cardigan. But there are other applications for this too—the simplest form of a "waterfall" cardigan is one with extra-wide cardigan fronts that are allowed to fall open. (Note: This requires a super-drapey fabric to be effective.) Draped-front cardigans with poncho-like fronts that can be pinned to a shoulder or either side of the neckline are also created with an overlapping allowance.

Trim height
equals allowance

Allowance more than
twice trim height

Separately from the allowance, you can adjust how tall the *trim height* is. For a traditionally buttoned cardigan, the trim height would equal the allowance: A 1" (2.5 cm) gap, combined with 1" (2.5 cm) of trim on each edge, means they can fully overlap and button without gapping. A traditional open cardigan might use an allowance that's more than twice the trim height to leave a bit of open space: a 5" (12.5 cm) allowance and a 2" (5 cm) trim height, for example.

If you're going to button a cardigan (double-breasted or otherwise), a trim height of 1¼–2½" (3–6.5 cm) is typical. If you'd like to work a slimmer button placket, consider trimming both edges with I-cord and creating buttonholes by detaching the I-cord (working it separately from your picked-up stitches) for a few rows for each buttonhole.

If you'd like your button band to be more substantial, you can make the trim however tall you like! But if you're making it wider than around 2½" (6.5 cm), you'll probably want to locate the buttonholes close to the edge for stability. *(On the other hand, remember: There is no knitting police! Swatch what you're thinking, and see how it goes.)*

Finally, if your cardigan is going to close, you have choices for how to close it! Buttons, zippers, hooks-and-eyes, frog closures, fancy screw-in closures that require no adjustments to your knitting . . .

*Buttonhole advice. There are a few different ways to work buttonholes, and different people prefer different types. You can see them in a single swatch below.*

- The simplest to work, and the most appropriate if you're using a strong, fairly fine yarn, is the **(yo, k2tog)** buttonhole. It's neat, easy to work, and over in a single row. I tend to use it when I'm making a sweater with lots of small buttons.

- The next-easiest to work is the **bind-off/cast-on** buttonhole. On the first buttonhole row, you bind off 2, 3, or 4 stitches (depending on the size of your button—it should be slightly difficult to put the button through the hole). On the following row, cast on the same number of stitches you've bound off.

- The third kind of buttonhole you'll likely find reference to is a **one-row** buttonhole. There are lots of tutorials online with great photographs, but the main idea is that you both bind off and cast on, on the same row. You'll need this buttonhole to be one stitch larger, generally speaking,

than a two-row buttonhole to achieve the same size. For the swatch shown here, I worked the one-row buttonhole this way: Work to your buttonhole, and slip the next two stitches with your yarn in the back, without knitting them. Pass the first slipped stitch over the second; repeat until buttonhole is as wide as you desire. Then, using the backwards-loop cast-on, cast on the same number of stitches. Work to your next buttonhole, and repeat.

I personally prefer a standard two-row buttonhole with the edges neatened up. There are a few tricks to making this buttonhole sturdy and lovely. I like to end the bind-offs with a k2tog instead of a bind-off; it makes for a neater closure. I also work the bound-off stitches and cast-on stitches through the back loop, twisting them to make them stiffer.

## POCKETS

There are a few different ways to work a pocket in a knitted garment—and I've used them all in the designs in this book.

*Patch pocket.* Patch pockets, like the ones in the Penobscot Pullover (page 147), are the simplest to work: Once you're finished with the sweater, knit pieces of fabric that are the size and shape you'd like

From bottom: eyelet, two-row, and
one-row buttonholes

Patch pocket

Afterthought pocket

(underside of pocket)

your pockets to be. Pin them and sew them to the front of your sweater using mattress stitch.

These can be rectangular, but are also a great way to make a kangaroo pocket for a hoodie or sweatshirt. I love patch pockets; I think they're a great blend of strength and a slim line for knitwear, and they're the kind of pocket I use most often.

***"Afterthought" pocket.*** Afterthought pockets, as their name implies, can be added to a garment after it's completely finished. But you can also plan ahead for them, as I did in the Campfire Cardigan on page 181: Once you reach the top edge of where you want the pocket to sit, change to a waste yarn and work the number of stitches you'd like to use for the pocket (see left swatch above); finish the garment.

When you're finished with the rest of the garment and are ready to add the pockets, put the pocket stitches in the rows above and below your waste yarn onto separate needles (I like to use circulars, letting the unused stitches rest on their cables, but

dpns (as used in the middle swatch) would work as well). Then remove the waste yarn (or cut out the stitches in your original yarn, if you're working a true afterthought pocket).

Join the pocket stitches for working in the round and work even in Stockinette (knit side on the interior of the pocket) until the pocket is the desired depth. You can work the outermost pocket stitches in reverse Stockinette for that first row to make picking up the pocket trim easier, if you like. Once your pocket is sufficiently deep, use a 3-needle bind-off to close the bottom. Pick up at the top of the pocket, on the outside (using the purl bumps if you set it up this way) and make the pocket's trim; sew the side edges of the trim in place with mattress stitch (see right swatch above).

Afterthought pockets have an entirely separate pocket lining, which is nice and strong but can be a bit bulky. You can reduce the bulk by working the lining in a much smaller yarn, or even lining the pocket with fabric if you prefer—it's up to you!

***Diagonal pocket.*** Pockets with a diagonal edge opening, like the Meadowbrook Cowl on page 159, are fussier but so beautiful that I think they're worth it. This is something of a hybrid of the patch and afterthought pockets; like a patch pocket, there are just two layers of fabric in this part of your garment, but like an afterthought pocket, the fabric of the pocket itself lies *inside* the garment rather than on the outside.

To work one, start by marking the stitches that will form the bottom edge of your pocket, placing the stitches to the right and/or left of the pocket (i.e., between the pocket and the side edge of the piece) on a holder:

Work the stitches of the pocket front along with the stitches between the pocket and the center front, straight until you're ready to shape the diagonal. Then shape the side(s) of the pocket in whatever curve you like. Optionally, once the shaping is complete, work straight for a bit more until you've reached the desired pocket height. Either way, when you're done working the pocket itself, your knitting will look something like this:

Now go back to the held stitches: Either work them, and then cast on the pocket-lining stitches, or cast on the pocket lining, and then work them, depending on which way the pocket opens. Work the pocket lining stitches, along with whatever stitches are to the right and/or left of the pocket until the pocket lining matches the front of the garment:

To close the pocket, work the stitches inside the pocket until you've reached the pocket marker, then hold the two needles next to each other and **knit the pocket lining stitches together with the top-of-pocket stitches as you might in a 3-needle bind-off (but don't bind off the stitches!).** Work the remainder of the pocket lining stitches to the side seam and remove all markers.

During finishing, trim the pocket opening however you like. I prefer an Applied I-cord, as in the Meadowbrook Cowl on page 159, but I've also seen lovely slipped-stitch edges, ribbing, and Garter trims. There is no edging on the sample pocket shown here. Carefully sew the cast-on bottom edge of the pocket lining [and the long side edge(s) if you've made a separate pocket on each side] to the WS of the piece, making sure that the stitches don't show on the RS.

## NECKLINE EMBELLISHMENTS

We covered the basics of neck *shaping* in part 2, and it's completely fine to add some basic trim to your neckline and stop there! But if you'd like to make a neckline that's a bit more special, I've got you covered.

Most of what you think of as a "neckline" actually gets created in the finishing stage, with trim:

**Turtlenecks and cowls** are built off of crew and scoop necks, respectively. Pick up stitches around the neckline and then work the edge stitch for 7-9" (18-23 cm) for a turtleneck, or 8-14" (20.5-35.5 cm) for a cowl, increasing your needle size by one every 4" (10 cm) or so.

**Hoods** are built off of crew necks. For the simplest hood, pick up stitches around the neckline and work back and forth until the pieces comfortably meet at the top of the head (with some extra head room). Then work a 3-needle bind-off to seal the hood. To tone down the hood's point a bit, work a few inches of soft decrease rows [working the decreases to either side of the center 1 or 2 stitches], an inch (2.5 cm) or so of every-RS-row decreases, and then an inch or so of every-row decreases, before working your bind-off. I like hoods trimmed with simple Applied I-cord (see page 135), but they look great with Garter or ribbing, too.

**Henleys** are variations on a round neckline somewhere in between a crew and a scoop in depth. Around 2" (5 cm) before the neck shaping begins, bind off around ½-1" (1.5-2.5 cm) of stitches at the center of the neck. Work straight to the round neck shaping and proceed as written, except eliminate the "notch" stitches from your initial bind-off. During finishing, edge the "notch" with a small placket and buttons.

**Shawl collars** are built off of V necklines. For a pullover, you'll need to bind off 2-3" (5-7.5 cm) of stitches at the bottom of the V to create a place to seam the shawl collar edge. Once you pick up stitches around the neckline, work flat for just under half the width of the neck trim. Then use short rows to ensure the back part of the neck trim measures twice the front neck trim width. Close your short rows and work until each front trim is the correct height, then bind off. The short rows should ensure the collar flips over properly.

# Recipe: Penobscot Pullover

This incredibly warm, incredibly soft pullover incorporates several of the embellishments discussed in this chapter. I started with the Basic Pullover (Yoke Construction) on page 65, changing the length and adding extra-long, fingerless-mitt sleeves, patch pockets, and an asymmetrical collar. I'm also a sucker for a good stripe, so I threw some in. I've already got plans for a version with dart-style waist shaping on the back, *and* an extra-long A-line version I can wear with my favorite boots!

**MATERIALS:** Blue Sky Fibers Baby Alpaca in Licorice (MC) and Toasted Almond (A); 12 (12, 13, 14, 14, 15, 16, 17, 18, 19, 20, 22) hanks MC and 2 (2, 2, 2, 2, 2, 3, 3, 3, 4, 4, 4) hanks A for sizes 33¼ (36, 38, 40, 42, 44, 46, 48, 52, 56, 60, 64)" [84.5 (91.5, 96.5, 101.5, 106.5, 112, 117, 122, 132, 142, 152.5, 162.5) cm] chest

**SAMPLE SHOWN** in size 42" (106.5 cm)

## PENOBSCOT STRIPE SEQUENCES

**STRIPE SEQUENCE 1:** Work 12 rounds in A; 8 rounds in MC; 8 rounds in A; 8 rounds in MC; 4 rounds in A; 8 rounds in MC; 2 rounds in A; 8 rounds in MC; 1 round in A; switch to MC. You will work a total of 59 rounds before final switch to MC.

**STRIPE SEQUENCE 2:** Work 14 rounds in A; 8 rounds in MC; 10 rounds in A; 8 rounds in MC; 6 rounds in A; 8 rounds in MC; 4 rounds in A; 8 rounds in MC; 2 rounds in A; switch to MC. You will work a total of 68 rounds before final switch to MC.

**STRIPE SEQUENCE 3:** Work 16 rounds in A; 8 rounds in MC; 12 rounds in A; 8 rounds in MC; 8 rounds in A; 8 rounds in MC; 6 rounds in A; 8 rounds in MC; 3 rounds in A; 4 rounds in MC; 1 round in A; switch to MC. You will work a total of 82 rounds before final switch to MC.

- I worked all trims in 1x1 Rib instead of 2x2 Rib (see Basic Stitch Patterns, page 187)
- I lengthened the body by 2½" (5 cm) before working yoke shaping.
- Beginning 1" (2.5 cm) before joining the yoke, I started Stripe Sequence 1 (1, 1, 1, 2, 2, 2, 2, 3, 3, 3, 3) (see above) and continued until complete, then switching to MC.

- I lengthened the sleeves by 5" (13 cm) to make the fingerless mitts, as follows:
  - I began with ½" (1.5 cm) of 1x1 Rib in MC, then switched to Stockinette stitch until sleeves measured 1" (2.5 cm).
  - I worked 4 rounds even in A, then switched back to MC.
  - When sleeve measured 1¾" (4.5 cm), I inserted a thumbhole by binding off 2 sts one-quarter of the way around the sleeve on the left sleeve, and three-quarters of the way around the right sleeve. I worked flat on the remaining stitches for 1¾" (4.5 cm) and then re-joined for working in the round, casting on the 2 sts I had removed.
  - Once the sleeve measured 7" (18 cm), I shaped as in the basic pattern. (Make sure, when you join, that the sleeves are lined up correctly!)
- During finishing, I made the following changes:
  - I trimmed the thumbholes with a few rounds of reverse Stockinette.
  - To make the collar, I picked up stitches around the neckline starting 1½" (4 cm) down from the left shoulder, and worked flat on those stitches, with 1" (2.5 cm) of 1x1 Rib on each edge, for 3" (7.5 cm). I went up one needle size and worked until the collar measured 5" (12.5 cm), then added stripes: 2 rows in A, 4 rows in MC, 4 rows in A, 2 rows in MC. I finished the collar off with ¾" (2 cm) of 1x1 Rib. I bound off with needles one size larger, so that I could block the collar nice and wide.
  - I made patch pockets that were 6" (15 cm) wide and tall, with a 1" (2.5 cm) (8-row) A stripe at the top and 1" (2.5 cm) of MC ribbing above that.

........................................................

# PART FOUR

# THE GARMENTS

Sometimes it's hard to look through pages and pages of technical knitting instructions and really *see* how things can play out in an actual piece of clothing. The design process, for most of us, can start in a number of different places: the yarn, the stitch pattern, a silhouette detail, something you saw a few years ago . . .

So in this section, I've worked up a collection of stand-alone patterns to provide some concrete starting points. (At least I hope you'll use them as starting points for your own inspiration—it's the spirit of this book!) There are eight—two patterns for each construction in part I—and they incorporate all the techniques from the rest of the book.

For each design, I talk a little bit about why I combined silhouette, fabric, construction, and stitch pattern the way I did. I hope these notes give you the confidence to steal ideas you like and make your own perfect garment—and then to share them with me online!

# Baxter Turtleneck

Sweaters are for keeping you warm and cozy during cold days, and I like to include an ultra-fuzzy sweater in each book. This time, I'm making it a soft, luscious turtleneck, with a graphic diagonal eyelet pattern on the sweater's body and sleeves. The modified drop-shoulder silhouette combines with the lace to feel simultaneously dressed-up and sit-on-the-couch-comfy; the size of the yarn makes the simple eyelets very eye-catching. I hope you'll wear this one all the time.

## FINISHED MEASUREMENTS

37½ (39½, 41½, 43½, 46, 48, 50, 52½, 56½, 61, 65, 69½)" [95.5 (100.5, 105.5, 110.5, 117, 122, 127, 133.5, 143.5, 155, 165, 176.5) cm] chest

*Note: Sweater is intended to be worn with 4–6" (10–15 cm) ease in the bust; shown in size 39½" (100.5 cm).*

## YARN

Blue Sky Fibers Techno [68% baby alpaca / 22% silk / 10% extra fine merino; 120 yards (109 meters) / 50 grams]: 9 (9, 10, 10, 11, 11, 12, 12, 13, 15, 16, 16) hanks #1970 Fame

## NEEDLES

One pair straight needles and one 16" (40 cm) long circular needle (for Turtleneck), size US 9 (5.5 mm)

One 16" (40 cm) long circular needle (for Turtleneck), size US 10 (6 mm)

One 16" (40 cm) long circular needle (for Turtleneck), size US 10½ (6.5 mm)

Change needle size if necessary to obtain correct gauge.

## NOTIONS

Stitch markers; removable stitch markers, cable needle

## GAUGE

15 sts and 23 rows = 4" (10 cm) in St st

## NOTES

If your size gives the number 0 for a particular instruction, skip that instruction and proceed to the next instruction.

Unless otherwise specified, decreases should be worked to match the slant of the edge being shaped, as follows: For left-slanting edges: On RS rows, k1, ssk, work to end; on WS rows, p1, p2tog, work to end. For right-slanting edges: On RS rows, work to last 3 sts, k2tog, k1; on WS rows, work to last 3 sts, ssp, p1. Increases should also be worked to match the slant of the edge being shaped, as follows: For right-slanting edges: On RS rows, k1, M1R, work to end; on WS rows, p1, M1PR, work to end. For left-slanting edges: On RS rows, work to last st, M1L, k1; on WS rows, p1, M1PL, work to end.

When working Back and Front neck shaping and Sleeve shaping, do not work a yo without a corresponding decrease and vice versa. If you can't work a complete 2/1 RC or 2/1 LC at side edges, work affected sts in St st.

Once Back, Front, and Sleeve ribbing is complete, maintain at least 1 st in St st at each edge of pieces.

## BACK

CO 70 (74, 78, 82, 86, 90, 94, 98, 106, 114, 122, 130) sts.

**ROW 1 (RS):** K0 (2, 0, 2, 0, 2, 0, 2, 2, 2, 2, 2), [p2, k2] 8 (8, 9, 9, 10, 10, 11, 11, 12, 13, 14, 15) times, p1, pm, p1, k2, p1, pm, p1, [k2, p2] 8 (8, 9, 9, 10, 10, 11, 11, 12, 13, 14, 15) times, k0 (2, 0, 2, 0, 2, 0, 2, 2, 2, 2, 2).

**ROW 2:** Knit the knit sts and purl the purl sts as they face you. Work even until piece measures 2" (5 cm), ending with a WS row.

**ROW 1 (RS):** Knit to marker, sm, p1, k2, p1, sm, knit to end. Work even, working sts between markers as established and remaining sts in St st, until piece measures 13 (13½, 13, 12½, 13, 12, 11½, 10½, 10, 10, 10, 10)" [33 (34.5, 33, 32, 33, 30.5, 29, 26.5, 25.5, 25.5, 25.5, 25.5) cm] from the beginning, ending with a RS row.

**NEXT ROW (WS):** Purl to 2 sts before marker, pm, p2, remove marker, k1, p1, pm for center, p1, k1, remove marker, p2, pm, purl to end.

### BEGIN LACE PATTERN

**ROW 1 (RS):** Knit to marker, sm, work Body Chart over 8 sts, slipping center marker, sm, knit to end.

**ROW 2:** Purl to marker, work to last marker, sm, purl to end.

**ROW 3:** Knit to 1 st before marker, pm, work Body Chart over 10 sts (removing original chart edge markers as you come to them and leaving center marker in place), pm, knit to end.

**ROW 4:** Purl to marker, work to last marker, sm, purl to end.

Continue working chart as established, moving markers 1 st to the outside on every RS row to bring 1 more st into the chart on each side, until piece measures 17 (17, 17, 17, 17, 17, 17, 17, 17, 16½, 16½, 16½)" ` [43 (43, 43, 43, 43, 43, 43, 43, 43, 42, 42, 42) cm] from the beginning, ending with a WS row.

### SHAPE ARMHOLES

Continuing to work in patterns as established, BO 2 sts at the beginning of the next 2 rows—66 (70, 74, 78, 82, 86, 90, 94, 102, 110, 118, 126) sts remain.

Work even until armholes measure 7 (7½, 8, 8½, 9, 9, 9½, 9½, 10, 10½, 11, 11)" [18 (19, 20.5, 21.5, 23, 23, 24, 24, 25.5, 26.5, 28, 28) cm], ending with a WS row.

### SHAPE NECK

**NEXT ROW (RS):** Work 22 (23, 25, 26, 28, 30, 31, 32, 36, 40, 44, 47) sts, join a second ball of yarn, BO center 22 (24, 24, 26, 26, 26, 28, 30, 30, 30, 30, 32) sts, work to end.

Working both sides at the same time, decrease 1 st at each neck edge every RS row twice—20 (21, 23, 24, 26, 28, 29, 30, 34, 38, 42, 45) sts remain each shoulder.

Work even until armholes measure 8 (8½, 9, 9½, 10, 10, 10½, 10½, 11, 11½, 12, 12)" [20.5 (21.5, 23, 24, 25.5, 25.5, 26.5, 26.5, 28, 29, 30.5, 30.5) cm], ending with a WS row.

### SHAPE SHOULDERS

BO 10 (11, 12, 12, 13, 14, 15, 15, 17, 19, 21, 23) sts at each armhole edge once, then 10 (10, 11, 12, 13, 14, 14, 15, 17, 19, 21, 22) sts once.

## FRONT

Work as for Back until armholes measure 4¾ (5¼, 5¾, 6¼, 6¾, 6¾, 7¼, 7¼, 7¾, 8¼, 8¾, 8¾)" [12 (13.5, 14.5, 16, 17, 17, 18.5, 18.5, 19.5, 21, 22, 22) cm], ending with a WS row—66 (70, 74, 78, 82, 86, 90, 94, 102, 110, 118, 126) sts remain.

### SHAPE NECK

**NEXT ROW (RS):** Work 25 (27, 29, 30, 32, 34, 36, 37, 41, 45, 49, 53) sts, join a second ball of yarn, BO center 16 (16, 16, 18, 18, 18, 18, 20, 20, 20, 20, 20) sts, work to end.

Working both sides at the same time, decrease 1 st at each neck edge every row 3 (4, 4, 4, 4, 4, 5, 5, 5, 5, 5, 5) times, then every RS row 2 (2, 2, 2, 2, 2, 2, 2, 2, 2, 2, 3) times—20 (21, 23, 24, 26, 28, 29, 30, 34, 38, 42, 45) sts remain each shoulder.

Work even until armholes measure 8 (8½, 9, 9½, 10, 10, 10½, 10½, 11, 11½, 12, 12)" [20.5 (21.5, 23, 24, 25.5, 25.5, 26.5, 26.5, 28, 29, 30.5, 30.5) cm], ending with a WS row.

### SHAPE SHOULDERS

BO 10 (11, 12, 12, 13, 14, 15, 15, 17, 19, 21, 23) sts at each armhole edge once, then 10 (10, 11, 12, 13, 14, 14, 15, 17, 19, 21, 22) sts once.

## SLEEVES

CO 34 (34, 34, 34, 34, 34, 38, 38, 38, 42, 46, 46) sts.
Begin 2x2 Rib; work even until piece measures 3" (7.5 cm), ending with a WS row.

### *RIGHT SLEEVE ONLY:*

**ROW 1 (RS):** K1, [yo, ssk (place removable marker on ssk; move marker up as you work), k9] 3 (3, 3, 3, 3, 3, 3, 3, 3, 3, 4, 4) times, k0 (0, 0, 0, 0, 0, 4, 4, 4, 8, 1, 1).

**ROW 2:** Purl.

**ROW 3:** *Knit to marked st, yo, ssk (marked st); repeat from * through last marked st, knit to end.

**ROW 4:** Purl.

### *LEFT SLEEVE ONLY:*

**ROW 1 (RS):** K0 (0, 0, 0, 0, 0, 4, 4, 4, 8, 1, 1), [k9, k2tog (place removable marker on k2tog; move marker up as you work), yo] 3 (3, 3, 3, 3, 3, 3, 3, 3, 3, 4, 4) times, k1.

**ROW 2:** Purl.

**ROW 3:** *Knit to 1 st before marked st, k2tog (marked st), yo; repeat from * through last marked st, knit to end.

**ROW 4:** Purl.

### SHAPE BOTH SLEEVES

Continuing to work openwork columns as established, then changing to St st across all sts once each openwork column has reached the side edge, increase 1 st each side this row, then every 5 (5, 4, 4, 3, 3, 3, 3, 3, 3, 3, 3) rows 12 (14, 16, 18, 20, 20, 20, 20, 22, 22, 21, 21) times—60 (64, 68, 72, 76, 76, 80, 80, 84, 88, 90, 90) sts.

Work even until piece measures 17½ (18, 18, 18, 18½, 18½, 18½, 18½, 18½, 19, 19, 19)" [44.5 (45.5, 45.5, 45.5, 47, 47, 47, 47, 47, 48.5, 48.5, 48.5) cm] from the beginning, ending with a WS row. BO all sts.

## FINISHING

Block pieces as desired. Sew shoulder seams. Sew in Sleeves, sewing BO edge at top of Sleeve to straight edge of armhole and upper side edges of Sleeve to BO edges of armhole; sew side and Sleeve seams.

### TURTLENECK

With RS facing, using smallest 16" (40 cm) circular needle and beginning at right shoulder, pick up and knit approximately 1 st in each BO st, 3 sts for every 4 rows along vertical edges, and 4 sts for every 5 rows along diagonal edges. You will pick up approximately 76 (76, 76, 80, 80, 80, 84, 88, 88, 88, 88, 92) sts. *Note: Exact st count is not essential, but be sure to end with a multiple of 4 sts + 2 for ribbing to work out evenly.* Join for working in the rnd; pm for beginning of rnd. Begin 2x2 Rib in the Rnd; work even until turtleneck measures 8" (20.5 cm), going up 1 needle size every 3" (7.5 cm). BO all sts in pattern.

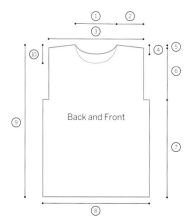

Back and Front

Sleeve

### Body Chart

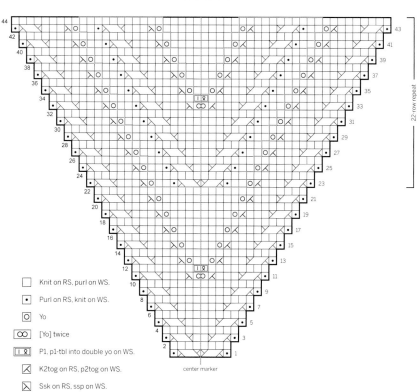

22-row repeat

center marker

| | |
|---|---|
| ☐ | Knit on RS, purl on WS. |
| • | Purl on RS, knit on WS. |
| O | Yo |
| ∞ | [Yo] twice |
| 1 ☿ ∞ | P1, p1-tbl into double yo on WS. |
| ╱ | K2tog on RS, p2tog on WS. |
| ╲ | Ssk on RS, ssp on WS. |
| ╱ | 2/1 RC (2/1 Right Cross): Slip 1 st to cable needle, hold to back, k2, k1 from cable needle. |
| ╲ | 2/1 LC (2/1 Left Cross): Slip 2 sts to cable needle, hold to front, k1, k2 from cable needle. |
| ☐ | Pattern repeat. Once Row 44 of chart is complete, continue to work in pattern as established and, AT THE SAME TIME, begin to work a new instance of red-outlined pattern repeat across the center 12 sts (6 sts on either side of center marker), beginning with Row 23 of pattern repeat. |

1  7 (7½, 7½, 8, 8, 8½, 9, 9, 9, 9, 9½)"
   18 (19, 19, 20.5, 20.5, 20.5, 21.5, 23, 23, 23, 23, 24) cm

2  5¼ (5½, 6¼, 6½, 7, 7½, 7¾, 8, 9, 10¼, 11¼, 12)"
   13.5 (14, 16, 16.5, 18, 19, 19.5, 20.5, 23, 26, 28.5, 30.5) cm

3  17½ (18¾, 19¾, 20¾, 21¾, 23, 24, 25, 27¼, 29¼, 31½, 33½)"
   44.5 (47.5, 50, 52.5, 55, 58.5, 61, 63.5, 69, 74.5, 80, 85) cm

4  1½"
   4 cm

5  ½"
   1.5 cm

6  8 (8½, 9, 9½, 10, 10, 10½, 10½, 11, 11½, 12, 12)"
   20.5 (21.5, 23, 24, 25.5, 25.5, 26.5, 26.5, 28, 29, 30.5, 30.5) cm

7  17 (17, 17, 17, 17, 17, 17, 17, 17, 16½, 16½, 16½)"
   43 (43, 43, 43, 43, 43, 43, 43, 43, 42, 42, 42) cm

8  18¾ (19¾, 20¾, 21¾, 23, 24, 25, 26¼, 28¼, 30½, 32½, 34¾)"
   47.5 (50, 52.5, 55, 58.5, 61, 63.5, 66.5, 72, 77.5, 82.5, 88.5) cm

9  25½ (26, 26½, 27, 27½, 27½, 28, 28, 28½, 28½, 29, 29)"
   65 (66, 67.5, 68.5, 70, 70, 71, 71, 72.5, 72.5, 73.5, 73.5) cm

10  3¾"
    9.5 cm

11  16 (17, 18¼, 19¼, 20¼, 20¼, 21¼, 21¼, 22½, 23½, 24, 24)"
    40.5 (43, 46.5, 49, 51.5, 51.5, 54, 54, 57, 59.5, 61, 61) cm

12  17½ (18, 18, 18, 18½, 18½, 18½, 18½, 18½, 19, 19, 19)"
    44.5 (45.5, 45.5, 45.5, 47, 47, 47, 47, 47, 48.5, 48.5, 48.5) cm

13  9 (9, 9, 9, 9, 9, 10¼, 10¼, 10¼, 11¼, 12¼, 12¼)"
    23 (23, 23, 23, 23, 23, 26, 26, 26, 28.5, 31, 31) cm

# Fiddler's Reach Cardigan

I love the way even a fairly complicated stitch pattern looks textural when worked all-over, in a small yarn. This open cardigan uses a lovely fingering wool-silk blend in an allover lace-and-cable pattern that's simpler than it looks. An A-line shape and modified drop-shoulder silhouette keep things from being too fussy; a deep, soft rolled collar makes the sweater versatile in the closet, as well. Fiddler's Reach is worked in pieces from the bottom up, then seamed, for stability. The neckband/collar is picked up and worked perpendicular to the main work. The body has an A-line shape and tapered three-quarter sleeves. To change the sleeves or body shape, please see chapters 7 and 8.

## FINISHED MEASUREMENTS

35½ (39, 42, 45½, 48½, 51½, 58, 61½, 64½)" [90 (99, 106.5, 115.5, 123, 131, 147.5, 156, 164) cm] chest, with Fronts overlapped

*Note: Sweater is intended to be worn with 4–8" (10–20.5 cm) ease in the bust; shown in size 42" (106.5 cm).*

## YARN

Quince and Co. Tern [75% American wool / 25% silk; 221 yards (202 meters) / 50 grams]: 11 (12, 13, 14, 15, 16, 17, 19, 19) hanks Columbine

## NEEDLES

One pair straight needles and one 40" (100 cm) or longer circular needle (for Front Bands/Collar), size US 2 (2.75 mm)

Change needle size if necessary to obtain correct gauge.

## NOTIONS

Stitch markers, cable needle

## GAUGE

30 sts and 42½ rows = 4" (10 cm) in Lace and Cable pattern

## NOTES

If your size gives the number 0 for a particular instruction, skip that instruction and proceed to the next instruction.

Unless otherwise specified, decreases should be worked to match the slant of the edge being shaped, as follows: For left-slanting edges: On RS rows, k2, ssk, work to end; on WS rows, p2, p2tog, work to end. For right-slanting edges: On RS rows, work to last 4 sts, k2tog, k2; on WS rows, work to last 4 sts, ssp, p2. Increases should also be worked to match the slant of the edge being shaped,

as follows: For right-slanting edges: On RS rows, k1, M1R, knit to end; on WS rows, p1, M1PR, purl to end. For left-slanting edges: On RS rows, knit to last st, M1L, k1; on WS rows, p1, M1PL, purl to end.

When working Back and Front neck shaping and Sleeve shaping, do not work a yo without a corresponding decrease and vice versa. If you can't work a complete 6-st cable cross, work affected sts in St st.

Once Back, Front, and Sleeve ribbing is complete, maintain at least 1 st in St st at each edge of pieces.

## BACK

CO 158 (170, 182, 194, 206, 218, 230, 254, 266) sts.
Begin 1x1 Rib Flat; work even until piece measures 1¾" (4.5 cm), ending with a WS row.
**SET-UP ROW (RS):** K1, work Lace and Cable Pattern (beginning as indicated in chart) to last st, k1.
Work even, working first and last sts in St st and remaining sts in Lace and Cable Pattern, until piece measures 2¼" (5.5 cm) from the beginning, ending with a WS row.

### SHAPE SIDES

Decrease 1 st each side this row, then every 11 (11, 12, 12, 12, 12, 23, 11, 11) rows 11 (11, 11, 11, 11, 11, 5, 11, 11) times—134 (146, 158, 170, 182, 194, 218, 230, 242) sts remain.
Work even until piece measures 17 (17, 17½, 17¾, 17½, 17½, 17, 17, 17)" [43 (43, 44.5, 45, 44.5, 44.5, 43, 43, 43) cm] from the beginning, ending with a RS row.

### SHAPE ARMHOLES

BO 6 sts at the beginning of the next 2 rows—122 (134, 146, 158, 170, 182, 206, 218, 230) sts remain.

Work even until armholes measure 7 (7½, 8½, 9, 9½, 10, 10½, 11, 11)" [18 (19, 21.5, 23, 24, 25.5, 26.5, 28, 28) cm], ending with a WS row.

### SHAPE NECK

**NEXT ROW (RS):** Work 37 (42, 46, 51, 56, 60, 71, 77, 82) sts, join a second ball of yarn, BO center 48 (50, 54, 56, 58, 62, 64, 64, 66) sts, work to end.

Working both sides at the same time, decrease 1 st at neck edge every RS row twice—35 (40, 44, 49, 54, 58, 69, 75, 80) sts for shoulder.

Work even until armholes measure 8 (8½, 9½, 10, 10½, 11, 11½, 12, 12)" [20.5 (21.5, 24, 25.5, 26.5, 28, 29, 30.5, 30.5) cm], ending with a WS row.

BO 18 (20, 22, 25, 27, 29, 35, 38, 40) sts at each armhole edge once, then 17 (20, 22, 24, 27, 29, 34, 37, 40) sts once.

## LEFT AND RIGHT FRONTS

CO 80 (86, 92, 98, 104, 110, 116, 128, 134) sts.

Begin 1x1 Rib Flat; work even until piece measures 1¾" (4.5 cm), ending with a WS row.

**SET-UP ROW (RS):** K1, work Lace and Cable Pattern (beginning as indicated in chart) to last st, k1.

Work even, working first and last sts in St st and remaining sts in Lace and Cable Pattern, until piece measures 2¼" (5.5 cm) from the beginning, ending with a WS row.

### SHAPE SIDE

Decrease 1 st at side edge this row, then every 11 (11, 12, 12, 12, 12, 23, 11, 11) rows 11 (11, 11, 11, 11, 11, 5, 11, 11) times—68 (74, 80, 86, 92, 98, 110, 116, 122) sts remain.

Work even until piece measures 17 (17, 17½, 17¾, 17½, 17½, 17, 17, 17)" [43 (43, 44.5, 45, 44.5, 44.5, 43, 43, 43) cm] from the beginning, ending at the armhole edge.

### SHAPE ARMHOLE

**NEXT ROW:** BO 6 sts, work to end—68 (74, 80, 86, 92, 98, 110, 116, 122) sts remain.

*LEFT FRONT:*

Work 3 rows even.

*RIGHT FRONT:*

Work 2 rows even.

### SHAPE NECK

Decrease 1 st at neck edge this row, then every 2 (3, 3, 3, 3, 3, 3, 3, 3) rows 26 (27, 29, 30, 31, 33, 34, 34, 35) times—35 (40, 44, 49, 54, 58, 69, 75, 80) sts remain.

Work even until armhole measures 8 (8½, 9½, 10, 10½, 11, 11½, 12, 12)" [20.5 (21.5, 24, 25.5, 26.5, 28, 29, 30.5, 30.5) cm], ending at armhole edge row.

### SHAPE SHOULDER

BO 18 (20, 22, 25, 27, 29, 35, 38, 40) sts at armhole edge once, then 17 (20, 22, 24, 27, 29, 34, 37, 40) sts once.

## SLEEVES

CO 78 (82, 88, 92, 92, 100, 104, 108, 116) sts.

Begin 1x1 Rib Flat; work even until piece measures 2" (5 cm), ending with a WS row.

**SET-UP ROW (RS):** K1, work Lace and Cable Pattern (beginning as indicated in chart) to last st, k1.

Work 2 rows even, working first and last sts in St st and remaining sts in Lace and Cable Pattern.

### SHAPE SLEEVE

Working new sts into pattern, increase 2 sts this row, then every 4 (4, 3, 3, 3, 3, 3, 3, 3) rows 20 (22, 27, 28, 32, 32, 34, 35, 31) times—120 (128, 144, 150, 158, 166, 174, 180, 180) sts. Work even until piece measures 12 (12½, 12½, 13, 13, 13, 13½, 13¼, 13¼)" [30.5 (32, 32, 33, 33, 33, 34.5, 33.5, 33.5) cm] from the beginning, ending with a WS row. BO all sts.

## FINISHING

Block pieces as desired. Sew shoulder seams. Sew in Sleeves, sewing BO edge at top of Sleeve to straight edge of armhole and upper side edges of Sleeve to BO edges of armhole; sew side and Sleeve seams.

### FRONT BANDS/COLLAR

With RS facing, using circular needle, beginning at lower Right Front edge and ending at lower Left Front edge, pick up and knit approximately 1 st in each BO st, 2 sts for every 3 rows along vertical edges, and 3 sts for every 4 rows along diagonal edges. You will pick up approximately 133 (132, 135, 137, 136, 136, 133, 133, 133) sts along the straight edges of the Fronts, 62 (66, 73, 77, 81, 85, 89, 93, 93) sts along each shaped Front neck edge, and 63 (65, 69, 69, 71, 75, 77, 77, 81) sts along the Back neck edge, and will have approximately 453 (461, 485, 497, 505, 517, 521, 529, 533) sts. *Note: Exact st count is not essential, but be sure to end with an odd number of sts for ribbing to work out evenly.* Begin St st; work even for 4" (10 cm). Change to 1x1 Rib Flat; work even for 1" (2.5 cm). BO all sts in pattern.

## Lace and Cable Pattern

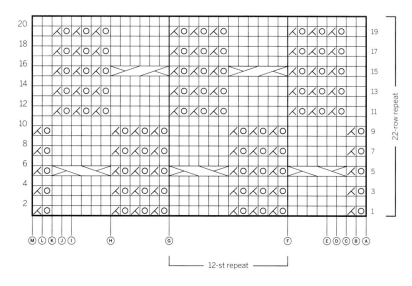

- Ⓐ Begin Sleeve size 61½" (156 cm)
- Ⓑ Begin Sleeve size 39" (99 cm)
- Ⓒ Begin Right Front sizes 35½, 42, 48½, 58, 61½" (90, 106.5, 123, 147.5, 156 cm); begin Sleeve sizes 45½, 48½, 58, 64½" (115.5, 123, 147.5, 164 cm)
- Ⓓ Begin Sleeve size 35½" (90 cm)
- Ⓔ Begin Sleeve sizes 42 and 51½" (106.5 and 131 cm)
- Ⓕ Begin Back all sizes; begin Left and Right Fronts sizes 39, 45½, 51½, 64½" (99, 115.5, 131, 164 cm)
- Ⓖ End Back all sizes; end Right Front sizes 35½, 42, 48½, 58, 61½" (90, 106.5, 123, 147.5, 156 cm)
- Ⓗ End Left Sleeve sizes 39, 45½, 51½, 64½" (99, 115.5, 131, 164 cm)
- Ⓘ End Sleeve sizes 42 and 51½" (106.5 and 131 cm)
- Ⓙ End Sleeve size 35½" (90 cm)
- Ⓚ End Sleeve sizes 45½, 48½, 58, 64½" (115.5, 123, 147.5, 164 cm)
- Ⓛ End Sleeve size 39" (99 cm)
- Ⓜ End Sleeve size 61½" (156 cm)

|  | Knit on RS, purl on WS. |
|---|---|
| O | Yo |
| ⤸ | K2tog on RS, p2tog on WS. |
| ⬅ | Slip 3 sts to cn, hold to back, k3, k3 from cn. |
| ➡ | Slip 3 sts to cn, hold to front, k3, k3 from cn. |

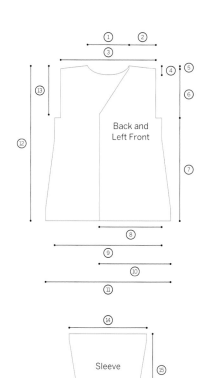

Back and Left Front

Sleeve

1 7 (7¼, 7¾, 8, 8¼, 8¾, 9, 9, 9¼)"
18 (18.5, 19.5, 20.5, 21, 22, 23, 23, 23.5) cm

2 4¾ (5¼, 5¾, 6½, 7¼, 7¾, 9¼, 10, 10¾)"
12 (13.5, 14.5, 16.5, 18.5, 19.5, 23.5, 25.5, 27.5) cm

3 16¼ (17¾, 19½, 21, 22¾, 24¼, 27½, 29, 30¾)"
41.5 (45, 49.5, 53.5, 58, 61.5, 70, 73.5, 78) cm

4 1½"
4 cm

5 ½"
1.5 cm

6 8 (8½, 9½, 10, 10½, 11, 11½, 12, 12)"
20.5 (21.5, 24, 25.5, 26.5, 28, 29, 30.5, 30.5) cm

7 17 (17, 17½, 17¾, 17½, 17½, 17, 17, 17)"
43 (43, 44.5, 45, 44.5, 44.5, 43, 43, 43) cm

8 9 (9¾, 10¾, 11½, 12¼, 13, 14¾, 15½, 16¼)"
23 (25, 27.5, 29, 31, 33, 37.5, 39.5, 41.5) cm

9 17¾ (19½, 21, 22¾, 24¼, 25¾, 29, 30¾, 32¼)"
45 (49.5, 53.5, 58, 61.5, 65.5, 73.5, 78, 82) cm

10 10¾ (11½, 12¼, 13, 13¾, 14¾, 15½, 17, 17¾)"
27.5 (29, 31, 33, 35, 37.5, 39.5, 43, 45) cm

11 21 (22¾, 24¼, 25¾, 27½, 29, 30¾, 33¾, 35½)"
53.5 (58, 61.5, 65.5, 70, 73.5, 78, 85.5, 90) cm

12 25½ (26, 27½, 28¼, 28½, 29, 29, 29½, 29½)"
65 (66, 70, 72, 72.5, 73.5, 73.5, 75, 75) cm

13 8 (8½, 9½, 10, 10½, 11, 11½, 12, 12)"
20.5 (21.5, 24, 25.5, 26.5, 28, 29, 30.5, 30.5) cm

14 16 (17, 19¼, 20, 21, 22¼, 23¼, 24, 24)"
40.5 (43, 49, 51, 53.5, 56.5, 59, 61, 61) cm

15 12 (12½, 12½, 13, 13, 13, 13½, 13¼, 13¼)"
30.5 (32, 32, 33, 33, 33, 34.5, 33.5, 33.5) cm

16 10½ (11, 11¾, 12¼, 12¼, 13¼, 13¾, 14½, 15½)"
26.5 (28, 30, 31, 31, 33.5, 35, 37, 39.5) cm

# Meadowbrook Cowl

Who says raglans can't be polished?! For this A-line cowl, I've turned the "luxe" dial to 11 with a linen-silk-merino combination and a soft, tweedy texture. I've added deep diagonal pockets and a cable pattern to the front, and left the back and three-quarter sleeves plain. (P.S. I've worn this with jeans and a pair of knee-high boots, too, and it works just as well in a casual outfit.)

Meadowbrook is worked in pieces from the bottom up and then seamed, with the neckline picked up and worked in the round to the end. The Sleeves and Back are in Stockinette, but a cable panel adorns the Front, between the diagonally slanted pockets.

## FINISHED MEASUREMENTS

32 (34½, 36, 38½, 40, 42½, 44, 48, 52, 56, 60, 64)" [81.5 (87.5, 91.5, 98, 101.5, 108, 112, 122, 132, 142, 152.5, 162.5) cm] chest

*Note: Sweater is intended to be worn with 3–4" (7.5–5 cm) ease in the bust; shown in size 42½" (108 cm).*

## YARN

Shibui Knits Staccato [70% superwash merino / 30% silk; 191 yards (175 meters)/ 50 grams]: 7 (7, 7, 8, 8, 9, 9, 10, 11, 12, 13, 14) hanks #115 Brick (A)

Shibui Knits Twig [46% linen / 42% recycled silk / 12% wool; 190 yards (174 meters) 50 grams]: 7 (7, 7, 8, 8, 9, 9, 10, 11, 12, 13, 14) hanks #115 Brick (B)

*Note: Sweater is worked with 1 strand each of A and B held together throughout.*

## NEEDLES

One pair straight needles, one 16" (40 cm) long circular needle (for Cowl), and one pair of double-pointed needles (for Applied I-cord), size US 7 (4.5 mm)

Change needle size if necessary to obtain correct gauge.

## NOTIONS

Stitch markers, stitch holders, cable needle

## GAUGE

20 sts and 28 rows = 4" (10 cm) in St st with 1 strand of A and B held together

45 sts from Cable Pattern chart measure 6¾" (17 cm) wide with 1 strand of A and B held together

## NOTES

If your size gives the number 0 for a particular instruction, skip that instruction and proceed to the next instruction.

Unless otherwise specified, decreases should be worked to slant the opposite direction of the edge being shaped, as follows: For left-slanting edges, k1, k2tog, work to end; for right-slanting edges, work to last 3 sts, ssk, k1. Increases should be worked to match the slant of the edge being shaped, as follows: For right-slanting edges: On RS rows, k1, M1R, knit to end; on WS rows, p1, M1PR, purl to end. For left-slanting edges: On RS rows, knit to last st, M1L, k1; on WS rows, p1, M1PL, purl to end.

## SPECIAL ABBREVIATIONS

**2/1 LPC (2 OVER 1 LEFT PURL CROSS):** Slip 2 sts to cn, hold in front, p1, k2 from cn.

**2/1 RPC (2 OVER 1 RIGHT PURL CROSS):** Slip 1 st to cn, hold to back, k2, p1 from cn.

**2/2 LC (2 OVER 2 LEFT CROSS):** Slip 2 sts to cn, hold to front, k2, k2 from cn.

**2/2 RC (2 OVER 2 RIGHT CROSS):** Slip 2 sts to cn, hold to back, k2, k2 from cn.

**3/3 LC (3 OVER 3 LEFT CROSS):** Slip 3 sts to cn, hold to front, k3, k3 from cn.

**3/3 RC (3 OVER 3 RIGHT CROSS):** Slip 3 sts to cn, hold to back, k3, k3 from cn.

### STITCH PATTERN

#### CABLE PATTERN (SEE CHART)

(panel of 34 sts; increases to 45 sts; 16-row repeat)

**SET-UP ROW 1 (RS):** P3, M1P, p1, k1, M1L, [k1, p1, M1P] twice, k4, p1, M1P, k2, M1P, p1, k4, [M1P, p1, k2] twice, M1P, p2, M1P, p1, k1, M1L, k1, p2—45 sts.

**SET-UP ROW 2:** Knit the knit sts and purl the purl sts as they face you.

**ROW 1:** P2, 3/3 RC, p4, 2/1 RPC, 2/1 LPC, [p1, k1] twice, 2/1 RPC, 2/1 LPC, p4, 2/1 RPC, p2, 3/3 RC, p2.

**ROW 2:** K2, p4, k1, p1, k3, p2, k4, p3, k1, p2, k1, p1, k1, p3, k2, p2, k4, p4, k1, p1, k2.

**ROW 3:** P3, k1, p1, k3, p3, 2/1 RPC, p2, 2/1 LPC, k1, p1, 2/1 RPC, k1, p1, 2/1 LPC, p2, 2/1 RPC, p4, k1, p1, k3, p2.

**ROW 4:** K2, p4, k1, p4, k4, p2, k2, p2, k1, p1, k1, p4, k1, p2, k4, p2, k3, p4, k1, p1, k2.

**ROW 5:** P3, k1, p1, k3, p2, 2/1 RPC, p4, 2/1 LPC, 2/1 RPC, [p1, k1] twice, 2/1 LPC, 2/1 RPC, p5, k1, p1, k3, p2.

**ROW 6:** K2, p4, k1, p1, k5, p5, k1, [p1, k1] twice, p4, k6, p2, k2, p4, k1, p1, k2.

**ROW 7:** P3, k1, p1, k3, p2, k2, p6, 2/2 LC, [k1, p1] 3 times, 2/2 LC, p6, k1, p1, k3, p2.

**ROW 8:** K2, p4, k1, p1, k5, p5, k1, [p1, k1] twice, p4, k6, p2, k2, p4, k1, p1, k2.

**ROW 9:** P2, 3/3 RC, p2, 2/1 LPC, p4, 2/1 RPC, 2/1 LPC, [p1, k1] twice, 2/1 RPC, 2/1 LPC, p4, 3/3 RC, p2.

**ROW 10:** K2, p1, k1, p4, k4, p2, k2, p2, k1, p1, k1, p4, k1, p2, k4, p2, k3, p1, k1, p4, k2.

**ROW 11:** P2, k3, p1, k1, p4, 2/1 LPC, p2, 2/1 RPC, k1, p1, 2/1 LPC, k1, p1, 2/1 RPC, p2, 2/1 LPC, p3, k3, p1, k1, p3.

**ROW 12:** K2, p1, k1, p4, k3, p2, k4, p3, k1, p2, k1, p1, k1, p3, k2, p2, k4, p1, k1, p4, k2.

**ROW 13:** P2, k3, p1, k1, p5, 2/1 LPC, 2/1 RPC, [p1, k1] twice, 2/1 LPC, 2/1 RPC, p4, 2/1 LPC, p2, k3, p1, k1, p3.

**ROW 14:** K2, p1, k1, p4, k2, p2, k6, p5, k1, [p1, k1] twice, p4, k5, p1, k1, p4, k2.

**ROW 15:** P2, k3, p1, k1, p6, 2/2 RC, [k1, p1] 3 times, 2/2 RC, p6, k2, p2, k3, p1, k1, p3.

**ROW 16:** K2, p1, k1, p4, k2, p2, k6, p5, k1, [p1, k1] twice, p4, k5, p1, k1, p4, k2.

Repeat Rows 1–16 for Cable Pattern.

## BACK

With 1 strand of A and B held together, CO 98 (104, 110, 110, 116, 122, 128, 140, 146, 158, 170, 176) sts.

**ROW 1 (RS):** K1, *k3, p3; rep from * to last st, k1.

**ROW 2:** P1, *k3, p3; rep from * to last st, p1.

Work even until piece measures 1¼" (3 cm), ending with a WS row.

Change to St st; work even until piece measures 3" (7.5 cm) from the beginning, ending with a WS row.

### SHAPE SIDES

Decrease 1 st each side this row, then every 10 (10, 9, 13, 12, 12, 10, 9, 12, 11, 10, 12) rows 8 (8, 9, 6, 7, 7, 8, 9, 7, 8, 9, 7) times—80 (86, 90, 96, 100, 106, 110, 120, 130, 140, 150, 160) sts remain.

Work even until piece measures 18 (18½, 18½, 18½, 19, 19, 19, 19, 19½, 19½, 19½, 19½)" [45.5 (47, 47, 47, 48.5, 48.5, 48.5, 48.5, 49.5, 49.5, 49.5, 49.5) cm] from the beginning, ending with a WS row.

### SHAPE RAGLAN ARMHOLES

BO 5 (5, 6, 7, 7, 7, 7, 7, 8, 9, 11) sts at the beginning of the next 2 rows. Decrease 1 st each side every RS row 3 (5, 4, 6, 5, 7, 5, 8, 12, 14, 15, 17) times, then every other RS row 9 (8, 9, 8, 10, 8, 12, 9, 5, 4, 4, 2) times, then every RS row 3 (4, 4, 5, 4, 6, 4, 8, 12, 14, 15, 17) times—40 (42, 44, 44, 48, 50, 54, 56, 58, 60, 64, 66) sts remain. Armholes measure 7¼ (7½, 7¾, 8, 8½, 8½, 9¾, 10, 10, 10½, 11¼, 11¼)" [18.5 (19, 19.5, 20.5, 21.5, 21.5, 25, 25.5, 25.5, 26.5, 28.5, 28.5) cm]. Work 1 WS row even. BO all sts.

## FRONT

With 1 strand of A and B held together, CO 98 (104, 110, 110, 116, 122, 128, 140, 146, 158, 170, 176) sts.

**ROW 1 (RS):** K2 (5, 2, 2, 5, 2, 5, 5, 2, 2, 2, 5), [p3, k3] 5 (5, 6, 6, 6, 7, 7, 8, 9, 10, 11, 11) times, pm, p4, k2, p1, k1, p1, k4, p1, k2, p1, k4, [p1, k2] twice, p3, k2, p2, pm, [k3, p3] 5 (5, 6, 6, 6, 7, 7, 8, 9, 10, 11, 11) times, k2 (5, 2, 2, 5, 2, 5, 5, 2, 2, 2, 5).

**ROW 2:** Knit the knit sts and purl the purl sts as they face you. Work 8 rows even.

**SET-UP ROW 1 (RS):** Work to marker, sm, work Set-Up Row 1 of Cable Pattern to marker, sm, work to end—109 (115, 121, 121, 127, 133, 139, 151, 157, 169, 181, 187) sts; 45 sts between markers.

**SET-UP ROW 2:** Work to marker, sm, work Set-Up Row 2 of Cable Pattern to marker, sm, work to end.

**ROW 1 (RS):** Knit to marker, sm, work Row 1 of Cable Pattern to marker, sm, knit to end.

**ROW 2:** Purl to marker, sm, work Row 2 of Cable Pattern to marker, sm, purl to end.
Work 2 rows even.

## MAKE POCKET FACING

**NEXT ROW (RS):** K6 and place on holder, k24 (26, 28, 28, 30, 30, 30, 30, 30, 30, 30, 30), pm, [work to marker, sm] twice, k2 (3, 4, 4, 5, 8, 11, 17, 20, 26, 32, 35), pm, knit to end. Break yarn. Place last 6 sts on holder.

With WS facing, rejoin yarn to center 97 (103, 109, 109, 115, 121, 127, 139, 145, 157, 169, 175) sts; work even on these sts only until Pocket Facing measures 5" (12.5 cm) from the beginning, ending with a WS row.

## SHAPE POCKET FACING

BO 3 (4, 5, 5, 5, 5, 5, 5, 5, 5, 5, 5) sts at the beginning of the next 2 rows, then 2 (3, 3, 3, 3, 3, 3, 3, 3, 3, 3) sts at the beginning of the following 2 rows. Decrease 1 st each side every row 8 (8, 6, 6, 10, 10, 10, 10, 10, 10, 10, 10) times, then every RS row 7 (7, 8, 8, 6, 6, 6, 6, 6, 6, 6, 6) times, ending with a WS row—57 (59, 65, 65, 67, 73, 79, 91, 97, 109, 121, 127) sts remain; 4 (4, 6, 6, 6, 6, 6, 6, 6, 6, 6, 6) sts remain on either side of chart markers. Pocket Facing measures approximately 8¾" [22 cm]. Place sts and markers on circular needle and set aside; break yarn.

## LEFT POCKET LINING

With RS facing, knit across 6 sts from first holder, pm, CO 24 (26, 28, 28, 30, 30, 30, 30, 30, 30, 30) sts using Backward Loop CO (see Special Techniques, page 188)—30 (32, 34, 34, 36, 36, 36, 36, 36, 36, 36, 36) sts.

Working in St st, work even until Pocket Lining measures 3" (7.5 cm), ending with a WS row.

## SHAPE POCKET LINING

Decrease 1 st at beginning of this row, then every 10 (10, 9, 13, 12, 12, 10, 9, 12, 11, 10, 12) rows 3 (3, 4, 3, 3, 3, 3, 4, 3, 3, 3, 3) times—26 (28, 29, 30, 32, 32, 32, 31, 32, 32, 32, 32) sts remain.
Work 9 (9, 3, 0, 3, 3, 9, 3, 3, 6, 9, 3) rows even. Place sts on holder and set aside; do not break yarn.

## RIGHT POCKET LINING

With RS facing, join yarn to 6 sts from holder at opposite side of Front, CO 24 (26, 28, 28, 30, 30, 30, 30, 30, 30, 30) sts in front of these 6 sts, knit across CO sts, pm, knit across sts from holder—30 (32, 34, 34, 36, 36, 36, 36, 36, 36, 36, 36) sts.

Working in St st, work even until Pocket Lining measures 3" (7.5 cm), ending with a WS row.

## SHAPE POCKET LINING

Decrease 1 st at end of this row, then every 10 (10, 9, 13, 12, 12, 10, 9, 12, 11, 10, 12) rows 3 (3, 4, 3, 3, 3, 3, 4, 3, 3, 3) times—26 (28, 29, 30, 32, 32, 32, 31, 32, 32, 32, 32) sts remain.
Work 9 (9, 3, 0, 3, 3, 9, 3, 3, 6, 9, 3) rows even. Leave sts on needle; break yarn.

## JOIN POCKET FACING AND LININGS

*SIZES 32 (34½, –, –, –, –, 44, –, –, –, 60, –)" [81.5 (87.5, –, –, –, 112, –, –, –, 152.5, –) CM] ONLY:*

**NEXT ROW (RS):** With yarn attached to Left Pocket Lining, k1, ssk, knit across Left Pocket Lining to last 4 (4, –, –, –, –, 6, –, –, –, 6, –) sts; holding Pocket Facing sts on circular needle in front of Left Pocket Lining, [k2tog (1 st from Pocket Facing together with 1 st from Left Pocket Lining)] 4 (4, –, –, –, –, 6, –, –, –, 6, –) times, work across Pocket Facing to marker, remove marker; holding Right Pocket Lining sts behind Pocket Facing, [k2tog (1 st from Pocket Facing together with 1 st from Right Pocket Lining)] 4 (4, –, –, –, –, 6, –, –, –, 6, –) times, knit across Right Pocket Lining to last 3 sts, k2tog, k1—99 (105, –, –, –, –, 129, –, –, –, 171, –) sts.

*SIZES – (–, 36, 38½, 40, 42½, –, 48, 52, 56, –, 64)" [– (–, 91.5, 98, 101.5, 108, –, 122, 132, 142, –, 162.5) CM] ONLY:*

**NEXT ROW (RS):** With yarn attached to Left Pocket Lining, knit across Left Pocket Lining to last 6 sts; holding Pocket Facing sts on circular needle in front of Left Pocket Lining, [k2tog (1 st from Pocket Facing together with 1 st from Left Pocket Lining)] 6 times, work across Pocket Facing to marker, remove marker; holding Right Pocket Lining sts behind Pocket Facing, [k2tog (1 st from Pocket Facing together with 1 st from Right Pocket Lining)] 6 times, knit across Right Pocket Lining to end: – (–, 111, 113, 119, 125, –, 141, 149, 161, –, 179) sts.

*ALL SIZES:*

Work 9 (9, 4, 11, 7, 7, 9, 4, 7, 3, 9, 7) rows even.

## SHAPE SIDES

Decrease 1 st each side this row, then every 10 (10, 9, 13, 12, 12, 10, 9, 12, 11, 10, 12) rows 3 (3, 4, 2, 3, 3, 3, 4, 3, 4, 4, 3) times—91 (97, 101, 107, 111, 117, 121, 131, 141, 151, 161, 171) sts remain.

Work even until piece measures 18 (18½, 18½, 18½, 19, 19, 19, 19, 19½, 19½, 19½, 19½)" [45.5 (47, 47, 47, 48.5, 48.5, 48.5, 48.5, 49.5, 49.5, 49.5, 49.5) cm] from the beginning, ending with a RS row.

**NEXT ROW (WS):** Work 39 (41, 42, 45, 45, 47, 47, 51, 55, 59, 62, 66) sts, pm, work 13 (15, 17, 17, 21, 23, 27, 29, 31, 33, 37, 39) sts, pm, work to end.

### SHAPE RAGLAN ARMHOLES AND NECK

*Note: Armholes and neck are shaped at the same time; please read entire section through before beginning.*

BO 5 (5, 6, 7, 7, 7, 7, 7, 8, 9, 11) sts at the beginning of the next 2 rows. Decrease 1 st each side every RS row 3 (5, 4, 6, 5, 7, 5, 8, 12, 14, 15, 17) times, then every other RS row 9 (8, 9, 8, 10, 8, 12, 9, 5, 4, 4, 2) times, then every RS row 3 (4, 4, 5, 4, 6, 4, 8, 12, 14, 15, 17) times. AT THE SAME TIME, when you have completed 18 (20, 22, 24, 28, 28, 36, 38, 38, 42, 46, 46) rows from the beginning of armhole shaping, shape neck as follows:

**NEXT ROW (RS):** Continuing to work armhole shaping as established, work to marker, join a second ball of yarn, BO total of 13 (15, 17, 17, 21, 23, 27, 29, 31, 33, 37, 39) center sts [working k2tog 2 (2, 2, 2, 2, 4, 4, 4, 5, 6, 6) times across cables as you BO to keep edge from flaring, counting each k2tog as 2 sts when counting BO sts], work to end.

Working both sides at the same time, decrease 1 st at each neck edge every row 9 times, then every RS row 5 times, then every other RS row 3 times, ending with a WS row.

**NEXT ROW (RS):** On left neck edge, k2tog; on right neck edge, ssk. Fasten off.

Armholes measure same as for Back.

## SLEEVES

With 1 strand of A and B held together, CO 50 (50, 50, 50, 50, 50, 56, 56, 62, 74, 80, 86) sts.

**ROW 1 (RS):** K4, p3, *k3, p3; repeat from * to last st, k1.
**ROW 2:** P1, *k3, p3; repeat from * to last st, p1.
Work even until piece measures 1½" (4 cm) from the beginning, ending with a WS row.
Change to St st; work 2 rows even.

### SHAPE SLEEVE

Increase 1 st each side this row, then every 21 (15, 12, 9, 7, 6, 6, 4, 4, 4, 3, 3) rows 2 (3, 4, 6, 8, 10, 10, 14, 16, 15, 17, 19) times—56 (58, 60, 64, 68, 72, 78, 86, 96, 106, 116, 126) sts.
Work even until piece measures 11½ (11½, 11½, 12, 12, 12, 12½, 12½, 12½, 12, 12, 11½)" [29 (29, 29, 30.5, 30.5, 30.5, 32, 32, 32, 30.5, 30.5, 29) cm] from the beginning, ending with a WS row.

### SHAPE RAGLAN CAP

BO 5 (5, 6, 7, 7, 7, 7, 7, 8, 9, 11) sts at the beginning of the next 2 rows. Decrease 1 st each side every RS row 3 (5, 4, 4, 5, 7, 5, 8, 12, 14, 15, 17) times, then every other RS row 8 (8, 9, 11, 11, 9, 10, 7, 2, 1, 1, 0) time(s), then every RS row 5 (4, 4, 1, 2, 4, 8, 12, 18, 20, 21, 21) time(s)—14 (14, 14, 18, 18, 18, 18, 18, 18, 20, 24, 28) sts remain. Cap measures same as for Back armholes. Work 1 WS row even. BO all sts.

## FINISHING

Block pieces as desired. Sew in Sleeves. Sew side and Sleeve seams. Carefully sew side edges of Pocket Facing to Front. Using dpns, work Applied I-cord (see page 135) along shaped edge of each Pocket Facing.

### COWL

With RS facing, using circular needle and 1 strand each of A and B held together, and beginning at right shoulder, pick up and knit approximately 1 st in each BO st, and 3 sts for every 4 rows along diagonal edges. You will pick up approximately 138 (138, 144, 150, 162, 162, 174, 174, 180, 186, 204, 216) stitches. *Note: Exact st count is not essential, but be sure to end with a multiple of 6 sts for ribbing to work out evenly.* Join for working in the rnd; pm for beginning of rnd. Next Rnd: *K3, p3; repeat from * to end. Work even for 6½" (16.5 cm). BO all sts in pattern.

Chart legend

| | |
|---|---|
| ☐ | Knit on RS, purl on WS. |
| • | Purl on RS, knit on WS. |
| ⅄ | M1L |
| ⅄ | M1P |
| ⟍ | 2/1 LPC |
| ⟋ | 2/1 RPC |
| ⟍ | 2/2 LC |
| ⟋ | 2/2 RC |
| ⟍ | 3/3 RC |

## Cable Pattern

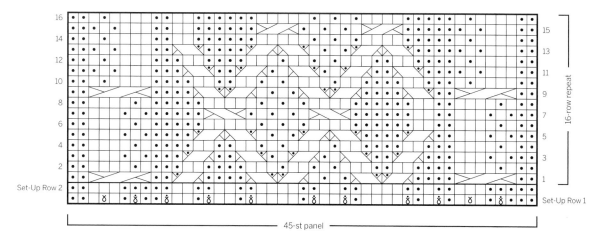

45-st panel

16-row repeat

Set-Up Row 2
Set-Up Row 1

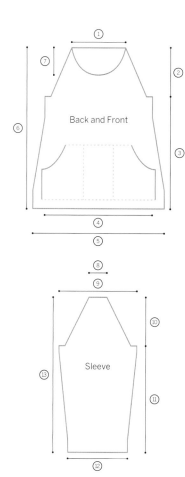

Back and Front

Sleeve

1   8 (8½, 8¾, 8¾, 9½, 10, 10¾, 11¼, 11½, 12, 12¾, 13¼)"
    20.5 (21.5, 22, 22, 24, 25.5, 27.5, 28.5, 29, 30.5, 32.5, 33.5) cm

2   7¼ (7½, 7¾, 8, 8½, 8½, 9¾, 10, 10, 10½, 11¼, 11¼)"
    18.5 (19, 19.5, 20.5, 21.5, 21.5, 25, 25.5, 25.5, 26.5, 28.5, 28.5) cm

3   18 (18½, 18½, 18½, 19, 19, 19, 19, 19½, 19½, 19½, 19½)"
    45.5 (47, 47, 47, 48.5, 48.5, 48.5, 48.5, 49.5, 49.5, 49.5, 49.5) cm

4   16 (17¼, 18, 19¼, 20, 21¼, 22, 24, 26, 28, 30, 32)"
    40.5 (44, 45.5, 49, 51, 54, 56, 61, 66, 71, 76, 81.5) cm

5   19½ (20¾, 22, 22, 23¼, 24½, 25½, 28, 29¼, 31½, 34, 35¼)"
    49.5 (52.5, 56, 56, 59, 62, 65, 71, 74.5, 80, 86.5, 89.5) cm

6   25¼ (26, 26¼, 26½, 27½, 27½, 28¾, 29, 29½, 30, 30¾, 30¾)"
    64 (66, 66.5, 67.5, 70, 70, 73, 73.5, 75, 76, 78, 78) cm

7   4¾ (4¾, 4½, 4½, 4½, 4½, 4½, 4½, 4½, 4½, 4¾, 4¾)"
    12 (12, 11.5, 11.5, 11.5, 11.5, 11.5, 11.5, 11.5, 11.5, 12, 12) cm

8   2¾ (2¾, 2¾, 3½, 3½, 3½, 3½, 3½, 3½, 4, 4¾, 5½)"
    7 (7, 7, 9, 9, 9, 9, 9, 9, 10, 12, 14) cm

9   11¼ (11½, 12, 12¾, 13½, 14½, 15½, 17¼, 19¼, 21¼, 23¼, 25¼)"
    28.5 (29, 30.5, 32.5, 34.5, 37, 39.5, 44, 49, 54, 59, 64) cm

10  7¼ (7½, 7¾, 8, 8½, 8½, 9¾, 10, 10, 10½, 11¼, 11¼)"
    18.5 (19, 19.5, 20.5, 21.5, 21.5, 25, 25.5, 25.5, 26.5, 28.5, 28.5) cm

11  11½ (11½, 11½, 12, 12, 12, 12½, 12½, 12½, 12, 12, 11½)"
    29 (29, 29, 30.5, 30.5, 30.5, 32, 32, 32, 30.5, 30.5, 29) cm

12  10 (10, 10, 10, 10, 10, 11¼, 11¼, 12½, 14¾, 16, 17¼)"
    25.5 (25.5, 25.5, 25.5, 25.5, 25.5, 28.5, 28.5, 32, 37.5, 40.5, 44) cm

13  18¾ (19, 19¼, 20, 20½, 20½, 22¼, 22½, 22½, 22½, 23¼, 22¾)"
    47.5 (48.5, 49, 51, 52, 52, 56.5, 57, 57, 57, 59, 58) cm

# Jump Shot Hoodie

Is there anything more comfortable, familiar, and throw-it-on-all-the-time than a hoodie? This one features a zipper opening, kicky ribbed details, and simple I-cord edgings. I've worked it up in a soft, hardwearing heathered wool and a more body-conscious fit, but it would look equally great worn oversize and cozy. The sleeve and body ribbing continues into the raglan shaping, highlighting this construction feature. (Variation idea: Add kangaroo patch pockets to the fronts!)

Jump Shot is worked in pieces from the bottom up, and then seamed for stability. The hood is picked up and added from the neckline; it is worked flat until the top, at which point the stitches are folded in half and joined using a 3-needle bind-off (see Special Techniques, page 188). After the hood is complete, I-cord is used to make facings for a zipper. For other closure options, see pages 140–142.

## FINISHED MEASUREMENTS

30 (31¾, 34¼, 36, 37½, 40¼, 41¾, 44, 47¾, 52, 56¼, 60)" [76 (80.5, 87, 91.5, 95.5, 102, 106, 112, 121.5, 132, 143, 152.5) cm] chest, zipped

*Note: Sweater is intended to be worn with 3–4" (7.5–10 cm) ease in the bust; shown in size 36" (91.5 cm).*

## YARN

Blue Sky Fibers Woolstok [100% fine highland wool; 370 yards (338 meters) / 150 grams]: 4 (4, 5, 5, 5, 6, 6, 6, 7, 7, 8) hanks #1302 Gravel Road

## NEEDLES

One pair straight needles, one 24" (60 cm) long or longer circular needle (for Hood), and one pair of double-pointed needles (for Applied I-cord), size US 6 (4 mm)

Change needle size if necessary to obtain correct gauge.

## NOTIONS

Stitch markers, separating zipper approximately 22 (22, 24, 24, 24, 26, 26, 26, 26, 28, 28, 28)" [56 (56, 61, 61, 61, 66, 66, 66, 66, 71, 71, 71) cm] long

## GAUGE

22 sts and 32 rows = 4" (10 cm) in St st

## NOTES

If your size gives the number 0 for a particular instruction, skip that instruction and proceed to the next instruction.

Unless otherwise specified, raglan decreases should be worked to match the slant of the edge being shaped, as follows: For left-slanting edges: [K1, p1] twice, ssk, knit to end; for right-slanting edges: knit to last 6 sts, k2tog, [p1, k1] twice. Increases should also be worked to match the slant of the edge being shaped, as follows: For right-slanting edges: On RS rows, k1, M1R, knit to end on; WS rows, p1, M1PR, purl to end. For left-slanting edges: On RS rows, knit to last st, M1L, k1; on WS rows, p1, M1PL, purl to end.

## BACK

CO 83 (89, 95, 99, 105, 111, 117, 121, 133, 143, 155, 165) sts.
Begin 1x1 Rib Flat; work even until piece measures 2½" (6.5 cm), ending with a WS row.
**NEXT ROW (RS):** Work in rib as established for 6 sts, pm, knit to last 6 sts, pm, work in rib as established to end.
Continuing to work in rib on first and last 6 sts, and in St st between markers, work even until piece measures 17 (17, 17½, 17½, 18, 18, 18, 18½, 18½, 18½, 18½, 19)" [43 (43, 44.5,

44.5, 45.5, 45.5, 45.5, 47, 47, 47, 47, 48.5) cm] from the beginning, ending with a WS row.

### SHAPE RAGLAN ARMHOLES

BO 7 sts at the beginning of the next 2 rows (removing markers). Decrease 1 st each side every RS row 2 (2, 4, 4, 6, 7, 7, 7, 11, 14, 17, 20) times, then every other RS row 12 (12, 11, 12, 11, 11, 12, 13, 9, 7, 5, 3) times, then every RS row 1 (2, 3, 3, 5, 6, 6, 6, 10, 13, 16, 19) time(s)—39 (43, 45, 47, 47, 49, 53, 55, 59, 61, 65, 67) sts remain. Armholes measure 7 (7¼, 7½, 8, 8½, 9, 9½, 10, 10, 10½, 11, 11½)" [18 (18.5, 19, 20.5, 21.5, 23, 24, 25.5, 25.5, 26.5, 28, 29) cm]. Work 1 WS row even. BO all sts in pattern.

## LEFT AND RIGHT FRONTS

CO 41 (43, 47, 49, 51, 55, 57, 61, 65, 71, 77, 83) sts.
Begin 1x1 Rib Flat; work even until piece measures 2½" (6.5 cm), ending with a WS row.

### LEFT FRONT:

**NEXT ROW (RS):** Work in rib as established for 6 sts, pm, knit to end.

### RIGHT FRONT:

**NEXT ROW (RS):** Knit to last 6 sts, pm, work in rib as established to end.

### BOTH FRONTS:

Continuing to work in rib on 6 sts at side edge, and in St st on remaining sts, work even until piece measures 17 (17, 17½, 17½, 18, 18, 18, 18½, 18½, 18½, 18½, 19)" [43 (43, 44.5, 44.5, 45.5, 45.5, 45.5, 47, 47, 47, 47, 48.5) cm] from the beginning, ending at the armhole edge.

### SHAPE RAGLAN ARMHOLE AND NECK

*Note: Armhole and neck are shaped at the same time; please read entire section through before beginning.*
BO 7 sts at armhole edge once (removing marker). Decrease 1 st at armhole edge every RS row 2 (2, 4, 4, 6, 7, 7, 7, 11, 14, 17, 20) times, then every other RS row 12 (12, 11, 12, 11, 11, 12, 13, 9, 7, 5, 3) times, then every RS row 1 (2, 3, 3, 5, 6, 6, 6, 10, 13, 16, 19) time(s).

### LEFT FRONT:

AT THE SAME TIME, when you have completed 35 (37, 39, 43, 47, 51, 55, 59, 63, 67, 71) rows from the beginning of armhole shaping, shape neck as follows:

**NEXT ROW (WS):** Continuing to work armhole shaping as established, BO 7 (8, 10, 11, 10, 12, 13, 16, 16, 18, 20, 22) sts, work to end.

### RIGHT FRONT:

AT THE SAME TIME, when you have completed 34 (36, 38, 42, 46, 50, 54, 58, 58, 62, 66, 70) rows from the beginning of armhole shaping, shape neck as follows:

**NEXT ROW (RS):** Continuing to work armhole shaping as established, BO 7 (8, 10, 11, 10, 12, 13, 16, 16, 18, 20, 22) sts, work to end.

### BOTH FRONTS:

Continuing to work armhole shaping as established, decrease 1 st at neck edge every RS row 4 times, then every other RS row 3 times, as follows: On Left Front, work to last 2 sts, k2tog; on Right Front, ssk, work to end—5 sts remain when all shaping is complete. Armhole measures same as for Back. Work 1 WS row even. BO all sts in pattern.

## SLEEVES

CO 45 (45, 45, 47, 47, 47, 51, 51, 51, 53, 53, 53) sts.
Begin 1x1 Rib Flat; work even until piece measures 3" (7.5 cm), ending with a WS row.
**NEXT ROW (RS):** K19 (19, 19, 19, 19, 19, 21, 21, 21, 23, 23, 23), pm, work in rib as established for 7 (7, 7, 9, 9, 9, 9, 9, 9, 7, 7, 7) sts, pm, knit to end.
Work 3 rows even, working sts between markers in rib as established, and remaining sts in St st.

### SHAPE SLEEVE

Increase 1 st each side this row, then every 15 (13, 10, 11, 9, 8, 8, 6, 5, 4, 3, 2) rows 6 (7, 9, 9, 11, 13, 13, 17, 21, 25, 31, 36) times—59 (61, 65, 67, 71, 75, 79, 87, 95, 105, 117, 127) sts.
Work even until piece measures 18 (18, 18, 18½, 18½, 18½, 18½, 18½, 18½, 18, 18, 17½)" [45.5 (45.5, 45.5, 47, 47, 47, 47, 47, 47, 45.5, 45.5, 44.5) cm] from the beginning, ending with a WS row.

### SHAPE RAGLAN CAP

BO 7 sts at the beginning of the next 2 rows. Decrease 1 st each side every RS row 2 (2, 4, 4, 6, 7, 7, 7, 11, 14, 17, 20) times, then every other RS row 12 (13, 12, 13, 13, 13, 14, 12, 9, 6, 2, 0) times, then every RS row 1 (0, 1, 1, 2, 2, 8, 10, 15, 22, 25) time(s)—15 (17, 17, 17, 17, 17, 19, 19, 21, 21, 21, 23) sts remain. Cap measures same as for Back armholes. Work 1 WS row even. BO all sts.

# FINISHING

Block pieces as desired. Sew in Sleeves. Sew side and Sleeve seams.

## HOOD

With RS facing, using circular needle and beginning at Right Front neck edge, pick up and knit approximately 1 st in each BO st and 3 sts for every 4 rows along diagonal edges, ending with an even number of sts. Begin St st; work even until piece measures 13" (33 cm) from pick-up row. Place marker at center of sts.

## SHAPE HOOD

Decrease 2 sts every RS row 5 times, as follows: Knit to 3 sts before marker, ssk, k1, sm, k1, k2tog, knit to end. Purl 1 WS row. Divide sts onto 2 needles and join halves using 3-Needle BO (see Special Techniques, page 188). (For more information on other hood options, see page 145.)

## ZIPPER FACING

With RS facing, using circular needle and beginning at lower Right Front edge, pick up and knit 4 sts for every 5 rows around entire neck opening, including along hood edge. Work a 4-st Applied I-cord around entire opening (see Applied I-cord, page 135).

Sew in zipper.

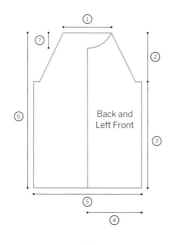

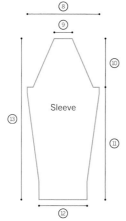

1   7 (7¾, 8¼, 8½, 8½, 9, 9¾, 10, 10¾, 11, 11¾, 12¼)"
    18 (19.5, 21, 21.5, 21.5, 23, 25, 25.5, 27.5, 28, 30, 31) cm

2   7 (7¼, 7½, 8, 8½, 9, 9½, 10, 10, 10½, 11, 11½)"
    18 (18.5, 19, 20.5, 21.5, 23, 24, 25.5, 25.5, 26.5, 28, 29) cm

3   17 (17, 17½, 17½, 18, 18, 18, 18½, 18½, 18½, 18½, 19)"
    43 (43, 44.5, 44.5, 45.5, 45.5, 45.5, 47, 47, 47, 47, 48.5) cm

4   7½ (7¾, 8½, 9, 9¼, 10, 10¼, 11, 11¾, 13, 14, 15)"
    19 (19.5, 21.5, 23, 23.5, 25.5, 26, 28, 30, 33, 35.5, 38) cm

5   15 (16¼, 17¼, 18, 19, 20¼, 21¼, 22, 24¼, 26, 28¼, 30)"
    38 (41.5, 44, 45.5, 48.5, 51.5, 54, 56, 61.5, 66, 72, 76) cm

6   24 (24¼, 25, 25½, 26½, 27, 27½, 28½, 28½, 29, 29½, 30½)"
    61 (61.5, 63.5, 65, 67.5, 68.5, 70, 72.5, 72.5, 73.5, 75, 77.5) cm

7   2½"
    6.5 cm

8   10¾ (11, 11¾, 12¼, 13, 13¾, 14¼, 15¾, 17¼, 19, 21¼, 23)"
    27.5 (28, 30, 31, 33, 35, 36, 40, 44, 48.5, 54, 58.5) cm

9   2¾ (3, 3, 3, 3, 3, 3½, 3½, 3¾, 3¾, 3¾, 4¼)"
    7 (7.5, 7.5, 7.5, 7.5, 7.5, 9, 9, 9.5, 9.5, 9.5, 11) cm

10  7 (7¼, 7½, 8, 8½, 9, 9½, 10, 10, 10½, 11, 11½)"
    18 (18.5, 19, 20.5, 21.5, 23, 24, 25.5, 25.5, 26.5, 28, 29) cm

11  18 (18, 18, 18½, 18½, 18½, 18½, 18½, 18½, 18, 18, 17½)"
    45.5 (45.5, 45.5, 47, 47, 47, 47, 47, 47, 45.5, 45.5, 44.5) cm

12  8¼ (8¼, 8¼, 8½, 8½, 8½, 9¼, 9¼, 9¼, 9¾, 9¾, 9¾)"
    21 (21, 21, 21.5, 21.5, 21.5, 23.5, 23.5, 23.5, 25, 25, 25) cm

13  25 (25¼, 25½, 26½, 27, 27½, 28, 28½, 28½, 28½, 29, 29)"
    63.5 (64, 65, 67.5, 68.5, 70, 71, 72.5, 72.5, 72.5, 73.5, 73.5) cm

# Quiet Moment Cardigan

A bit of silence with my morning coffee is a ritual around these parts. For most of the year, you'll find me outside as I sip. Since I live in New England, that means sweaters! I designed this cardi with an asymmetric opening, long, belled sleeves, and a collar that can be worn either open or buttoned up into a loose cowl. I've added a wee bit of dart-style waist shaping to keep things from being too boxy, but I think this would also look great longer and straight, or with A-line shaping that echoes the sleeves. Quiet Moment is worked in 3 pieces (body, 2 sleeves) bottom up to the yoke shaping, and then in one piece to the neck. Pick up stitches for the button band firmly to add structure to the cardigan front.

## FINISHED MEASUREMENTS

34½ (37½, 38¾, 41½, 43¼, 44¾, 47½, 49, 53½, 57¾, 60¾, 65)" [87.5 (95.5, 98.5, 106, 110, 113.5, 120.5, 124.5, 136, 146.5, 154.5, 165) cm] chest, buttoned

*Note: Sweater is intended to be worn with 2–4" (5–10 cm) positive ease in the bust; shown in sample size 38¾" (98.5 cm).*

## YARN

The Fibre Company Arranmore Light [80% merino wool / 10% cashmere / 10% silk; 328 yards (300 meters) / 100 grams]: 4 (5, 5, 5, 6, 6, 6, 7, 7, 8, 8, 9) hanks River Esque

## NEEDLES

One 40" (100 cm) long circular needle and one set of double-pointed needles, size US 6 (4 mm)

Change needle size if necessary to obtain correct gauge.

## NOTIONS

Stitch markers, removable stitch markers, stitch holders or waste yarn, 13 (13, 13, 13, 13, 13, 14, 14, 14, 14, 14, 15) ¾-inch (19-mm) buttons

## GAUGE

22 sts and 32 rows = 4" (10 cm) in St st

## BODY

Using circular needle, CO 180 (196, 204, 220, 228, 236, 252, 260, 284, 308, 324, 348) sts.

**NEXT ROW (RS):** K30 (32, 34, 36, 38, 40, 42, 44, 48, 52, 54, 58), place marker for end of Right Front, k93 (101, 105, 113, 117, 121, 129, 133, 145, 157, 165, 177), pm for beginning of Left Front, knit to end.

**ROW 1:** P1, *p2, k2; repeat from * to last 3 sts, p3.

**ROW 2:** Knit.

Continuing in Broken Rib as established, work even until piece measures 2" (5 cm), ending with a WS row.

Change to St st; work even until piece measures 2¾" (7 cm) from the beginning, ending with a RS row.

**NEXT ROW (WS):** Purl to marker, sm, p31 (33, 35, 37, 39, 40, 43, 44, 48, 52, 55, 59) sts, pm for shaping, p31 (35, 35, 39, 39, 41, 43, 45, 49, 53, 55, 59) sts, pm for shaping, purl to marker, sm, purl to end.

## SHAPE WAIST

Decrease 2 sts this row, then every 6 rows 5 times, as follows: Knit to 2 sts before first shaping marker, ssk, sm, knit to next shaping marker, sm, k2tog, knit to end—168 (184, 192, 208, 216, 224, 240, 248, 272, 296, 312, 336) sts remain; 81 (89, 93, 101, 105, 109, 117, 121, 133, 145, 153, 165) sts remain for Back. Work even until piece measures 8" (20.5 cm) from the beginning, ending with a WS row.

Increase 2 sts this row, then 8 rows 5 times, as follows: Knit to first shaping marker, M1R, sm, knit to next shaping marker, sm, M1L, knit to end—180 (196, 204, 220, 228, 236, 252, 260, 284, 308, 324, 348) sts.

Work even until piece measures 17" (43 cm) from the beginning, removing shaping markers on first row (leaving side markers in place).

**DIVIDING ROW (RS):** [Knit to 7 (7, 9, 9, 9, 10, 10, 10, 11, 11, 13, 13) sts before marker, BO 14 (14, 18, 18, 18, 20, 20, 20, 22, 22, 26, 26) sts (removing marker)] twice, knit to end—23 (25, 25, 27, 29, 30, 32, 34, 37, 41, 41, 45) sts remain for Right Front, 79 (87, 87, 95, 99, 101, 109, 113, 123, 135, 139, 151) sts remain for Back, and 50 (56, 56, 62, 64, 65, 71, 73, 80, 88, 92, 100) sts remain for Left Front. Break yarn transfer sts to holders or waste yarn.

## SLEEVES

Using dpns, CO 68 (68, 76, 80, 84, 92, 96, 100, 108, 112, 120, 128) sts. Join for working in the rnd, being careful not to twist sts; pm for beginning of rnd.

**RND 1:** Knit.

**RND 2:** *P2, k2; repeat from * to end.

Continuing in Broken Rib as established, work even until piece measures 2" (5 cm).

Change to St st; work 2 rnds even.

### SHAPE SLEEVE

Decrease 2 sts this rnd, then every 12 rnds 1 (0, 2, 3, 2, 3, 3, 2, 3, 2, 4, 2) time(s), as follows: K2, ssk, knit to last 4 sts, k2tog, k2—64 (66, 70, 72, 78, 84, 88, 94, 100, 106, 110, 122) sts remain.

Work even until piece measures 18 (18, 18, 18½, 18½, 19, 19, 19, 18½, 18½, 18, 18)" [45.5 (45.5, 45.5, 47, 47, 48.5, 48.5, 48.5, 47, 47, 45.5, 45.5) cm] from the beginning.

**NEXT RND:** BO 7 (7, 9, 9, 9, 10, 10, 10, 11, 11, 13, 13) sts, knit to last 7 (7, 9, 9, 9, 10, 10, 10, 11, 11, 13, 13) sts, BO to end—50 (52, 52, 54, 60, 64, 68, 74, 78, 84, 84, 96) sts remain. Break yarn; transfer sts to holder or waste yarn.

## YOKE

**JOINING ROW (RS):** Using circular needle, knit across 23 (25, 25, 27, 29, 30, 32, 34, 37, 41, 41, 45) Right Front sts, pm, 50 (52, 52, 54, 60, 64, 68, 74, 78, 84, 84, 96) Right Sleeve sts, pm, 79 (87, 87, 95, 99, 101, 109, 113, 123, 135, 139, 151) Back sts, pm, 50 (52, 52, 54, 60, 64, 68, 74, 78, 84, 84, 96) Left Sleeve sts, pm, then 50 (56, 56, 62, 64, 65, 71, 73, 80, 88, 92, 100) Left Front sts—252 (272, 272, 292, 312, 324, 348, 368, 396, 432, 440, 488) sts.

*SIZES 34½ (−, −, −, 43¼, 44¾, 47½, −, 53½, 57¾, −, −)" [87.5 (−, −, −, 110, 113.5, 120.5, −, 136, 146.5, −, −) CM] ONLY:*

Work 1 row even.

*SIZES − (37½, 38¾, −, −, −, −, 49, −, −, 60¾, 65)" [− (95.5, 98.5, −, −, −, −, 124.5, −, −, 154.5, 165) CM] ONLY:*

**INCREASE ROW (WS):** [Purl to marker, M1P, sm, purl to marker, sm, M1P] twice, purl to end—4 sts increased.

*SIZE 41¾" (106 CM) ONLY:*

**DECREASE ROW (WS):** [Purl to 2 sts before marker, p2tog, sm, purl to marker, sm, p2tog] twice, purl to end—4 sts decreased.

*ALL SIZES:*

252 (276, 276, 288, 312, 324, 348, 372, 396, 432, 444, 492) sts.

Work 23 (25, 27, 29, 31, 31, 33, 35, 35, 37, 39, 41) rows even, ending with a RS row.

**NEXT ROW (WS):** *P12, pm; repeat from * to last 12 sts, purl to end.

### SHAPE YOKE

**YOKE DECREASE ROW (RS):** *K2tog, knit to marker, sm; repeat from * to last marker, sm, k2tog, knit to end—21 (23, 23, 24, 26, 27, 29, 31, 33, 36, 37, 41) sts decreased.

Work 5 (7, 7, 7, 7, 7, 9, 9, 9, 9, 11) rows even.

Repeat Yoke Decrease Row.

Work 5 (5, 5, 5, 3, 3, 3, 3, 5, 5, 5) rows even.

Repeat Yoke Decrease Row.

*SIZES − (−, −, −, 43¼, 44¾, 47½, 49, 53½, 57¾, 60¾, 65)" [− (−, −, −, 110, 113.5, 120.5, 124.5, 136, 146.5, 154.5, 165) CM] ONLY:*

Work 3 rows even.

Repeat Yoke Decrease Row.

*ALL SIZES:*

189 (207, 207, 216, 208, 216, 232, 248, 264, 288, 296, 328) sts remain.

Work 3 (3, 5, 5, 5, 5, 5, 5, 5, 5, 5) rows even.

Repeat Yoke Decrease Row.

Work 3 (3, 3, 3, 3, 5, 5, 5, 5, 3, 5, 5) rows even.

Repeat Yoke Decrease Row.

Work 3 (3, 3, 3, 3, 3, 3, 5, 3, 3, 3) rows even.

Repeat Yoke Decrease Row.

*SIZES − (−, −, −, −, −, −, −, −, 57¾, 60¾, 65)" [− (−, −, −, −, −, −, −, −, 146.5, 154.5, 165) CM] ONLY:*

Work 3 rows even.

Repeat Yoke Decrease Row.

*ALL SIZES:*

126 (138, 138, 144, 130, 135, 145, 155, 165, 144, 148, 164) sts remain.

**NEXT ROW (RS):** Decrease 14 (18, 18, 16, 2, 7, 17, 27, 29, 8, 12, 28) sts evenly spaced to end—112 (120, 120, 128, 128, 128, 128, 128, 136, 136, 136, 136) sts remain. Place removable markers approximately three-quarters of the way through each Sleeve, placing markers closer to the Front than the Back. *Note: The position of the markers doesn't have to be exact, but they should be in the same relative position on either side.*

## SHAPE BACK NECK

*Note: Back neck is shaped using short rows (see Special Techniques, page 188).*

**SHORT ROW 1 (RS):** Knit to 1 st before Left Sleeve marker, w&t.

**SHORT ROW 2:** Purl to 1 st before Right Sleeve marker, w&t.

**SHORT ROW 3:** Knit to 6 sts before wrapped st from previous RS row, w&t.

**SHORT ROW 4:** Purl to 6 sts before wrapped st from previous WS row, w&t.

**SHORT ROWS 5–8:** Repeat Short Rows 3 and 4 twice.

Knit to end, working wraps together with wrapped sts as you come to them.

## COLLAR

Work even for 4" (10 cm), working remaining wraps together with wrapped sts as you come to them on first row, and ending with a WS row.

**ROW 1 (RS):** Knit.

**ROW 2:** P1, *p2, k2; repeat from * to last 3 sts, p3.

Work in Broken Rib as established for 1" (2.5 cm). BO all sts in pattern.

## FINISHING

Block piece as desired. Sew underarm seams.

### BUTTON BAND

With RS facing, beginning at top of Left Collar, pick up and knit approximately 3 sts for every 4 rows along Left Front edge. You will have approximately 158 (158, 162, 162, 166, 166, 170, 170, 174, 174, 178, 182) sts. *Note: Exact st count is not essential, but be sure to end with a multiple of 4 sts + 2 for ribbing to work out evenly.*

**ROW 1 (WS):** P2, *k2, p2; repeat from * to end.

**ROW 2:** Knit.

Repeat Rows 1 and 2 six times. BO all sts in pattern.

### BUTTONHOLE BAND

With RS facing, beginning at lower Right Front edge, pick up and knit the same number of sts as for Button Band.

Work as for Button Band for 5 rows.

**BUTTONHOLE ROW (RS):** Work 7 (7, 9, 9, 11, 11, 7, 7, 9, 9, 11, 7) sts, [BO 2 sts, work 10 sts] 13 (13, 13, 13, 13, 13, 14, 14, 14, 14, 14, 15) times, work to end.

Work 8 rows even, CO 2 sts over BO sts on first row. BO all sts in pattern.

Sew buttons opposite buttonholes.

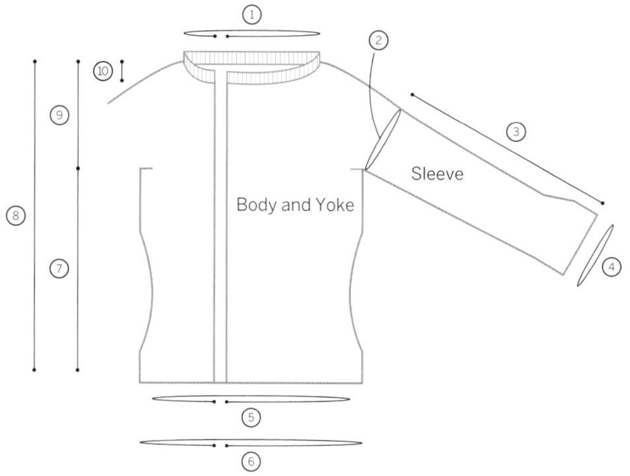

1   20¼ (21¾, 21¾, 23¼, 23¼, 23¼, 23¼, 23¼, 24¾, 24¾, 24¾, 24¾)"
    51.5 (55, 55, 59, 59, 59, 59, 59, 63, 63, 63, 63) cm

2   11¾ (12, 12¾, 13, 14¼, 15¼, 16, 17, 18¼, 19¼, 20, 22¼)"
    30 (30.5, 32.5, 33, 36, 38.5, 40.5, 43, 46.5, 49, 51, 56.5) cm

3   18 (18, 18, 18½, 18½, 19, 19, 19, 18½, 18½, 18, 18)"
    45.5 (45.5, 45.5, 47, 47, 48.5, 48.5, 48.5, 47, 47, 45.5, 45.5) cm

4   12¼ (12¼, 13¾, 14½, 15¼, 16¾, 17½, 18¼, 19¾, 20¼, 21¾, 23¼)"
    31 (31, 35, 37, 38.5, 42.5, 44.5, 46.5, 50, 51.5, 55, 59) cm

5   30½ (33½, 35, 37¾, 39¼, 40¾, 43¾, 45, 49½, 53¾, 56¾, 61)"
    77.5 (85, 89, 96, 99.5, 103.5, 111, 114.5, 125.5, 136.5, 144, 155) cm

6   32¾ (35¾, 37, 40, 41½, 43, 45¾, 47¼, 51¾, 56, 59, 63¼)"
    83 (91, 94, 101.5, 105.5, 109, 116, 120, 131.5, 142, 150, 160.5) cm

7   17"
    43 cm

8   24¾ (25¼, 25¾, 26, 26½, 26¾, 27, 27½, 27¾, 28½, 29, 29½)"
    63 (64, 65.5, 66, 67.5, 68, 68.5, 70, 70.5, 72.5, 73.5, 75) cm

9   7¾ (8¼, 8¾, 9, 9½, 9¾, 10, 10½, 10¾, 11½, 12, 12½)"
    19.5 (21, 22, 23, 24, 25, 25.5, 26.5, 27.5, 29, 30.5, 32) cm

10  1"
    2.5 cm

# Constellation Tunic

I love a traditional colorwork pullover. But for this sweater, worked up in Brooklyn Tweed's stunning colors, I wanted something a bit more modern. I played with the silhouette first, opting for a wide turtleneck, snug little elbow sleeves, and an A-line tunic length. I sketched up some space-inspired motifs. If this geometric patterning isn't quite your style, no fear! I kept the stitch pattern repeats at a very mix-and-match-friendly 12 stitches, so that you can play around to your heart's content.

Constellation is worked from the bottom up, with elbow sleeves and a short cowl. It's designed to let you easily swap out the color pattern for one of your own devising.

## FINISHED MEASUREMENTS

34¼ (36¼, 37¾, 40, 42¼, 44¼, 45¾, 48, 52¼, 56, 60¼, 64)"
[87 (92, 96, 101.5, 107.5, 112.5, 116, 122, 132.5, 142, 153, 162.5) cm] chest

*Note: Sweater is intended to be worn with 2–4" (5–10 cm) positive ease in the bust; shown in size 36¼" (92 cm).*

## YARN

Brooklyn Tweed Arbor [100% American Targhee Wool; 145 yards (132 meters) / 50 grams]: 11 (12, 13, 14, 14, 15, 16, 17, 19, 20, 22, 24) hanks Gale (MC), 2 hanks each Humpback (A) and Vintner (B), and 1 hank each Hammock (C), Crumb (D), and Rainer (E)

## NEEDLES

One 24" (60 cm) long circular needle and one set of double-pointed needles, size US 6 (4 mm)

One 24" (60 cm) long circular needle, size US 7 (4.5 mm) (for Cowl)

One 24" (60 cm) long circular needle, size US 8 (5 mm) (for Cowl)

Change needle size if necessary to obtain correct gauge.

## NOTIONS

Stitch markers, removable stitch markers, stitch holders or waste yarn

## GAUGE

22 sts and 32 rnds = 4" (10 cm) in St st, using smallest needle

## BODY

Using circular needle and MC, CO 228 (240, 252, 264, 276, 288, 300, 312, 336, 348, 372, 396) sts. Join for working in the rnd, being careful not to twist sts; pm for beginning of rnd and after 114 (120, 126, 132, 138, 144, 150, 156, 168, 174, 186, 198) sts for side.

Begin 1x1 Rib in the Rnd; work even until piece measures 1½" (4 cm).

Change to St st; knit 2 rnds.

Work Rnds 1–9 of Body Chart; break A, B, and C, and continue with MC only.

Knit 1 rnd.

### SHAPE BODY

Continuing in St st, decrease 4 sts this rnd, then every 12 (12, 11, 11, 11, 11, 11, 11, 13, 13, 12) rnds 9 (9, 10, 10, 10, 10, 11, 11, 11, 9, 9, 10) times, as follows: [K2, k2tog, knit to 4 sts before marker, ssk, k2, sm] twice—188 (200, 208, 220, 232, 244, 252, 264, 288, 308, 332, 352) sts remain.

Work even until piece measures 19 (19, 20, 20, 20, 20, 20½, 20½, 20½, 20½, 21, 21)" [48.5 (48.5, 51, 51, 51, 51, 52, 52, 52, 52, 53.5, 53.5) cm] from the beginning.

**DIVIDING RND:** BO 7 (7, 9, 9, 9, 10, 10, 10, 11, 11, 13, 13) sts, knit to 7 (7, 9, 9, 9, 10, 10, 10, 11, 11, 13, 13) sts before marker, BO 14 (14, 18, 18, 18, 20, 20, 20, 22, 22, 26, 26) sts (removing marker), knit to last 7 (7, 9, 9, 9, 10, 10, 10, 11, 11, 13, 13) sts, BO to end—80 (86, 86, 92, 98, 102, 106, 112, 122, 132, 140, 150) sts remain for Front and Back. Break yarn and transfer sts to holder or waste yarn.

## SLEEVES

Using dpns and MC, CO 60 (60, 66, 66, 72, 78, 84, 90, 96, 102, 102, 114) sts. Join for working in the rnd, being careful not to twist sts; pm for beginning of rnd.
Begin 1x1 Rib in the Rnd; work even until piece measures ½" (1.5 cm).
Change to St st; knit 2 rnds.
Work Rnds 1–3 of Sleeve Chart; break A and B and continue with MC only.
Knit 1 rnd.

### SHAPE SLEEVE

Increase 2 sts this rnd, then every 14 (9, 16, 10, 10, 10, 18, 18, 18, 20, 10, 11) rnds 1 (2, 1, 2, 2, 2, 1, 1, 1, 1, 3, 3) time(s), as follows: K2, M1R, knit to last 2 sts, M1L, knit to end—64 (66, 70, 72, 78, 84, 88, 94, 100, 106, 110, 122) sts.
Work even until piece measures 5½ (5½, 6, 6, 6, 6, 6½, 6½, 6½, 7, 7, 7½)" [14 (14, 15, 15, 15, 15, 16.5, 16.5, 16.5, 18, 18, 19) cm] from the beginning.
**NEXT RND:** BO 7 (7, 9, 9, 9, 10, 10, 10, 11, 11, 13, 13) sts, knit to last 7 (7, 9, 9, 9, 10, 10, 10, 11, 11, 13, 13) sts, BO to end—50 (52, 52, 54, 60, 64, 68, 74, 78, 84, 84, 96) sts remain. Break yarn; transfer sts to holder or waste yarn.

## YOKE

**JOINING RND:** Using MC, knit across 40 (43, 43, 46, 49, 51, 53, 56, 61, 66, 70, 75) Back sts, pm for beginning of rnd at center Back, knit to end of Back, pm, knit across 50 (52, 52, 54, 60, 64, 68, 74, 78, 84, 84, 96) Left Sleeve sts, pm, knit across 80 (86, 86, 92, 98, 102, 106, 112, 122, 132, 140, 150) Front sts, pm, knit across 50 (52, 52, 54, 60, 64, 68, 74, 78, 84, 84, 96) Right Sleeve sts, pm, knit to beginning of rnd—260 (276, 276, 292, 316, 332, 348, 372, 400, 432, 448, 492) sts.

*SIZES 34¼ (–, –, –, –, 44¼, –, –, –, –, –, –)" [87 (–, –, –, –, 112.5, –, –, –, –, –, –) CM] ONLY:*

**INCREASE RND:** [Knit to marker, M1L, sm, knit to marker, sm, M1L] twice, knit to end—4 sts increased.

*SIZES – (36¼, 37¾, –, –, –, 45¾, 48, –, 56, –, 64)" [– (92, 96, –, –, –, 116, 122, –, 142, –, 162.5) CM] ONLY:*

Knit 1 rnd.

*SIZES – (–, –, 40, 42¼, –, –, –, 52¼, –, 60¼, –)" [– (–, –, 101.5, 107.5, –, –, –, 132.5, –, 153, –) CM] ONLY:*

**DECREASE RND:** [Knit to 2 sts before marker, k2tog, sm, knit to marker, sm, k2tog], knit to end—4 sts decreased.

*ALL SIZES:*

264 (276, 276, 288, 312, 336, 348, 372, 396, 432, 444, 492) sts. Remove all markers except beginning-of-rnd marker.
**NEXT RND:** *K12, pm; repeat from * to last 12 sts, knit to end—21 (22, 22, 23, 25, 27, 28, 30, 32, 35, 36, 40) additional markers placed.
Knit 0 (4, 4, 4, 4, 4, 4, 4, 4, 4, 4, 4) rnds.
Work Rnds 1–52 of Yoke Chart—132 (138, 138, 144, 156, 168, 174, 186, 198, 216, 222, 246) sts remain when chart is complete. Break A, B, C, D, and E and continue with MC only.

*SIZES – (–, –, –, –, 44¼, 45¾, 48, 52¼, 56, 60¼, 64)" [– (–, –, –, –, 112.5, 116, 122, 132.5, 142, 153, 162.5) CM] ONLY:*

Knit – (–, –, –, –, 8, 12, 16, 18, 11, 12, 13) rnds.
**DECREASE RND:** *K2tog, knit to marker, sm; repeat from * to end.

*SIZES – (–, –, –, –, –, –, –, –, 56, 60¼, 64)" [– (–, –, –, –, –, –, –, –, 142, 153, 162.5) CM] ONLY:*

Knit – (–, –, –, –, –, –, –, 10, 11, 12) rnds.
**DECREASE RND:** *K2tog, knit to marker, sm; repeat from * to end.

*ALL SIZES:*

132 (138, 138, 144, 156, 140, 145, 155, 165, 144, 148, 164) sts remain.
Knit 1 (1, 3, 5, 7, 1, 1, 1, 1, 1, 1, 1) rnd(s), removing all markers except beginning-of-rnd marker on first rnd.
**DECREASE RND:** K0 (2, 0, 4, 2, 2, 5, 2, 15, 0, 0, 2), *k2tog, k64 (15, 21, 12, 5, 21, 18, 7, 4, 34, 35, 7); repeat from * to end—130 (130, 132, 134, 134, 134, 138, 138, 140, 140, 144, 146) sts remain. Place removable markers between the Front and Left and Right Sleeves. *Note: The position of the markers doesn't have to be exact, but they should be in the same relative position on either side.*

### SHAPE BACK NECK

*Note: Back neck is shaped using short rows (see Special Techniques, page 188).*

**SHORT ROW 1 (RS):** Knit to 1 st before Left Sleeve marker, w&t.
**SHORT ROW 2 (WS):** Purl to 1 st before Right Sleeve marker, w&t.
**SHORT ROW 3:** Knit to 5 sts before wrapped st from previous RS row, w&t.
**SHORT ROW 4:** Purl to 5 sts before wrapped st from previous WS row, w&t.

**SHORT ROWS 5 AND 6:** Repeat Short Rows 3 and 4.

Knit 2 rnds, working wraps together with wrapped sts as you come to them.

Change to size 7 (4.5 mm) needle. Begin 1x1 Rib in the Rnd; work even until rib measures 3" (7.5 cm).

Change to size 8 (5 mm) needle. Work even until rib measures 7" (18 cm). BO all sts loosely in pattern.

## FINISHING

Block piece as desired. Sew underarm seams.

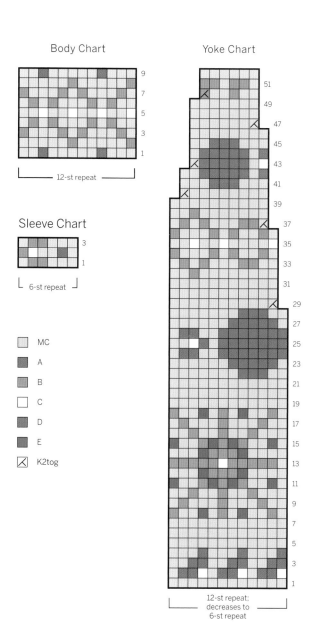

Body Chart

12-st repeat

Sleeve Chart

6-st repeat

MC
A
B
C
D
E
K2tog

Yoke Chart

12-st repeat;
decreases to
6-st repeat

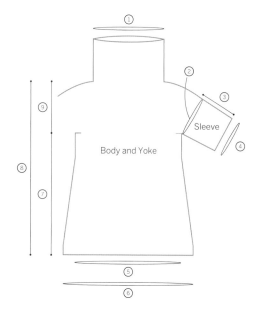

1   23¾ (23¾, 24, 24¼, 24¼, 24¼, 25, 25, 25½, 25½, 26¼, 26½)"
    60.5 (60.5, 61, 61.5, 61.5, 61.5, 63.5, 63.5, 65, 65, 66.5, 67.5) cm

2   11¾ (12, 12¾, 13, 14¼, 15¼, 16, 17, 18¼, 19¼, 20, 22¼)"
    30 (30.5, 32.5, 33, 36, 38.5, 40.5, 43, 46.5, 49, 51, 56.5) cm

3   5½ (5½, 6, 6, 6, 6, 6½, 6½, 6½, 7, 7, 7½)"
    14 (14, 15, 15, 15, 15, 16.5, 16.5, 16.5, 18, 18, 19) cm

4   11 (11, 12, 12, 13, 14¼, 15¼, 16¼, 17½, 18½, 18½, 20¾)"
    28 (28, 30.5, 30.5, 33, 36, 38.5, 41.5, 44.5, 47, 47, 52.5) cm

5   34¼ (36¼, 37¾, 40, 42¼, 44¼, 45¾, 48, 52¼, 56, 60¼, 64)"
    87 (92, 96, 101.5, 107.5, 112.5, 116, 122, 132.5, 142, 153, 162.5) cm

6   41½ (43¾, 45¾, 48, 50¼, 52¼, 54½, 56¾, 61, 63¼, 67¾, 72)"
    105.5 (111, 116, 122, 127.5, 132.5, 138.5, 144, 155, 160.5, 172, 183) cm

7   19 (19, 20, 20, 20, 20, 20½, 20½, 20½, 20½, 21, 21)"
    48.5 (48.5, 51, 51, 51, 51, 52, 52, 52, 52, 53.5, 53.5) cm

8   27½ (28, 29¼, 29½, 29¾, 30, 31, 31½, 31¾, 32¼, 33, 33¼)"
    70 (71, 74.5, 75, 75.5, 76, 78.5, 80, 80.5, 82, 84, 84.5) cm

9   8½ (9, 9¼, 9½, 9¾, 10, 10½, 11, 11¼, 11¾, 12, 12¼)"
    21.5 (23, 23.5, 24, 25, 25.5, 26.5, 28, 28.5, 30, 30.5, 31) cm

# Spring Rain Tee

The soft-as-a-breeze Merino Silk Sock from indigodragonfly has always made me think of a delicate little slip of a sweater, and when Kim sent me the most beautiful dusty pink, I started thinking of the first tulips of the season. I fiddled around with a little short-row overlap, and decided to use it both on the short sleeves and hem of this sweater. Spring Rain is worked from the bottom up with set-in sleeves. The sweater hems and sleeve cuffs are begun in two asymmetrical pieces, with thin Garter stitch trims and short rows to create the curves. After the curves are complete, the two pieces are knit together and each piece is worked in a single layer of fabric to the end.

**FINISHED MEASUREMENTS**
30½ (32, 34, 36½, 38½, 40, 42, 44½, 48, 52½, 56, 60½)" [77.5 (81.5, 86.5, 92.5, 98, 101.5, 106.5, 113, 122, 133.5, 142, 153.5) cm] chest

*Note: Sweater is intended to be worn with 1–2" (2.5–5 cm) ease in the bust; shown in size 36½" (92.5 cm).*

**YARN**
indigodragonfly Merino Silk 4-Ply Sock [50% superwash merino, 50% silk; 430 yards (393 meters) / 100 grams]: 3 (3, 3, 3, 3, 4, 4, 4, 5, 5, 6) hanks Sarcastic Unicorn

**NEEDLES**
One pair straight needles and one 24" (60 cm) long circular needle (for Neckband) size US 2 (2.75 mm)

Change needle size if necessary to obtain correct gauge.

**NOTIONS**
Stitch markers

**GAUGE**
30 sts and 38 rows = 4" (10 cm) in St st

**NOTES**
If your size gives the number 0 for a particular instruction, skip that instruction and proceed to the next instruction.

Unless otherwise specified, decreases should be worked to match the slant of the edge being shaped, as follows: For left-slanting edges: On RS rows, k1, k2tog, knit to end; on WS rows, p1, ssp, purl to end. For right-slanting edges: On RS rows, knit to last 3 sts, ssk, k1; on WS rows, purl to last 3 sts, p2tog, p1.

## BACK

### FIRST HEM PIECE
CO 114 (120, 128, 136, 144, 150, 158, 166, 180, 196, 210, 226) sts.
Begin Garter st; work even for ½" (1.5 cm), ending with a WS row.
Change to St st, beginning with a RS row; work 3 rows even.

### SHAPE PIECE
*Note: Piece is shaped using short rows (see Special Techniques, page 188).*
**SHORT ROW 1 (WS):** Purl to last 8 sts, w&t.
**SHORT ROW 2:** Knit to end.
**SHORT ROW 3:** Purl to 7 (7, 7, 8, 8, 9, 9, 10, 10, 11, 12, 13) sts before wrapped st from previous WS row, w&t.
**SHORT ROW 4:** Knit to end.
**SHORT ROWS 5–10:** Repeat Short Rows 3 and 4 three times.
Work 3 rows even across all sts, working wraps together with wrapped sts on first row. Leave sts on needle and set aside; do not break yarn.

### SECOND HEM PIECE
Using circular needle and second ball of yarn, CO 36 (36, 36, 40, 40, 44, 44, 48, 48, 52, 56, 60) sts.
Begin Garter st; work even for ½" (1.5 cm), ending with a WS row.

Change to St st, beginning with a RS row; work 4 rows even.

### SHAPE PIECE

**SHORT ROW 1 (RS):** Knit to last 7 (7, 7, 8, 8, 9, 9, 10, 10, 11, 12, 13) sts, w&t.

**SHORT ROW 2:** Purl to end.

**SHORT ROW 3:** Knit to 7 (7, 7, 8, 8, 9, 9, 10, 10, 11, 12, 13) sts before wrapped st from previous RS row, w&t.

**SHORT ROW 4:** Purl to end.

**SHORT ROWS 5–10:** Repeat Short Rows 3 and 4 three times. Work 2 rows even across all sts, working wraps together with wrapped sts on first row. Leave sts on needle; break yarn.

### JOIN HEM PIECES

**JOINING ROW (RS):** With RSs of pieces facing, holding second (narrower) piece behind first (wider) piece, *k2tog (1 st from first piece together with 1 st from second piece); repeat from * until all second piece sts have been worked, knit to end—114 (120, 128, 136, 144, 150, 158, 166, 180, 196, 210, 226) sts. Work even in St st until piece measures 3¼" (8.5 cm) from the beginning, ending with a WS row.

### SHAPE WAIST

**DECREASE ROW (RS):** Decrease 2 sts this row, then every 6 rows 5 times—102 (108, 116, 124, 132, 138, 146, 154, 168, 184, 198, 214) sts remain. Work even until piece measures 8" (20.5 cm) from the beginning, ending with a WS row.

### SHAPE BUST

Increase 2 sts this row, then every 8 rows 5 times, as follows: K1, M1L, knit to last st, M1R, k1—114 (120, 128, 136, 144, 150, 158, 166, 180, 196, 210, 226) sts. Work even until piece measures 16 (16, 16½, 16½, 17, 17, 17½, 17½, 17½, 17½, 17½, 17½)" [40.5 (40.5, 42, 42, 43, 43, 44.5, 44.5, 44.5, 44.5, 44.5, 44.5) cm] from the beginning, ending with a WS row.

### SHAPE ARMHOLES

BO 10 (10, 10, 12, 12, 12, 12, 12, 14, 14, 15, 19) sts at the beginning of the next 2 rows, then 0 (0, 4, 4, 4, 4, 4, 4, 6, 8, 10, 12) sts at the beginning of the following 2 rows. Decrease 1 st each side every RS row 3 (5, 4, 4, 6, 5, 6, 8, 10, 14, 16, 16) times—88 (90, 92, 96, 100, 108, 114, 118, 120, 124, 128, 132) sts remain. Work even until armholes measure 5½ (5¾, 6, 6½, 7, 7¼, 7½, 8, 8½, 9, 9¾, 10½)" [14 (14.5, 15, 16.5, 18, 18.5, 19, 20.5, 21.5, 23, 25, 26.5) cm], ending with a WS row.

### SHAPE NECK

**NEXT ROW (RS):** K15 (16, 15, 16, 17, 18, 19, 20, 20, 20, 21, 22), join a second ball of yarn, BO center 58 (58, 62, 64, 66, 72, 76, 78, 80, 84, 86, 88) sts, knit to end.

Working both sides at the same time, decrease 1 st at each

neck edge every RS row twice—13 (14, 13, 14, 15, 16, 17, 18, 18, 19, 20) sts remain each shoulder.

Work even until armholes measure 6½ (6¾, 7, 7½, 8, 8¼, 8½, 9, 9½, 10, 10¾, 11½)" [16.5 (17, 18, 19, 20.5, 21, 21.5, 23, 24, 25.5, 27.5, 29) cm], ending with a WS row.

### SHAPE SHOULDERS

BO 7 (7, 7, 7, 8, 8, 9, 9, 9, 10, 10) sts at each armhole edge once, then 6 (7, 6, 7, 7, 8, 8, 9, 9, 9, 10) sts once.

## FRONT

Work as for Back until armholes measure 4 (4¼, 4½, 5, 5½, 5¾, 6, 6½, 7, 7½, 8¼, 9)" [10 (11, 11.5, 12.5, 14, 14.5, 15, 16.5, 18, 19, 21, 23) cm], ending with a WS row—88 (90, 92, 96, 100, 108, 114, 118, 120, 124, 128, 132) sts remain.

### SHAPE NECK

**NEXT ROW (RS):** K17 (18, 17, 18, 19, 20, 21, 22, 22, 22, 23, 24), join a second ball of yarn, BO center 54 (54, 58, 60, 62, 68, 72, 74, 76, 80, 82, 84) sts, knit to end.

Working both sides at the same time, decrease 1 st at each neck edge every RS row 4 times—13 (14, 13, 14, 15, 16, 17, 18, 18, 18, 19, 20) sts remain each shoulder.

Work even until armholes measure 6½ (6¾, 7, 7½, 8, 8¼, 8½, 9, 9½, 10, 10¾, 11½)" [16.5 (17, 18, 19, 20.5, 21, 21.5, 23, 24, 25.5, 27.5, 29) cm], ending with a WS row.

### SHAPE SHOULDERS

BO 7 (7, 7, 7, 8, 8, 9, 9, 9, 10, 10) sts at each armhole edge once, then 6 (7, 6, 7, 7, 8, 8, 9, 9, 9, 10) sts once.

## SLEEVES

### FIRST CUFF PIECE

CO 80 (84, 88, 90, 96, 102, 108, 118, 128, 144, 158, 174) sts. Begin Garter st; work even for ½" (1.5 cm), ending with a WS row.

Change to St st, beginning with a RS row; work 3 rows even.

### SHAPE PIECE

**SHORT ROW 1 (WS):** Purl to last 24 (26, 28, 25, 28, 31, 34, 35, 40, 44, 47, 51) sts, w&t.

**SHORT ROW 2:** Knit to end.

**SHORT ROW 3:** Purl to 4 (4, 4, 5, 5, 5, 5, 6, 6, 7, 8, 9) sts before wrapped st from previous WS row, w&t.

**SHORT ROW 4:** Knit to end.

**SHORT ROWS 5–18:** Repeat Short Rows 3 and 4 seven times. Work 1 row even across all sts, working wraps together with wrapped sts. Leave sts on needle and set aside; do not break yarn.

## SECOND CUFF PIECE

Using circular needle and second ball of yarn, CO 80 (84, 88, 90, 96, 102, 108, 118, 128, 144, 158, 174) sts.

Begin Garter st; work even for ½" (1.5 cm), ending with a WS row.

Change to St st; work 2 rows even.

## SHAPE PIECE

**SHORT ROW 1 (RS):** Knit to last 24 (26, 28, 25, 28, 31, 34, 35, 40, 44, 47, 51) sts, w&t.

**SHORT ROW 2:** Purl to end.

**SHORT ROW 3:** Knit to 4 (4, 4, 5, 5, 5, 6, 6, 7, 8, 9) sts before wrapped st from previous RS row, w&t.

**SHORT ROW 4:** Purl to end.

**SHORT ROWS 5–18:** Repeat Short Rows 3 and 4 seven times.

Work 2 rows even across all sts, working wraps together with wrapped sts on first row. Leave sts on needle; break yarn.

## JOIN HEM PIECES

**JOINING ROW (RS):** With RSs of pieces facing, holding second piece (on circular needle) behind first piece (on straight needle), *k2tog (1 st from first piece together with 1 st from second piece); repeat from * to end—80 (84, 88, 90, 96, 102, 108, 118, 128, 144, 158, 174) sts.

Work even in St st until piece measures 4" (10 cm) from the beginning, ending with a WS row.

## SHAPE CAP

BO 10 (10, 10, 12, 12, 12, 12, 14, 14, 15, 19) sts at the beginning of the next 2 rows, then 0 (0, 4, 4, 4, 4, 4, 6, 8, 8, 8) sts at the beginning of the following 2 rows. Decrease 1 st each side every third RS row 1 (1, 2, 4, 4, 3, 2, 1, 3, 1, 1, 2) time(s), then every other RS row 1 (0, 1, 1, 1, 1, 1, 1, 0, 1, 0, 0) time(s), then every RS row 14 (17, 12, 9, 11, 14, 17, 21, 19, 24, 28, 29) times. BO 3 (3, 3, 3, 3, 3, 4, 4, 5, 6, 7, 8) sts at the beginning of the next 4 rows. BO remaining 16 (16, 18, 18, 20, 22, 20, 24, 24, 24, 26, 26) sts.

# FINISHING

Block pieces as desired. Sew shoulder seams. Set in Sleeves; sew side and Sleeve seams.

## NECKBAND

With RS facing, using circular needle and beginning at right shoulder, pick up and knit approximately 1 st in each BO st and 3 sts for every 4 rows along diagonal edges. Join for working in the rnd; pm for beginning of rnd. Work even in Garter st (purl 1 rnd, knit 1 rnd) for ¾" (2 cm). BO all sts.

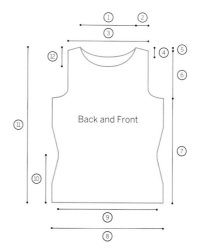

Back and Front

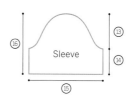

Sleeve

1   8¼ (8¼, 8¾, 9, 9¼, 10¼, 10¾, 11, 11¼, 11¾, 12, 12¼)"
    21 (21, 22, 23, 23.5, 26, 27.5, 28, 28.5, 30, 30.5, 31) cm

2   1¾ (1¾, 1¾, 1¾, 2, 2¼, 2¼, 2½, 2½, 2½, 2½, 2¾)"
    4.5 (4.5, 4.5, 4.5, 5, 5.5, 5.5, 6.5, 6.5, 6.5, 6.5, 7) cm

3   11¾ (12, 12¼, 12¾, 13¼, 14½, 15¼, 15¾, 16, 16½, 17, 17½)"
    30 (30.5, 31, 32.5, 33.5, 37, 38.5, 40, 40.5, 42, 43, 44.5) cm

4   1½"
    4 cm

5   ½"
    .5 cm

6   6½ (6¾, 7, 7½, 8, 8¼, 8½, 9, 9½, 10, 10¾, 11½)"
    16.5 (17, 18, 19, 20.5, 21, 21.5, 23, 24, 25.5, 27.5, 29) cm

7   16 (16, 16½, 16½, 17, 17, 17½, 17½, 17½, 17½, 17½, 17½)"
    40.5 (40.5, 42, 42, 43, 43, 44.5, 44.5, 44.5, 44.5, 44.5, 44.5) cm

8   15¼ (16, 17, 18¼, 19¼, 20, 21, 22¼, 24, 26¼, 28, 30¼)"
    38.5 (40.5, 43, 46.5, 49, 51, 53.5, 56.5, 61, 66.5, 71, 77) cm

9   13½ (14½, 15½, 16½, 17½, 18½, 19½, 20½, 22½, 24½, 26½, 28½)"
    34.5 (37, 39.5, 42, 44.5, 47, 49.5, 52, 57, 62, 67.5, 72.5) cm

10  3½"
    19 cm

11  22½ (22¾, 23½, 24, 25, 25¼, 26, 26½, 27, 27½, 28¼, 29)"
    57 (58, 59.5, 61, 63.5, 64, 66, 67.5, 68.5, 70, 72, 73.5) cm

12  3"
    7.5 cm

13  4½ (4¾, 5, 5½, 6, 6, 6, 6¼, 6¾, 6¾, 7¼, 8)"
    11.5 (12, 12.5, 14, 15, 15, 15, 16, 17, 17, 18.5, 20.5) cm

14  4"
    10 cm

15  10¾ (11¼, 11¾, 12, 12¾, 13½, 14½, 15¾, 17, 19¼, 21, 23¼)"
    27.5 (28.5, 30, 30.5, 32.5, 34.5, 37, 40, 43, 49, 53.5, 59) cm

16  8½ (8¾, 9, 9½, 10, 10, 10, 10¼, 10¾, 10¾, 11¼, 12)"
    21.5 (22, 23, 24, 25.5, 25.5, 25.5, 26, 27.5, 27.5, 28.5, 30.5) cm

# Campfire Cardigan

This unisex, shawl-collar, super-cabled, fantastically pocketed cardigan is the sweater of my childhood: I saw them all the time in Maine, where I grew up. Of course, those were made out of scratchy, rough wool (dare I say it?), and this version is like buddah. (Promise not to tell?) I loaded this cardigan up with cozy touches and tweed—and can't wait to make one for myself!

Campfire is worked in pieces from the bottom up and then seamed, with set-in sleeves. The fronts are worked with afterthought pockets (for more information on pockets, see pages 142–144), and no waist shaping is included. A shawl collar is worked with short rows.

## FINISHED MEASUREMENTS
31¼ (33, 34¾, 36½, 39¼, 40¾, 42½, 44¼, 49, 52¼, 57, 60¼)" [79.5 (84, 88.5, 92.5, 99.5, 103.5, 108, 112.5, 124.5, 132.5, 145, 153) cm] chest, buttoned

*Note: Sweater is intended to be worn with 2–3" (5–7.5 cm) ease in the bust; shown in size 36½" (92.5 cm).*

## YARN
Berroco Tuscan Tweed [65% wool / 25% viscose / 10% mohair; 120 yards (110 meters) / 50 grams]: 10 (10, 11, 12, 13, 14, 15, 15, 17, 19, 20, 22) balls #9055 Cherries

## NEEDLES
One pair straight needles, one 40" (100 cm) long circular needle (for Neckband/Collar), one set of double-pointed needles (for Pockets), size US 6 (4 mm)

Change needle size if necessary to obtain correct gauge.

## NOTIONS
Stitch markers, cable needle, waste yarn, seven ¾-inch (19-mm) buttons

## GAUGE
20 sts and 28 rows = 4" (10 cm) in St st

## NOTES
If your size gives the number 0 for a particular instruction, skip that instruction and proceed to the next instruction.

Unless otherwise specified, decreases should be worked to match the slant of the edge being shaped, as follows: For left-slanting edges: On RS rows, k2, ssk, work to end; on WS rows, p2, p2tog, work to end. For right-slanting edges: On RS rows, work to last 4 sts, k2tog, k2; on WS rows, work to last 4 sts, ssp, p2. Increases should also be worked to match the slant of the edge being shaped, as follows: For right-slanting edges: On RS rows, k1, M1R, knit to end on WS rows, p1, M1PR, purl to end. For left-slanting edges: On RS rows, knit to last st, M1L, k1; on WS rows, p1, M1PL, purl to end.

## SPECIAL ABBREVIATIONS
**2/2 LC (2 OVER 2 LEFT CROSS):** Slip 2 sts to cn, hold to front, k2, k2 from cn.

**2/2 RC (2 OVER 2 RIGHT CROSS):** Slip 2 sts to cn, hold to back, k2, k2 from cn.

**LC (LEFT CROSS):** Slip 1 st to cn, hold to front, k1, k1 from cn. To work LC without a cn, knit second st on needle and then, without slipping the just-knit st off, knit first st on needle. Slip both sts off.

## STITCH PATTERNS
**SIDE CABLE PATTERN (SEE CHART)**
(panel of 20 sts; 18-row repeat)
**ROW 1 (RS):** LC, p4, 2/2 RC, L, p4, LC.
**ROW 2 AND ALL WS ROWS:** Knit the knit sts and purl the purl sts as they face you.
**ROW 3:** LC, p2, 2/2 RC, k4, L, p2, LC.
**ROW 5:** LC, p2, k2, 2/2 RC, L, k2, p2, LC.

**ROW 7:** Repeat Row 3.

**ROW 9:** LC, p2, k12, p2, LC.

**ROW 11:** LC, p2, L, k4, 2/2 RC, p2, LC.

**ROW 13:** LC, p2, k2, L, 2/2 RC, k2, p2, LC.

**ROW 15:** Repeat Row 11.

**ROW 17:** LC, p4, L, 2/2 RC, p4, LC.

**ROW 18:** Repeat Row 2.

Repeat Rows 1–18 for Side Cable Pattern.

**CENTER CABLE PATTERN (SEE CHART)**

(multiple of 8 sts; 8-row repeat)

**ROW 1 (RS):** 2/2 RC, L.

**ROW 2 AND ALL WS ROWS:** Purl.

**ROW 3:** Knit.

**ROW 5:** L, 2/2 RC.

**ROW 7:** Knit.

**ROW 8:** Purl.

Repeat Rows 1–8 for Center Cable Pattern.

## BACK

CO 96 (100, 108, 112, 120, 124, 132, 136, 148, 158, 170, 180) sts.

**ROW 1 (RS):** P0 (0, 1, 0, 0, 0, 0, 1, 1, 0, 0, 0), k0 (1, 2, 0, 1, 1, 2, 2, 2, 2, 2, 2), [p2, k2] 3 (3, 3, 4, 4, 4, 4, 4, 5, 6, 7, 8) times, pm, p1, [k2, p2] twice, k4, [p2, k2] twice, p1, pm, p4 (5, 3, 4, 3, 5, 4, 5, 3, 5, 3, 4), k4, [p4, k4] 2 (2, 3, 3, 4, 4, 5, 5, 6, 6, 7, 7) times, p4 (5, 3, 4, 3, 5, 4, 5, 3, 5, 3, 4), pm, p1, [k2, p2] twice, k4, [p2, k2] twice, p1, pm, [k2, p2] 3 (3, 3, 4, 4, 4, 4, 4, 5, 6, 7, 8) times, k0 (1, 2, 0, 1, 1, 2, 2, 2, 2, 2, 2), p0 (0, 1, 0, 0, 0, 0, 1, 1, 0, 0, 0).

**ROW 2:** Knit the knit sts and purl the purl sts as they face you. Work even until piece measures 2½" (6.5 cm), ending with a WS row.

### BEGIN CABLE PATTERNS

**ROW 1 (RS):** Knit to marker, sm, p1, work Row 1 of Side Cable Pattern to 1 st before marker, p1, sm, p2 (3, 1, 2, 1, 3, 2, 3, 1, 3, 1, 2), work Row 1 of Center Cable Pattern 3 (3, 4, 4, 5, 5, 6, 6, 7, 7, 8, 8) times, purl to marker, sm, p1, work Row 1 of Side Cable Pattern to 1 st before marker, p1, sm, knit to end.

**ROW 2:** Purl to marker, sm, k2, work Row 2 of Side Cable Pattern to 2 sts before marker, k2, sm, k1 (2, 1, 1, 1, 2, 1, 2, 1, 2, 1, 1), work Row 2 of Center Cable Pattern 3 (3, 4, 4, 5, 5, 6, 6, 7, 7, 8, 8) times, knit to marker, sm, k2, work Row 2 of Side Cable Pattern to 2 sts before marker, k2, sm, purl to end.

Work even until piece measures 16 (16, 16½, 16½, 17, 17, 17, 17½, 17½, 17½, 17½, 18)" [40.5 (40.5, 42, 42, 43, 43, 43, 44.5, 44.5, 44.5, 44.5, 45.5) cm] from the beginning, ending with a WS row.

### SHAPE ARMHOLES

BO 7 (7, 7, 8, 8, 8, 8, 9, 9, 10, 13) sts at the beginning of the next 2 rows, then 0 (0, 3, 3, 3, 3, 3, 3, 4, 5, 7, 8) sts at the beginning of the following 2 rows. Decrease 1 st each side every RS row 2 (3, 2, 2, 3, 3, 4, 5, 7, 9, 10, 10) times as follows: K2, ssk, work to last 4 sts, k2tog, k2—78 (80, 84, 86, 92, 96, 102, 104, 108, 112, 116, 118) sts remain.

Work even until armholes measure 5½ (6, 6¼, 6½, 7, 7¼, 7½, 8, 8½, 9½, 10, 11)" [14 (15, 16, 16.5, 18, 18.5, 19, 20.5, 21.5, 24, 25.5, 28) cm], ending with a WS row.

### SHAPE NECK

**NEXT ROW (RS):** Work 25 (26, 26, 27, 25, 26, 27, 27, 28, 29, 29, 30) sts, join a second ball of yarn, BO total of 28 (28, 32, 32, 42, 44, 48, 50, 52, 54, 58, 58) center sts [working k2tog 4 (4, 5, 5, 6, 6, 7, 8, 8, 9, 9) times across cables as you BO to keep edge from flaring, counting each k2tog as 2 sts when counting BO sts], work to end.

Working both sides at the same time, decrease 1 st at each neck edge every RS row twice—23 (24, 24, 25, 23, 24, 25, 25, 26, 27, 27, 28) sts remain each shoulder.

Work even until armhole measures 6½ (7, 7¼, 7½, 8, 8¼, 8½, 9, 9½, 10½, 11, 12)" [16.5 (18, 18.5, 19, 20.5, 21, 21.5, 23, 24, 26.5, 28, 30.5) cm], ending with a WS row.

### SHAPE SHOULDERS

BO 12 (12, 12, 13, 12, 12, 13, 13, 13, 14, 14, 14) sts at each armhole edge once, then 11 (12, 12, 12, 11, 12, 12, 12, 13, 13, 13, 14) sts once.

## LEFT FRONT

CO 42 (44, 46, 48, 52, 54, 56, 58, 64, 68, 74, 78) sts.

**ROW 1 (RS):** P0 (0, 1, 0, 0, 0, 0, 1, 1, 0, 0, 0), k0 (1, 2, 0, 1, 1, 2, 2, 2, 2, 2, 2), [p2, k2] 3 (3, 3, 4, 4, 4, 4, 4, 5, 6, 7, 8) times, pm, p1, [k2, p2] twice, k4, [p2, k2] twice, p1, pm, [k2, p2] 2 (2, 2, 2, 3, 3, 4, 4, 4, 5, 5, 5) times, k0 (1, 1, 2, 1, 2, 0, 1, 2, 0, 2, 2), p0 (0, 0, 0, 0, 1, 0, 0, 1, 0, 0, 0).

**ROW 2:** Knit the knit sts and purl the purl sts as they face you. Work even until piece measures 2½" (6.5 cm), ending with a WS row.

### BEGIN CABLE PATTERN

**ROW 1 (RS):** Knit to marker, sm, p1, work Row 1 of Side Cable Pattern to 1 st before marker, p1, sm, knit to end.

**ROW 2:** Purl to marker, sm, k1, work Row 2 of Side Cable Pattern to 1 st before marker, k1, sm, k2 (3, 1, 2, 1, 3, 2, 3, 1, 1, 2), work Row 2 of Center Cable Pattern 3 (3, 4, 4, 5, 5, 6, 6, 7, 7, 8, 8) times, knit to marker, sm, k1, work Row 2 of Side Cable Pattern to 1 st before marker, k1, sm, purl to end.

**PLACE POCKET OPENING**

**NEXT ROW (RS):** Work 10 (11, 11, 12, 13, 11, 12, 13, 17, 20, 24, 28) sts, change to waste yarn, k26 (26, 30, 30, 30, 34, 34, 34, 34, 34, 34, 34), break waste yarn and slide these 26 (26, 30, 30, 30, 34, 34, 34, 34, 34, 34, 34) sts back to left-hand needle, change to working yarn and knit across these sts again, then work to end.

Work even until piece measures 14½ (14½, 15, 15, 15½, 15½, 15½, 16, 16, 16, 16, 16½)" [37 (37, 38, 38, 39.5, 39.5, 39.5, 40.5, 40.5, 40.5, 40.5, 42) cm] from the beginning, ending with a WS row.

**SHAPE NECK AND ARMHOLE**

*Note: Neck and armhole shaping are worked at the same time. Neck shaping begins first, and will not be completed until after armhole shaping is complete. Please read entire section through before beginning.*

Decrease 1 st at neck edge this row, then every 5 (5, 6, 6, 4, 4, 4, 4, 4, 4, 4, 4) rows 9 (9, 9, 9, 14, 15, 15, 16, 17, 17, 19, 18) times, as follows: On RS rows, work to last 4 sts, k2tog, k2; on WS rows, p2, p2tog, work to end.

AT THE SAME TIME, when piece measures 16 (16, 16½, 16½, 17, 17, 17, 17½, 17½, 17½, 17½, 18)" [40.5 (40.5, 42, 42, 43, 43, 43, 44.5, 44.5, 44.5, 44.5, 45.5) cm] from the beginning, ending with a RS row, shape armhole as follows:

BO 7 (7, 7, 8, 8, 8, 8, 9, 9, 10, 13) sts at armhole edge once, then 0 (0, 3, 3, 3, 3, 3, 4, 5, 7, 8) sts once. Decrease 1 st at armhole edge every RS row 2 (3, 2, 2, 3, 3, 4, 5, 7, 9, 10, 10) times, as follows: K2, ssk, work to end—23 (24, 24, 25, 23, 24, 25, 25, 26, 27, 27, 28) sts remain when all shaping is complete.

Work even until armhole measures 6½ (7, 7¼, 7½, 8, 8¼, 8½, 9, 9½, 10½, 11, 12)" [16.5 (18, 18.5, 19, 20.5, 21, 21.5, 23, 24, 26.5, 28, 30.5) cm], ending with a WS row.

BO 12 (12, 12, 13, 12, 12, 13, 13, 13, 14, 14, 14) sts at armhole edge once, then 11 (12, 12, 12, 11, 12, 12, 12, 13, 13, 13, 14) sts once.

## RIGHT FRONT

CO 42 (44, 46, 48, 52, 54, 56, 58, 64, 68, 74, 78) sts.

**ROW 1 (RS):** P0 (0, 0, 0, 1, 0, 0, 1, 0, 0, 0, 0), k0 (1, 1, 2, 1, 2, 0, 1, 2, 0, 2, 2), [p2, k2] 1 (2, 2, 2, 3, 3, 3, 4, 4, 4, 5, 5) time(s), pm, p1, [k2, p2] twice, k4, [p2, k2] twice, p1, pm, [k2, p2] 3 (3, 3, 4, 4, 4, 4, 5, 6, 7, 8) times, k0 (1, 2, 0, 1, 1, 2, 2, 2, 2, 2, 2), p0 (0, 1, 0, 0, 0, 0, 1, 1, 0, 0, 0).

**ROW 2:** Knit the knit sts and purl the purl sts as they face you.

Work even until piece measures 2½" (6.5 cm), ending with a WS row.

**BEGIN CABLE PATTERN**

**ROW 1 (RS):** Knit to marker, sm, p1, work Row 1 of Side Cable Pattern to 1 st before marker, p1, sm, knit to end.

**ROW 2:** Purl to marker, sm, k1, work Row 2 of Side Cable Pattern to 1 st before marker, k1, sm, purl to end.

Work even until piece measures 9" (23 cm) from the beginning, ending with a WS row.

**PLACE POCKET OPENING**

**NEXT ROW (RS):** Work 6 (7, 5, 6, 9, 9, 10, 11, 13, 14, 16, 16) sts, change to waste yarn, k26 (26, 30, 30, 30, 34, 34, 34, 34, 34, 34, 34), break waste yarn and slide these 26 (26, 30, 30, 30, 34, 34, 34, 34, 34, 34, 34) sts back to left-hand needle, change to working yarn and knit across these sts again, then work to end.

Work even until piece measures 14½ (14½, 15, 15, 15½, 15½, 15½, 16, 16, 16, 16, 16½)" [37 (37, 38, 38, 39.5, 39.5, 39.5, 40.5, 40.5, 40.5, 40.5, 42) cm], ending with a WS row.

**SHAPE NECK AND ARMHOLE**

*Note: Neck and armhole shaping are worked at the same time. Neck shaping begins first, and will not be completed until after armhole shaping is complete. Please read entire section through before beginning.*

Decrease 1 st at neck edge this row, then every 5 (5, 6, 6, 4, 4, 4, 4, 4, 4, 4, 4) rows 9 (9, 9, 9, 14, 15, 15, 16, 17, 17, 19, 18) times, as follows: On RS rows, k2, ssk, work to; on WS rows, work to last 4 sts, ssp, p2.

AT THE SAME TIME, when piece measures 16 (16, 16½, 16½, 17, 17, 17, 17½, 17½, 17½, 17½, 18)" [40.5 (40.5, 42, 42, 43, 43, 43, 44.5, 44.5, 44.5, 44.5, 45.5) cm] from the beginning, ending with a WS row, shape armhole as follows:

BO 7 (7, 7, 8, 8, 8, 8, 9, 9, 10, 13) sts at armhole edge once, then 0 (0, 3, 3, 3, 3, 3, 4, 5, 7, 8) sts once. Decrease 1 st at armhole edge every RS row 2 (3, 2, 2, 3, 3, 4, 5, 7, 9, 10, 10) times, as follows: Work to last 4 sts, k2tog, k2—23 (24, 24, 25, 23, 24, 25, 25, 26, 27, 27, 28) sts remain when all shaping is complete.

Work even until armhole measures 6½ (7, 7¼, 7½, 8, 8¼, 8½, 9, 9½, 10½, 11, 12)" [16.5 (18, 18.5, 19, 20.5, 21, 21.5, 23, 24, 26.5, 28, 30.5) cm], ending with a RS row.

BO 12 (12, 12, 13, 12, 12, 13, 13, 13, 14, 14, 14) sts at armhole edge once, then 11 (12, 12, 12, 11, 12, 12, 12, 13, 13, 13, 14) sts once.

## SLEEVES

CO 42 (42, 42, 46, 46, 46, 50, 50, 50, 50, 50, 50) sts.

Begin 2x2 Rib Flat; work even until piece measures 3½" (9 cm), ending with a WS row.

Change to St st; work 2 rows even.

### SHAPE SLEEVE

Increase 1 st each side this row, then every 15 (13, 11, 12, 10, 8, 9, 7, 5, 4, 3, 3) rows 5 (6, 7, 7, 8, 10, 10, 13, 17, 22, 27, 32) times—54 (56, 58, 62, 64, 68, 72, 78, 86, 96, 106, 116) sts.

Work even until piece measures 18 (18, 18, 18½, 18½, 18½, 19, 19, 19, 19, 19, 19)" [45.5 (45.5, 45.5, 47, 47, 47, 48.5, 48.5, 48.5, 48.5, 48.5, 48.5) cm] from the beginning, ending with a WS row.

### SHAPE CAP

BO 7 (7, 7, 8, 8, 8, 8, 9, 9, 10, 13) sts at the beginning of the next 2 rows, then 0 (0, 3, 3, 3, 3, 3, 3, 4, 5, 5, 5) sts at the beginning of the following 2 rows. Decrease st each side every third RS row 1 (2, 3, 3, 3, 3, 2, 2, 2, 2, 2, 3) time(s), then every other RS row 1 (0, 0, 1, 1, 0, 1, 0, 1, 0, 0, 1) time(s), then every RS row 9 (9, 6, 5, 6, 8, 10, 13, 12, 16, 18, 16) times. BO 2 (2, 2, 2, 2, 2, 3, 3, 3, 4, 4, 5) sts at the beginning of the next 4 rows. BO remaining 10 (12, 12, 14, 14, 16, 12, 14, 18, 16, 20, 20) sts.

## FINISHING

Block pieces as desired. Sew shoulder seams. Set in Sleeves; sew side and Sleeve seams.

### NECKBAND/COLLAR

With RS facing, using circular needle, beginning at lower Right Front edge and ending at lower Left Front edge, pick up and knit approximately 1 st in each BO st, 2 sts for every 3 rows along vertical edges, and 3 sts for every 4 rows along diagonal edges. You will pick up approximately 73 (73, 75, 75, 78, 78, 78, 80, 80, 80, 80, 83) sts along the straight edges of the Fronts, 42 (44, 45, 47, 50, 52, 53, 56, 58, 63, 66, 71) sts along each shaped Front neck edge, and 32 (32, 34, 34, 42, 46, 48, 50, 50, 52, 54, 54) sts along the Back neck edge, and will have approximately 262 (266, 274, 278, 298, 306, 310, 322, 326, 338, 346, 362) sts. *Note: Exact st count is not essential, but be sure to end with a multiple of 4 sts + 2 for ribbing to work out evenly.*

Begin 2x2 Rib Flat; work even for 1 row, placing a marker at beginning of neck shaping on each Front on second row.

### SHAPE COLLAR

**SHORT ROW 1 (RS):** Work to 1 st before second marker, w&t.

**SHORT ROW 2:** Work to 1 st before marker, w&t.

**SHORT ROW 3:** Work to 3 (3, 3, 3, 3, 3, 3, 4, 4, 4, 4, 5) sts before wrapped st from previous RS row, w&t.

**SHORT ROW 4:** Work to 3 (3, 3, 3, 3, 3, 3, 4, 4, 4, 4, 5) sts before wrapped st from previous WS row, w&t.

**SHORT ROWS 5–28:** Repeat Short Rows 3 and 4 twelve times.

**SHORT ROW 29:** Work to end, working wraps together with wrapped sts as you come to them.

**NEXT ROW:** Work to end, working remaining wraps together with wrapped sts as you come to them, and removing markers.

Work even for 2 rows.

**BUTTONHOLE ROW (RS):** [Work 8 (8, 8, 9, 9, 9, 9, 9, 9, 9, 9) sts, BO 2 sts] 7 times, work to end.

Work 7 rows even, CO 2 sts over BO sts on first row using Backward Loop CO (see Special Techniques, page 188). BO all sts in pattern.

### POCKETS

With RS facing, carefully unravel waste yarn from Pocket opening sts and place top and bottom sts onto dpns, being careful not to twist sts, and picking up 1 additional st with bottom needle so that you have the same number of sts on both needles—52 (52, 60, 60, 60, 68, 68, 68, 68, 68, 68, 68). Redistribute sts among 3 or 4 needles. Join working yarn to bottom sts. Purl across bottom sts, knit across top sts; join for working in the rnd; pm for beginning of rnd. Work in St st (knit every rnd) until piece measures 6½" (16.5 cm) from pick-up row. Redistribute sts so that all bottom sts are on one needle and all top sts are on a second needle. Turn Pocket inside out and, using 3-Needle BO (see Special Techniques, page 188), join sides.

### POCKET RIBBING

With RS facing, using dpn, pick up and knit 1 st in each purl bump along top edge of front of Pocket—26 (26, 30, 30, 30, 34, 34, 34, 34, 34, 34, 34) sts. Begin 2x2 Rib Flat; work even for 1" (2.5 cm). BO all sts in pattern. Carefully sew side edges of ribbing to Front.

Sew buttons opposite buttonholes.

## Side Cable Pattern

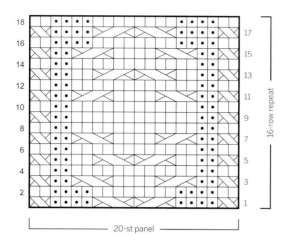

16-row repeat

20-st panel

## Center Cable Pattern

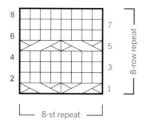

8-row repeat

8-st repeat

| | |
|---|---|
| ☐ | Knit on RS, purl on WS. |
| • | Purl on RS, knit on WS. |
| ⬕ | LC |
| ⬕ | 2/2 RC |
| ⬕ | 2/2 LC |

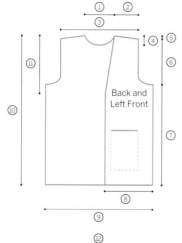

Back and Left Front

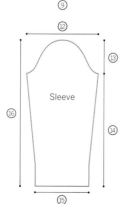

Sleeve

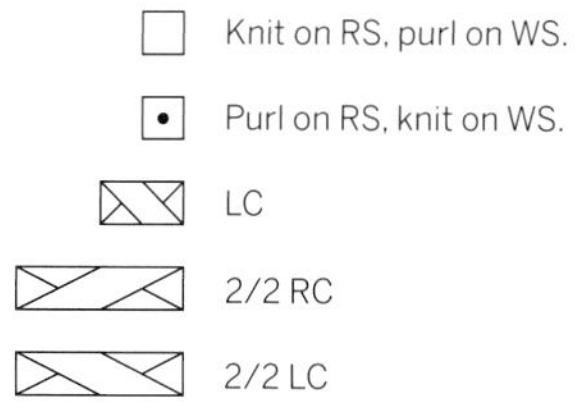

1    4¾ (4¾, 5¼, 5¼, 6¾, 7, 7½, 7¾, 8¼, 8½, 9, 9)"
     12 (12, 13.5, 13.5, 17, 18, 19, 19.5, 21, 21.5, 23, 23) cm

2    3½ (3¾, 3½, 3¾, 3½, 3¾, 3¾, 3¾, 4, 4¼, 4, 4¼)"
     9 (9.5, 9, 9.5, 9, 9.5, 9.5, 9.5, 10, 11, 10, 11) cm

3    11¾ (12, 12½, 12¾, 13½, 14¼, 15¼, 15½, 16, 16¾, 17, 17½)"
     30 (30.5, 32, 32.5, 34.5, 36, 38.5, 39.5, 40.5, 42.5, 43, 44.5) cm

4    1½"
     4 cm

5    ½"
     1.5 cm

6    6½ (7, 7¼, 7½, 8, 8¼, 8½, 9, 9½, 10½, 11, 12)"
     16.5 (18, 18.5, 19, 20.5, 21, 21.5, 23, 24, 26.5, 28, 30.5) cm

7    16 (16, 16½, 16½, 17, 17, 17, 17½, 17½, 17½, 17½, 18)"
     40.5 (40.5, 42, 42, 43, 43, 43, 44.5, 44.5, 44.5, 44.5, 45.5) cm

8    7 (7½, 8, 8¼, 9, 9½, 10, 10¼, 11½, 12¼, 13½, 14¼)"
     18 (19, 20.5, 21, 23, 24, 25.5, 26, 29, 31, 34.5, 36) cm

9    15¼ (16, 17¼, 18, 19¼, 20, 21¼, 22, 24, 26, 27¾, 29¾)"
     38.5 (40.5, 44, 45.5, 49, 51, 54, 56, 61, 66, 70.5, 75.5) cm

10   23 (23½, 24¼, 24½, 25½, 25¾, 26, 27, 27½, 28½, 29, 30½)"
     58.5 (59.5, 61.5, 62, 65, 65.5, 66, 68.5, 70, 72.5, 73.5, 77.5) cm

11   8½ (9, 9¼, 9½, 10, 10¼, 10½, 11, 11½, 12½, 13, 14)"
     21.5 (23, 23.5, 24, 25.5, 26, 26.5, 28, 29, 32, 33, 35.5) cm

12   10¾ (11¼, 11½, 12½, 12¾, 13½, 14½, 15½, 17¼, 19¼, 21¼, 23¼)"
     27.5 (28.5, 29, 32, 32.5, 34.5, 37, 39.5, 44, 49, 54, 59) cm

13   4¾ (5, 5¼, 5½, 5¾, 5¾, 6¼, 6½, 6¾, 7¼, 7¾, 8¾)"
     12 (12.5, 13.5, 14, 14.5, 14.5, 16, 16.5, 17, 18.5, 19.5, 22) cm

14   18 (18, 18, 18½, 18½, 18½, 19, 19, 19, 19, 19½, 19½)"
     45.5 (45.5, 45.5, 47, 47, 47, 48.5, 48.5, 48.5, 48.5, 49.5, 49.5) cm

15   8½ (8½, 8½, 9¼, 9¼, 9¼, 10, 10, 10, 10, 10, 10)"
     21.5 (21.5, 21.5, 23.5, 23.5, 23.5, 25.5, 25.5, 25.5, 25.5, 25.5, 25.5) cm

16   22¾ (23, 23¼, 24, 24¼, 24¼, 25¼, 25½, 25¾, 26¼, 26¾, 27¾)"
     58 (58.5, 59, 61, 61.5, 61.5, 64, 65, 65.5, 66.5, 68, 70.5) cm

# MATERIALS AND RECOMMENDED READING

## GARMENT SOURCES

Shibui Knits

Elsebeth Lavold

Lana Grossa

Quince & Co.

indigodragonfly

Swans Island Company

Blue Sky Fibers

Harrisville Designs

Berroco

Kelbourne Woolens and The Fibre Company

Rowan

Brooklyn Tweed

Valley Yarns

Skacel (for buttons)

## READING LIST AND RESOURCES

Of course, I hope this book contains the answers to most of your sweater questions! But you may also find these books helpful—they're my own favorites.

- *A Treasury of Knitting Patterns* and *A Second Treasury of Knitting Patterns* by Barbara G. Walker
- *Vogue Knitting: The Ultimate Knitting Book* by the editors of *Vogue Knitting* magazine
- *Finishing School* by Deborah Newton
- *The Knitter's Book of Finishing Techniques* by Nancie M. Wiseman
- *The Knowledgeable Knitter* by Margaret Radcliffe
- *The Knitter's Book of Yarn* and *The Knitter's Book of Wool* by Clara Parkes

(And of course, I hope that if you haven't already, you'll explore style, fit, and flattering your figure through sweater knitting in my first three books: *You Can Knit That*, *Knit to Flatter*, and *Knit Wear Love*.)

# ABBREVIATIONS

**BO:** Bind off

**CO:** Cast on

**Cn:** Cable needle

**Dpn:** Double-pointed needle(s)

**K2tog:** Knit 2 stitches together.

**K:** Knit

**M1 or M1L (make 1-left slanting):** With the tip of the left-hand needle inserted from front to back, lift the strand between the 2 needles onto the left-hand needle; knit the strand through the back loop to increase 1 stitch.

**M1P or M1PR (make 1 purlwise-right slanting):** With the tip of the left-hand needle inserted from back to front, lift the strand between the 2 needles onto the left-hand needle; purl the strand through the front loop to increase 1 stitch.

**M1PL (make 1 purlwise-left slanting):** With the tip of the left-hand needle inserted from front to back, lift the strand between the 2 needles onto the left-hand needle; purl the strand through the back loop to increase 1 stitch.

**M1R (make 1-right slanting):** With the tip of the left-hand needle inserted from back to front, lift the strand between the 2 needles onto the left-hand needle; knit the strand through the front loop to increase 1 stitch.

**P2tog:** Purl 2 stitches together.

**Pm:** Place marker

**P:** Purl

**Rnd(s):** Round(s)

**RS:** Right side

**Sm:** Slip marker

**Ssk (slip, slip, knit):** Slip the next 2 stitches to the right-hand needle one at a time as if to knit; return them to the left-hand needle one at a time in their new orientation; knit them together through the back loops.

**Ssp (slip, slip, purl):** Slip the next 2 stitches to the right-hand needle one at a time as if to knit; return them to the left-hand needle one at a time in their new orientation; purl them together through the back loops.

**Sssk:** Same as ssk but worked on the next 3 stitches.

**St(s):** Stitch(es)

**WS:** Wrong side

**W&t:** Wrap and turn (see Special Techniques, Short-Row Shaping)

**Wyib:** With yarn in back

**Wyif:** With yarn in front

**Yo:** Yarnover (see Special Techniques)

# BASIC STITCH PATTERNS

## GARTER STITCH FLAT

(any number of sts; 1-row repeat)

**ALL ROWS:** Knit.

## GARTER STITCH IN THE RND

(any number of sts; 2-rnd repeat)

**RND 1:** Knit.

**RND 2:** Purl.

Repeat Rnds 1 and 2 for Garter stitch in the Rnd.

## 1X1 RIB FLAT

(multiple of 2 sts; 2-row repeat)

**ROW 1 (RS):** *K1, p1; repeat from * to end.

**ROW 2:** *P1, k1; repeat from * to end.

Repeat Rows 1 and 2 for 1x1 Rib Flat.

## 1X1 RIB IN THE RND

(multiple of 2 sts; 1-rnd repeat)

**ALL RNDS:** *K1, p1; repeat from * to end.

## 2X2 RIB FLAT

(multiple of 4 sts + 2; 1-row repeat)

**ROW 1 (RS):** K2, *p2, k2; repeat from * to end.

**ROW 2:** P2, *k2, p2; repeat from * to end.

Repeat Rows 1 and 2 for 2x2 Rib Flat.

## 2X2 RIB IN THE RND

(multiple of 4 sts; 1-rnd repeat)

**ALL RNDS:** *K2, p2; repeat from * to end.

## BROKEN RIB FLAT

(multiple of 4 sts + 2; 2-row repeat)

**ROW 1 (RS):** K2, *p2, k2; repeat from * to end.

**ROW 2:** Purl.

Repeat Rows 1 and 2 for Broken 2x2 Rib Flat.

## BROKEN RIB IN THE RND

(multiple of 4 sts; 2-rnd repeat)

**RND 1:** *K2, p2; repeat from * to end.

**RND 2:** Knit.

Repeat Rnds 1 and 2 for Broken 2x2 Rib in the Rnd

## SEED STITCH FLAT

(multiple of 2 sts; 2-row repeat)

**ROW 1 (RS):** *K1, p1; repeat from * to end.

**ROW 2:** *P1, k1; repeat from * to end.

Repeat Rows 1 and 2 for Seed stitch Flat.

## SEED STITCH IN THE RND

(multiple of 2 sts; 2-rnd repeat)

**RND 1:** *K1, p1; repeat from * to end.

**RND 2:** *P1, k1; repeat from * to end.

Repeat Rnds 1 and 2 for Seed stitch in the Rnd.

# SPECIAL TECHNIQUES

### 3-NEEDLE BO

Place the sts to be joined onto two same-size needles; hold the pieces to be joined with the right sides facing each other and the needles parallel, both pointing to the right. Holding both needles in your left hand, using working yarn and a third needle same size or one size larger, insert third needle into first st on front needle, then into first st on back needle; knit these two sts together; *knit next st from each needle together (two sts on right-hand needle); pass first st over second st to BO one st. Repeat from * until one st remains on third needle; cut yarn and fasten off.

### BACKWARD LOOP CO

Make a loop (using a slip knot) with the working yarn and place it on the right-hand needle (first st CO), *wind yarn around thumb clockwise, insert right-hand needle into the front of the loop on thumb, remove thumb and tighten st on needle; repeat from * for remaining sts to be CO, or for casting on at the end of a row in progress.

### SHORT-ROW SHAPING

Work the number of sts specified in the instructions, wrap and turn (w&t) as follows:

- To wrap a knit st, bring yarn to the front (purl position), slip the next st purlwise to the right-hand needle, bring yarn to the back of work, return the slipped st on the right-hand needle to the left-hand needle purlwise; turn, ready to work the next row, leaving the remaining sts unworked. To wrap a purl st, work as for wrapping a knit st, but bring yarn to the back (knit position) before slipping the st, and to the front after slipping the st.

When short rows are completed, or when working progressively longer short rows, work the wrap together with the wrapped st as you come to it as follows:

- If st is to be worked as a knit st, insert the right-hand needle into the wrap, from below, then into the wrapped st; k2tog; if st to be worked is a purl st, insert needle into the wrapped st, then down into the wrap; p2tog. (Wrap may be lifted onto the left-hand needle, then worked together with the wrapped st if this is easier.)

# ACKNOWLEDGMENTS

This book is dedicated to Jonathan, my amazing, steadfast partner through more crazy leaps and madcap ideas than either of us can count. May we never stop.

Books are all different, and whether it's one's first or fourth, there are bound to be challenges along the way. For this book, as always, I was surrounded and supported by an incredible group of people. Thank you all so very, very much.

First and always, thanks must go to my family: Jonathan, Jacob, and Daniel. However new and surprising *I* find each book, *they* are old pros, stepping in to make delicious meals, acting like it's completely normal for people to knit at the bus stop in the morning, and listening to endless waffling on design decisions with patience and grace. You make my life the most wonderful adventure, and I couldn't possibly love you more. Thank you so much for all that you do.

My team at Abrams is the foundation of everything great about my books: Thanks to my editors, Cristina Garces and Shawna Mullen, who patiently and thoughtfully shaped my words and ideas into something clear and helpful; to Deb Wood and Darilyn Carnes for their beautiful design; and to managing editor Annalea Manalili and production manager Katie Gaffney. Thanks to my technical editor, Sue McCain, for her attention to detail and the occasional (deserved!) reality check. Thanks to Burcu Avsar and Zach Desart for their inspiring photographs and keen eyes, and also to Fernando Soto. Thanks, too, to Melissa Morbillo and the entire team at the Sebasco Harbor Resort for sharing their stunning little piece of Maine with us. Thanks to Caron at Port City models and to our models Taylor, Meghan, and Aaliyah, for lending their beauty to these pages. Thanks to Tamara Savage and Heidi Andrews, for their beautiful styling, and to Natalie Cusson, for lovely makeup.

As usual, the materials donated to make the garments in this book represent the very finest our craft has to offer. Thank you so much to the amazing teams at Shibui Knits, Elsebeth Lavold, Lana Grossa, Quince & Co., indigodragonfly, Swans Island Company, Blue Sky Fibers, Harrisville Designs, Berroco, Kelbourne Woolens and The Fibre Company, Rowan, Brooklyn Tweed, and Valley Yarns. Further thanks to Deb, Jennifer, Julie T., Julie B., Erin, Anjeanette, Brooke, and Karen, for turning these materials into such beautiful fabric.

Thanks as always to Linda Roghaar, who has such a lovely way of turning my unformed half ideas into something wonderful. Thanks, too, to my knitting colleagues and friends Kate, Kim, and Beth—this would not exist without you, and I can never thank you enough for the patience, humor, and life you gave it.

Finally, this book has benefited more than most from the thousands of knitters who generously let me into their creative spaces. From email to classes to retreats to social media, your questions and creativity and beautiful, beautiful selves inspire me. Thank you for your lovely knitting, and for being there.

Let's get knitting.

# INDEX

....................................................................

Note: Page numbers in *italics* indicate
   patterns.

Editor: Shawna Mullen
Designer: Darilyn Lowe Carnes
Production Manager: Kathleen Gaffney

Library of Congress Control Number: 2017956868

ISBN: 978-1-4197-2670-5
eISBN: 978-1-68335-332-4

Printed and bound in China
10 9 8 7 6

Abrams books are available at special discounts when purchased
in quantity for premiums and promotions as well as fundraising
or educational use. Special editions can also be created to
specification. For details, contact specialsales@abramsbooks.com
or the address below.

Abrams® is a registered trademark of Harry N. Abrams, Inc.

**ABRAMS** The Art of Books
195 Broadway, New York, NY 10007
abramsbooks.com